First Edition: July 2023

Printed by Amazon

The Road to Kona

A Drive Half Done

Stuart Staples

Part of the Flawed but Resilient Series

www.flawedbutresilient.com

A Drive Half Done:
An Inquisitive Mind

'Dad?'

We were driving around the bypass not far from home. From his tone I could tell a deep question was coming.

'Tom?'

'How far is an Ironman?'

Phew, I had this, easy to answer. Ironman, this was my *Mastermind* specialist subject. It was the early Spring of 2023 and the previous summer I'd finished my thirtieth Ironman in Bolton, UK. This was my lane.

'Well you start with the swim. That's 2.4 miles which is 3.8 kilometres.'

I paused for dramatic effect. He was bound to be impressed.

'How far is that?'

It was early evening, maybe just before 7pm. Tom and I were in convoy following Linds, my wife, Ben, Tom's older brother and my in-laws for a local pub supper. In the second car with my younger son, it was time to bask in my patriarchal glory. I pressed the trip button on the car's dash.

'I'll start measuring from here and we can see how far we drive.'

As we drove under the railway, past allotments and a retirement home I explained how the start felt; the nerves before entering the water, the breathlessness in the first few minutes, close bodies, taking whacks from arms and legs across the shoulders and head. Continuing through two roundabouts and past the gliding school, I tried to convey what it felt like to be face down in often murky, weedy water, with two thousand other neoprene-clad triathletes. As the distance clicked through 2.4 miles I finished with a flourish.

'Can you imagine swimming for over an hour from where we started to here as fast as you possibly can?'

Glancing from the road for a split second, he looked unimpressed. Determined to wow him I pressed on,

'From here you cycle 112 miles which is 180 kilometres.'

Knowing this would be hard to comprehend for a teenage mind, I tried to give him a sense of the magnitude.

'It's a bit like driving from home to Granny and Grandad's.'

I knew from the back of our overloaded car, this was a long and boring journey for a young passenger.

'Or it's like when we go to the airport on holiday, but instead of parking we'd simply turn around and come straight home.'

Again, with a quick look across, I could see him indifferently taking all this in his stride. *Hey this makes me special.* I had to up the ante to earn my parental respect. It was time to play my ace card.

'Once you've done the swim and the bike, you run a full marathon, 26.2 miles, that's 42.2 kilometres.'

Tom was fourteen and running that sort of distance wouldn't compute.

'Basically, once you'd cycled to the airport and back, you'd then run about half the distance again to the airport.'

Nothing.

'Okay, it's like doing the five kilometre Parkrun eight times.'

We'd run these together and he'd been puffed out by the end of one loop. But like a young pretender absorbing a flurry of my best shots, I wasn't even getting a nod of approval. We were getting close to the pub, the fields and gateways flashing by, the suspension absorbing the undulations. He pushed his advantage, lining up his next sucker punch.

'Dad, are you a professional?'

2

Ouch!

'No.'

I smiled. Time to surrender to humility. My guard dropped, I wasn't going to win this bout. I hardly had the heart to shatter his illusions and confess I relied less on special athletic gifts, but rather a tenacity bordering on stupidity.

'I'm an Age Grouper. That means I compete in a category with people around my age and I don't get paid.'

This got a longer, puzzled look. He knew the net worth of every person famous for being famous; YouTube stars, gamers, influencers. The incredulity.

You do it all for no money?

'And how long does it take?'

'Well the professionals cover the distance in under eight hours on the fastest courses. But on a good day and when I was a lot younger, I could finish in just under eleven hours.'

A self-inflicted cuff, another dent to the battered ego. I was all too aware, I'd be celebrating my fiftieth birthday this November.

'But these days I'm somewhere around twelve and a half hours. For the harder races I'm up to and sometimes over fourteen hours.'

I could see he was trying to imagine these times. A whiff of victory, snatched from the jaws of defeat. Was this my last minute comeback before the final bell? With a killer jab I could have him rocking on his heels. With the vain glorious hubris of a waning champ, I wound up my knockout blow,

'It's like starting when you have breakfast before school and then swimming, biking and running non-stop, without a break until bedtime.'

I could win this yet. We were nearly there. I slowed for the sleeping policemen on the village boundary, taking them gently. The pub's warm entrance beckoned with its fairy lights, blackboards of Friday specials and I hoped to find an easy parking space. I looked at him, scanning for a glimmer of reverence.

3

His *coup de grace.*

Slow and dry.

'Why Dad? Why?'

Thunk!

Stars. My head was spinning. I was on the mat and I could hear the referee counting me out. I hadn't seen that blow coming.

For over twenty years, I'd trained and prepared for thousands of hours. I didn't dare think what they'd cost me in entry fees, travel, accommodation, equipment purchased and time. Guilt, untold opportunities missed, liberties taken while gripped and lost in my selfish, self-centred, single-minded daze.

Why Dad? Why?

The knockout punch. The haymaker. He had me there.

I pulled in next to Linds, her parents and Tom's older brother, Ben, now only a few months younger than I had been when I first met and fell for his mum. Tom was out in a flash, his tall frame stretched, the waist of his trousers in view as he bobbed, impatient with young excitement by the passenger window. His mind was already inside looking at the menu as his door closed. I could hear his muted voice behind the glass. His new deep tones of adolescence. The dreamer, the boy I had been, full of innocence and invincibility.

I stopped the engine and took in the silence. The air inside unmoving, unconsciously breathing. A wall, an invisible barrier. On the outside I was the imagined Iron-dad-hero, different from his friend's, bullish and exciting. On the inside, the many unspoken truths, fragile, the legions of cracks and imperfections. The obsessiveness and addictive behaviour hadn't escalated quickly. It was more an indiscernible creep, a gradual shift of thinking and new behaviours that became habit.

My first seismic dose was in 2001 at Ironman USA, Lake Placid where I experienced the intoxicating mix of endorphins, euphoria and exhilaration.

Powerless and searching for the next high, I was hooked and swept away for the next decade. From one, to two, to even three Ironman races in a year, plus ultramarathons, mountain bike events and 24-hour solo challenges to satisfy the receptor craving. In 2011, I upped my narcotic potency when the World Triathlon Corporation announced that any Age Grouper could race the Ironman World Championship in Kona, Hawaii, through a newly formed Legacy Programme. Four years later I stood on the beach in Kailua Bay at the start of the Ironman World Championship.

Inside the metal cocoon the quiet stillness stirred forgotten memories. I held my keys and moved my fingers to the door handle. Out of the window, my two boys with Linds and her parents. Beyond the glass, teenage energy, exuberance and limitless potential. When had I first dabbled, unconsciously taken an experimental toke? No pills were ingested, leaves inhaled or noxious hallucinogens. Instead the escalation was far more subtle and addictive for an impressionable adolescent brain.

The answers flitted about, eluding me. I had to get out of the car and step back into the world. I went to pull the handle. How had I found myself on the start line at Lake Placid in 2001? How had committing to the Legacy Programme involved way less deliberation than the weekly food shop? And how had I found myself with thirty Ironman medals yet unable to answer my son?

Why Dad? Why?

It wasn't only Tom, Ben and Linds who needed the truth. Somehow I'd found myself on an indiscernible slide towards an impulsive, obsessive, extreme and addictive life. Perhaps the answer might go some way to helping me find a way to step off, let go, stop the whirlwind in my mind and find some peace.

But did I really want to change? I had found a way, as an average age-grouper with a family and a full-time job, to the start line of the *friggin'* Ironman World

Championship. Could I have done this without my single-mindedness, endurance experience, my successes and failures?

Tap, tap.

With his knuckles.

'Dad. You coming?'

Woken from my dream I blinked, smiled and put on the game face. In the fold of my fingers the brushed metal handle, smooth and cool. *Pull.* I applied pressure but not enough yet. A few more moments with the memories, the stillness, the quiet.

Then it came to me. I'd made a decision when I was his age.

Physical! Let's Get Physical

I'm not sure you'd get away with it now but this was the 1980s. Dave, Jonathan and I were hanging from the wooden climbing bars in the school sports hall. We must have been fourteen. I can't quite remember how the challenge had come about, but there we were gripping with white fingers, arms extended above our heads, our feet probably two feet from the ground.

Mr Jones stood, timing how long we could last. He'd set a target of ten minutes. We all adored Mr Jones with his '80s mullet and thick rugby player legs. He was the best PE teacher in the world and definitely our hero. He was laughing and joking with us. But despite the humour, this was deadly serious. We all wanted his respect and high opinion. Me more than anyone. The game was to see who could hang the longest.

In the first five minutes I'd done some tactical arithmetic. Dave was the smallest and acknowledged as the sportiest in our year. He ran cross country for the county and was the hot favourite. But I fancied my chances against Jonathan.

The rest of the class had cleared out. It was only the three of us who'd taken the bait and were left with Mr Jones and Mr Payne. 'Bill Payne', as we called him out of ear shot, was equally idolised. Mr Payne taught geography but helped out with PE. We knew Mr Jones' real name was Tim, but in his presence we'd always call him 'Sir' or 'Mr Jones'.

They were our absolute favourite teachers. If we stepped out of line, they'd regularly give us detentions or send us to the corridor to consider the error of our ways. But if we were good, they were like mates, grown up kids who we called Mister. Instinctively we knew they enjoyed their time with us. It was more than a job, they believed in our potential.

'That's six minutes boys.'

Mr Jones gave us a time check. I could feel my hands getting slippery, sweaty, my grip giving way. This wasn't easy. I looked across at Dave and Jonathan. They looked in as much discomfort as me. I couldn't be the first to let go. I could take being beaten by Dave, but not by Jonathan. No way.

And then the inexplicable happened.

My hands gave up.

My fingers slipped.

I dropped to the floor.

I'd hardly put up a fight. Simply let go. I couldn't believe it. I stood blinking, humiliated, mortified. Feeling my cheeks redden, I wanted the hard green surface to swallow me whole. I longed to start again but it was too late. Dave and Jonathan had hung on longer than me. They'd beaten me and they'd done it in front of the two coolest teachers in the school. I was crushed and felt a long way from special. I'd failed in front of my heroes. A public loss of approval.

That was it. In an instant, something flipped in my head. My own physical prowess hadn't stood up to the test. Until that PE lesson I'd succeeded in sport through the sheer exuberance of being a kid. I expected to be good. For the first time ever my perceived powers fell short of where I'd pegged them. A line had been crossed and I no longer took my level of performance for granted.

It was as if a gauntlet had been thrown down and I was compelled to be better, and if not with natural exuberance, then what? I'd accepted Dave would beat me, but not Jonathan. I'm pretty confident that out of the five of us involved, no one else even remembers it. But I guess I have been training to beat Jonathan and get the approval and validation of my heroes ever since. For me it was an epiphany.

I made a decision.

That's when I first started to mix my potent cocktail.

'Mum, just going for a run,' became interchangeable with 'Just going for a bike ride.' At this point I had a lot of enthusiasm but really was quite clueless. I wasn't trying to find out how far I could push myself but unwittingly I was testing my limits.

Six months on from my sports hall humiliation I'd cut grass, cleaned cars and vacuumed the house to pull together enough money to buy a set of weights. These I'd thrown around vigorously without much science and no guidance as to what I should be doing. I'd do bicep curls and shoulder presses, unsure how effective it all was. But I'd build up a sweat in front of the mirror, sound-tracked by *The Cure* or *Bruce Springsteen*.

I'd also persuaded Dad to let me borrow his racer and started riding the five miles to and from school on a daily basis. I wore a cycling shirt, padded shorts, mirror glasses and finished my Tour de France look with rugby socks and a red plastic helmet. I looked like an extra on *Top of the Pops*, but felt like a cycling pro.

Before I left each morning I'd do a quick warm up playing a Madonna single, Paul Hardcastle's *19* or *Live is Life* by Opus on Dad's wooden cased Hifi stack. I'd get to school buzzing, quickly change and already be looking forward to the ride home. During a typical week I threw in some runs and found a comfortable seven mile loop.

With regular exercise I noticed the last remnants of puppy fat had either been stretched out or burned away. New behaviours and ways of thinking were becoming ingrained habits. Perhaps unwittingly for an impressionable teenage brain, I'd started soaking my cells in an addictive gateway dose of feeling great. Getting physical. Suffering was leading to enjoyment, the release of incredible hormones and endorphins.

It was about this time that triathlon first came into my peripheral vision. Paul, who lived three doors away and was as many years my senior, was into triathlon. He was taller than me, tanned and covered in lean muscle. He looked how I'd love to look. He instantly became my idol. I bought into the lifestyle advert and started swimming once or twice a week. Paul gave me a pile of old *220 Triathlon*

9

magazines and I pored over the pages reading about Dave Scott, Mike Pigg, Scott Tinley and Mark Allen. The pictures of them shoulder-to-shoulder running through Kona's lava fields became indelibly etched in my brain.

Paul took me under his wing, extending my boundaries on some longer rides. We did sixty miles one Saturday which was way more than I'd ever ridden before. He was much more experienced than me and when I was flagging, told me to sit in the draft of his wheel as he dragged me home. I dug deep, desperate to make a favourable impression. I'd unconsciously passed a test. The following weekend he invited me to join him for his Sunday triathlon club's swim and bike. In my private world I was rocking it, but this was a very public test of my new found superpowers.

As the appointed morning of my reckoning arrived, I was more than nervous. Knowing nothing of nutrition I filled my cycling jersey with Mars bars. Paul and I rode the fifteen miles to the pool. Locking our bikes outside we jumped in and did the session. I beasted myself determined not to disappoint his faith in me. To my teenage eyes, the members of Warwick Tri Club in the late 1980s were the real deal, cut straight out of the pictures of *220*. They had one-piece suits, all the gear, aero bars, bulging muscles and shaved legs. I looked down at my wispy teenage pins and scrunched up striped rugby socks. I felt very out of place.

Once the swim was out of the way it was time for the club bike ride. Following the hour-long pre-swim slog into Warwick and the thrashing in the pool, even I could tell I was low on my reserves. I surreptitiously gobbled two Mars bars from my precious stash and glugged at what was left of my drink.

Looking back I am amazed I lasted as long as I did. It was a fierce pace. No mercy for the new boy. I sat at the back of the group, but even out of the wind, the embers of my hastily devoured Mars bars quickly died. As the needle hit empty, so too did my chances of staying with the group up the next hill. I had more sickly chocolate in my pocket but couldn't face it. I was beyond help. To

10

his credit, Paul saw my plight and kindly offered to lead me home. As we gently rolled the last few miles we agreed I should continue to build my base. I wasn't invited the following Sunday. Of this I was mightily relieved.

I'd now seen what good looked like and rather than put me off, it turbo charged my enthusiasm. I was hooked on training and it felt great being in shape. My next purchase was a turbo trainer which became a permanent set up in our conservatory. Back in the eighties these were crude affairs. Mine was a simple metal frame where I removed my front wheel and clipped in the forks. My back wheel sat on a tyre chewing cylinder slowed by a very noisy fan. It was engineered perfectly to irreparably corrode its owner's bike. With some more car cleaning, grass cutting and other odd jobs I soon had the £50 needed to own this very unsophisticated torture device. Imagining I was leading a break in the Tour de France or the fictional 'Hell of the West' from *American Flyers,* I'd pedal to the beat of *Ozzy Osborne's Paranoid* and *Ironman.* I was obsessed with the feel good drug of being fit. A year on, now fifteen, I wasn't training to 'out-hang' Jonathan anymore, but to have the stamina and strength to stay with the adults from Warwick Triathlon Club.

These were my early formative, and often bumpy, endurance experiences. I was learning fast and hard, nearly always through my mistakes, and tumbling through degrees of suffering. I was to discover I'd merely 'bonked' on my sixty mile ride with Paul and my Sunday outing with Warwick Tri. Quickly I was finding my outer limits with swimming, biking and running. When I did finally hit 'the wall' it was different. I really turned myself inside out and fortunately I had the pleasure of doing it all alone.

I'd regularly been running ten miles and naturally in my ever-escalating-limit-probing mind wondered what it would be like to double the distance. Of course I didn't tell anyone, I just went out and did it, following a twenty mile loop that I frequently cycled on my bike. Perhaps my only sensible decision was to apply some Vaseline to the rubbing parts. Before closing the front door I yelled my familiar,

'Mum. Just going for a run.'

With that, I broke into my stride. With no notion of pacing, the first ten miles flew by. *I've got this*, I assured myself, *I'm a natural*. After this test, I was sure I'd be back with Warwick Tri ready to hustle with the real men. But then at about mile thirteen my legs started to feel heavy and my pace dropped away. By mile fifteen, I wanted it all to end and the ground to swallow me whole.

I was done. Empty. In the red.

But I was alone in the middle of nowhere. Even if there had been shops, I had no money. It was decades before mobile phones and, despite my cub scout badge collecting, I'd not even thought to bring ten pence for a phone box. My only option was to get home.

So I ran on. Well, it was more of a shuffle. One foot in front of the other. Deeper and deeper into energy depletion. Everything closed down. It didn't feel like a 'wall', more a loss of sensation and awareness. In the last two miles all I had was a letter box view, my peripheral vision in darkness. Like looking out of a knight's helmet. My hearing muted. Absolute emptiness.

My trainers crunched the shingle of the driveway. Such sweet relief to be home. Saved. Through the front door straight to the fridge. Bottle of milk. Push the foil cap. To the mouth. Tip up. Gone. I grabbed a big bar of Milka chocolate and a second bottle of milk and slumped into a chair. After fifteen minutes the chocolate was no more and two empty milk bottles sat in front of me.

I felt a million dollars. What a feeling. I'd survived. Suffering definitely equalled pleasure. Mum wandered in and found me in the midst of my impromptu picnic.

'You weren't out long. How was the run?'

Completely oblivious to my catastrophic breakdown. This was the parenting-philosophy of my childhood. If I was outside and doing stuff, the detail didn't matter. I was given absolute freedom. Strong values but no rules. As long as I was active and pushing myself, it earned approval, no questions asked.

But my power pack of unlimited energy did come with a few disruptive drawbacks, especially when it came to my schooling. I spent a lot of my early teenage years standing in corridors perplexed at why the teacher hadn't found my wisecrack as funny as the rest of the class. I guess I was labelled a nuisance and the chief troublemaker. If there was mischief, I was the boisterous ringleader. The filter and my ability to extrapolate consequences between spontaneous thoughts, actions and the words that fell out of my mouth were non-existent.

'Stuart is easily distracted,' read Mrs Taylor's pithy school report. She taught domestic science. 'Most of the distractions are set up by himself.'

Damning, but perhaps fair.

Others were less tolerant of my boundless adolescent exuberance.

'Mr Blunt wants to exclude you from the school.'

In the 80s it was easier to expel than empathise and manage.

Privileged And Feral

Dad and I were in his car and I must have been nearly fifteen. It was moving fast, the countryside a blur through the window.

'We've had a letter home from the headmaster.'

The car door was locked. We were doing 50mph and there was no escape. It was just Dad and me. I should have seen it coming. This was a setup and, like a schmuck, I'd walked straight into it. Dad *never* took me to town on a Saturday.

'Mr Blunt wants to exclude you from the school.'

Definitely no escape. Incredibly for once I had the sense to know this wasn't a time for me to speak. Inexplicably, I read the room, I was here to listen.

'I'm going to write back and say they should give you one more chance.'

He didn't take his eyes off the road. I wasn't driving and neither did I.

'I'll write, "If Stuart is excluded from school, we've all failed. We as parents and you as teachers".'

Stirring stuff but definitely still listening time for me.

'You're on your last life. We believe in you. You need to prove Mr Blunt wrong.'

I gave him my word I would. Mum and Dad believed in me. I wasn't going to let them down in front of Mr Blunt and the school. That moment was a watershed. I was going in the wrong direction and faced another public humiliation in front of the two people whose praise and approval I sought the most, my parents. They'd raised Josie, my sister, and I to unquestioningly believe we were special. Now I had to make a decision whether I wanted to achieve this potential. I realised what I did next would shape my future.

My parents were free-spirits and our family stories are laced with the values they taught us. Luckily for me they met at the Reading University Climbing Club.

There was some matchmaking at play as Mum is a few years younger than Dad. He was an accomplished climber and established member when she joined. The union was sealed while he was belaying the safety line. Mum, on the other end, was new to rock faces and when she reached the top called down,

'I'm up. What do I do now?'

'Jump!' came the mischievous reply. To Dad's surprise, the rope went tight and he flew from the ground as she did. They have been jumping together ever since. Humour and risk became a double-edged blade in their courtship. For their honeymoon, and with the backing of the Royal Geographic Society, they drove an ex-army lorry from London to the Hindu Kush in Afghanistan. This was the late 1960s, and with a rare window of peace in the Middle East, they travelled non-stop. But romance never got ahead of resourcefulness for these two lovebirds. To keep costs down the honeymoon was an expedition in the company of a group of hairy climbers wanting to bag some previously unscaled peaks.. It was far from a conventional nuptial start.

Dad was, and is, a worker. From his childhood he's grafted to make money. Not for material gain or avarice, never flash or extravagant. He came from an unstable home, grew up with my granny and his younger brother in a bedsit. They had nothing and he had to earn to eat. It was a childhood that would either break you, or in his case, build near limitless tenacity and resilience. He created a very simple formula,

Hard work makes money. Money makes security.

Dad worked hard, we had a stable family and I felt very secure.

They continued climbing until my sister, Josie, was born and although the risks on rock became irreconcilable with family life, their adventurous flame never died. When I was four we went sailing for the first time with some family friends. Shortly afterwards they bought their first boat. It was far from a yacht, more a big dingy with a cabin. Within a few years they upgraded to a slightly larger, but still cramped for a family of four, Contessa.

We sailed everywhere along the south coast of England; Cowes, Studland Bay, Lulworth Cove, Weymouth, around Portland Bill. With the inevitable escalation of adventures, we pushed further to Devon, Cornwall, France and the Channel Islands. Josie and I would trim sails, steer and tack. Jeopardy followed us constantly. We got caught in naval manoeuvres, becalmed, benighted and tossed in violent tidal races. We saw the world differently. When you drive to a harbour you're a tourist. When you sail there, you own it. We'd tootle in the dinghy, buzzing from pontoons to beaches, round moorings, topping up the outboard with petrol. Swashbucklers, not conforming.

When we sailed, Dad was no longer the worker. He'd grow a beard over our two week summer holiday. He'd show us knots, take us crabbing, cut bacon for bait, swim off the stern, drink oil from the mackerel tins. Dressed in his speedos, an old shirt and barefoot he'd catch fish, gutting them in the cockpit. Around him things never stopped, we were always doing something, on the go. He was definitely the stuff of heroes.

Mum kept things together. She was always there for us, our fearless protector, resourceful and unflappable. She was my rock, my friend, my confidant and had near inexhaustible patience and belief in us both. When we were young, she worked as a teacher, juggling school runs, packed lunches, encouragement and counselling. Generous beyond fault and selfless, we were always her absolute focus. However tired after a long day at work, she'd read to us, often for an hour or more before going to bed. Josie and I would snuggle in on either side urging her to do one more page. She'd always relent. We'd sing a lot too. Nothing sophisticated initially. *Two, four, six, eight, who do we appreciate?* as we stood on the landing, me in my blue muppet pyjamas, waiting for Dad's headlights to illuminate the long track to the house. When Mum sang, things were always safe.

It was an idyllic childhood.

***

'You're not as bright as your sister,' Mr Lewis, the Deputy Head and our Chemistry teacher, maliciously sneered. The petty dismissal of potential and individuality.

Barbed cuts that the tree remembers and the axe forgets.

I didn't want to but I believed him and it hurt. I told Mum and she was furious, exclaiming, 'What an idiot!' and reassured me with words like jealous, small-minded and petty. With her protection I was learning to mistrust authority.

My sister, Josie, is eleven months older and in many ways tougher than me. She was always my companion and before we became teenagers we did everything together. We are siblings and of course we'd argue and fight, but for the most part we were friends. I was definitely the younger brother. She would lead and I'd follow.

She was also way hardier than me and made me feel the wimpy younger brother on many occasions. In the depths of winter, she didn't hesitate to spontaneously strip and leap into a freezing mountain stream in Skye with Dad whilst I stood fully clothed shivering on the rocks. She wild-swims to this day. I go neck to ankle in neoprene and the water temperature always takes my breath away. She was definitely the boss; tougher, rebellious, independent, strong-willed, talented and I followed behind.

No rules, strong values.

We were privileged, and very feral kids.

***

The car sped on and now it was time for Dad's *lets convince the school they shouldn't expel you* plan. My parents weren't totally naive and had a strong sense of realism when it came to my imminent expulsion. They knew the chances of a boisterous boy successfully mending his ways with only a '*I-will-behave-honest*' promise and no outside assistance were slim to zero. They certainly weren't ready to gamble that my new found and untested self-control was strong enough to override my powerful teenage impulses.

'To assist the turnaround at school, I'm going to write to tell them we're looking at ways to help you with your emotions.'

For the first time I took my eyes off the road.

Say what?

I'd seen troublemakers on *Grange Hill* get therapy, counselling and, for the really out of control ones, even medication. I hadn't seen this coming. It didn't feel like their style.

'Mum and I think you should start TaeKwonDo.'

No way! I couldn't have been more delighted. My best friend Christian was already a black belt. Ralph Macchio had recently kicked ass in *The Karate Kid* and together we'd watched endless Jean Claude Van Damme, Bruce Lee and Chuck Norris movies. I was in trouble at school and was sent to learn martial arts. Straight out of the movies. Result!

I was obsessed from the first lesson, despite having my head almost taken off by a rather enthusiastic blue belt. He thought I'd move or block when he swung. I didn't. My jaw felt like it moved an inch sideways. My eyes watered from the searing crunching in my right ear and bone-stretch on my left. I'd been taught to be resilient. I was fourteen and the rest of the class were adults. No one was pulling punches for kids here and I was instantly absorbed.

Two years later when I was a blue belt my instructor, Liam, suggested I join the Friday 'Fight Night' run by the Chairman of the TaeKwonDo Association of

Great Britain, TAGB, Dave Oliver. The TAGB's national squad, legends of the time like Jackson White, Mick Keogh, Nigel Banks and Harjit Singh, were there. Up against these fighters, I was a punch bag. Slower, less flexible, out of my depth but also totally and utterly in awe. By simply being there, I was living my teenage dream.

I'd finish the session with my suit soaked through, ringing wet, jacked on adrenaline. I'd get hammered, but was always smiling and ready to take more. This earned me respect. I was accepted and part of the tribe, the TAGB family. I was with adults who spoke to me like an equal. These were my people and the TaeKwonDo therapy worked. It was an outlet that burned my teenage frustration, a juvenile hormone antidote. It gave me self-esteem and self-control and built an inner confidence. I have never been in an actual fight since.

I won't ever forget our drive. I hope if it's ever needed, I too can have the words, respect and wisdom to guide those I love. Mum and Dad believed in me, I couldn't fail them, and I didn't. I changed almost overnight. Eighteen months later I got the best results of my year. To Mr Blunt's credit he had the graciousness to congratulate me. We were both equally as surprised. I didn't think I had any talent but I *could* work hard and had achieved what I thought was impossible.

These lessons stayed lodged in my brain.

Now Get Out Of That

Our absolute favourite TV show as kids was *Now Get Out of That*.

Made in the early 80s, it was the original *Big Brother* and *SAS Who Dares Wins* rolled into one. It was outdoors, had real people involved in teamwork, but the only prize was the challenge. Together they'd make rafts and shelters, escape from islands, cross rivers and survive in the wilderness with bushcraft and problem solving. As the contestants lurched from disaster to catastrophe the narrator would intone, 'Now get out of that.' It felt like a mirror being held up to our childhood. When benighted in the Highlands, caught in naval manoeuvres, becalmed in a shipping lane, we'd cheer in chorus, 'Now get out of that!' looking for the cameras.

When we laughed at calamity it was never dangerous, always fun, a test of our resilience. Jeopardy was part of the family narrative. It definitely helped to be tough and have a sense of humour. Our toddler years in the wilds of Scotland gave us an incredible early perspective. We stood on frozen lakes, had the run of a farmyard, kept ferrets, battled rat infestations and were regularly entertained as we watched Hector, the local farmer, chase crazed bulls round the barn.

I sometimes wonder how I made it to adulthood. Hector's four collies set on me when I must have been about three years old. I can see them tearing towards me in the farmyard and then my memory goes dark. Instinctively protective, Mum weighed in, kicking and screaming until they yelped away. That pack of dogs had met their match mistaking me for an easy morsel. I came to in hospital. The scar on my eye was a badge of honour.

Despite the sailing, I definitely wasn't safe around water. Bizarrely for a triathlete, I couldn't even get into a swimming pool until I was five years old. At eighteen months I almost drowned in a garden centre pond. I was pulled out unconscious. I don't remember it but for years I couldn't put my head underwater in the bath. When we went to the local leisure centre I'd scream on the side. A deep, unremembered, pathological hatred of water was embedded. In the end it was Josie who coaxed me in as I saw her fearlessly gliding along the bottom and didn't want to be left behind.

'Come on Stuart, you can swim with me.'

I wouldn't say I was a clumsy kid but visits to the hospital were fairly frequent. My power to see the potentially painful consequences of my actions kept letting me down. How I shot myself in the thumb was quite predictable and, with hindsight, pretty dumb. So stupid in fact, it required a mild stretching of the honesty value. Technically, I didn't shoot myself in the thumb. Naveed did. He pulled the trigger. The 'shooting myself' is what we told our parents.

The three of us, Naveed, Christian and I, were fifteen and all wanted to be in the Army. I actually wanted to be a Royal Marine but let's not split hairs at this stage. Back then we didn't have the realistic graphics of modern first-person-shooter video games. When the accident happened we were living our real life version of *Call of Duty* in the countryside behind Christian's house. We had a campfire, had pitched our tent and laid out our sleeping bags. We'd crept around all night with *Rambo* style hunting knives, our air rifles, camo cream and olive drab fatigues. It was an altogether more innocent time. Thoughts of global terrorism and the lethal consequences of the potential police response to seeing three near adult sized boys fully tooled up hadn't crossed our minds. We'd made it through the night without Birmingham's armed-response descending on us and were doing a bit of early morning target practice. My thumb happened to cross over the end of Naveed's barrel at the exact moment he was about to demonstrate his marksmanship.

It was like being hit by a hammer and under my camo cream I went cold, clammy and turned as white as a sheet. Christian's parents, Maureen and Jerry, had their peaceful Sunday morning shattered as we rolled up to the back door looking like extras from *Platoon*. Maureen had the sense to scrub my face clean of waxy green and black cream to avoid difficult questions at Solihull's Accident & Emergency. Three hours later I was heading home with my thumb erect and fully bandaged. I had a neat entry hole on the underside and a rather messy cross a few millimetres behind my nail where they'd pulled the pellet out. It had almost gone clean through, narrowly missing the bone and luckily I swerved a potential end of digit amputation. A month later, I was back in hospital with a ruptured appendix. Worried about lead poisoning, my surgeon, Mr Levi, reassured me that the two visits were unrelated.

In my teenage years self-inflicted pain seemed to follow me and it definitely felt like there was an irreconcilable gap between my actions and my ability to consider their potential consequences. Fortunately most incidents were minor, however on occasion they were much more serious.

'I'm worried it's a spinal injury.'

This time I was in the back of an ambulance, neck brace on and feeling very scared. Dad was following in the car. For my A-levels I'd moved to a new school and made the first team rugby squad. The sixth form was bigger and so were the boys. In the summer months, with my routine of swimming, biking and running I was lean and trim. Most of my teammates and critically the opposition had gone up inches, got wider, bigger, grown beards and had fingers like thick sausages. It was the second game of the season and we were playing at home. With Dad on the touchline I was keen to put on a good show.

'Who's that lying on the floor?' he'd asked another parent, unsuccessfully scanning the field for his upright son.

'He's been out for a while,' came the reply.

I knew none of this and only put the pieces together afterwards. They brought me round in the time honoured way of medieval rugby medicine with a dose of cold water over the head. Things escalated quickly. They were worried I'd broken my neck.

Paralysed!

Not even seventeen.

As we sped through the traffic, blue lights on and siren wailing, big, wet tears trickled slowly, uncontrollably from my eyes. Lying horizontal and unable to move, the drops ran into my ears. It didn't hurt. I was numb and very afraid. The Trauma Team swept me through the waiting room and straight into x-ray. For the next two hours hospital orderlies carefully moved me as the radiologist took multiple shots of my neck and spine from every conceivable angle. I held my breath. My future was in limbo. I knew the potential consequences of a broken neck or back. Thoughts and memories swirled. I was caught between two worlds, a future of adventures and dreams, the other of darkness.

About a week before my unplanned rugby induced visit to A&E I'd sat in the school's career room to talk informally about the process of becoming a Royal Marine. The Navy's recruitment officer had had a white beard, a crisp, starched blue uniform and, to my adolescent brain, looked beyond active service age. I'd done my research and knew the selection process, the fitness test and the pathway to becoming a green beret commando. I was already doing more than the average teenager to keep in shape and I seemed to have a battery that never ran out.

Mum's family were mainly Navy and one of her cousin's husbands was in the Special Boat Service, SBS. We'd spent the day with 'Uncle' Richard a few years earlier and he exuded a strength, confidence and invincibility I'd never encountered before. His life seemed extraordinary. He was super fit and spent his time between endurance and warfare exercises, skiing in Norway and his speciality, underwater sabotage. I wondered whether I had the *strength of mind* to be a Royal Marine Commando like Richard. It would be a job where I'd get paid to stay fit, shoot guns, jump in and out of helicopters, drive speed boats and Land Rovers. It sounded pretty good to me.

Mum and Dad weren't at all keen. There was talk of getting a profession, being a solicitor, a barrister, having a career in law. That would get their approval. But it sounded really dull so I called the recruitment line to get the glossy overview pack anyway. When my form teacher asked what I'd like to be as I started my A-levels I replied,

'I'd like to be a Royal Marine Commando.'

And that's how I found myself having a preliminary chat with the Royal Navy's recruitment officer. He confirmed everything I thought it would be. It sounded perfect. We talked through fitness. He assured me with the sports I did, although I shouldn't underestimate how tough training could be, I would have a good chance.

'But before we go much further there are a couple of important questions you should think over.'

He looked straight at me.

'You don't need to answer them now but they will be asked of you and need consideration.'

He paused.

'These are the two fundamentals of the service.'

I listened with every fibre, desperate to impress.

'How do you feel about killing someone?'

I was glad I didn't have to answer because it hadn't crossed my mind. He paused again for effect.

'How do you feel about being killed?'

I knew instantly I didn't relish either of them.

'As I say, don't answer them now but consider both. Yes, it's an active life. It would suit someone like you. But the job boils down to these two questions. You and we have to be comfortable with how you answer.'

As I reflected, my perspective changed. I'd been looking at it like a child, playing war with Christian and Naveed with camo paint in the fields. After an hour with the Navy's recruitment officer I saw it for what it was. An adult's job, preparing for war, killing or being killed. In the days that followed, the dream slowly drifted away. I could be as fit as a Marine but not forced to follow a superior's orders, to take a life or have mine snuffed out. Those were two good questions to ask a sixteen year old boy attracted by the lifestyle who'd done little deep thinking about the *raison d'etre* of the service.

I hadn't told Mum and Dad about my big decision. They'd be happy.

On the gurney childhood memories swirled. Sailing trips with the family, long winter passages off the south coast, walking holidays in the Lake District and the wilds of Scotland with our smelly dog. My blasts down the canal on a mountain bike, getting lost on fun runs. Mum finding me in the medical tent on the seafront where I'd passed out delirious after riding the London to Brighton without enough food or drink.

I was unbelievably scared and also a little smelly. When you can smell yourself, you know it's bad. My rugby shirt had dried and the aroma of my sweat oozed through. But it wasn't only odour vapours that had become ingrained. In the years since I'd hung from the bars with Dave and Jonathan my brain had made a subtle, virtually invisible and likely irreversible shift. With a parental nudge in the right direction and the help of TaeKwonDo, I'd cracked the star-pupil formula. *Hard work trumps talent.* I had got myself together. What's more, the habit of exercise had gradually, indiscernibly morphed into something exceptionally addictive. Being very active settled my mind, gave me a buzz and helped me feel good.

25

As I lay on the hospital gurney slowly rotating like a pig on a spit for the radiographer's skeletal portraits, I no longer wanted to exercise. I *needed* to exercise. It shaped my identity, my thinking, it was what I did. The more I did, the more I wanted to do.

I was very afraid.

My future was hanging in the balance.

The Third Quarter

After my ride in the ambulance, fast track through the trauma unit, multiple x-rays and indeterminable wait, incredibly I walked out of the hospital that evening. My neck was in a brace but mercifully nothing was broken.

It had been a very long Saturday and I was in no doubt I'd been given a second life. As I crossed the car park with Dad, the sun felt brighter, the air fresher, my footsteps lighter. This time I'd really dodged a life-changing bullet. I'd survived but dark thoughts haunted me when I closed my eyes. I left some innocence on that hospital gurney.

The spinal specialist told me it was the end of my rugby playing career. Giving up scrums, the smell of Ralgex and cauliflower ears seemed like a small price to pay. I'd have taken anything not to be paralysed. Stiff as a plank and with limited upper body mobility from the whiplash, I saw the physiotherapist and started my rehab. I was determined to grab the lifeline I'd been thrown with both hands. Fitness was now more important than ever and, as soon as I could, I dropped back into my old routine of swimming, biking, running, TaeKwonDo and weights. Without the bruising, knocks and injuries of playing weekend rugby and mid-week practice, my training was far more consistent and my stamina grew.

The games master at sixth form, Mr Cowell, initially had me join hockey practice but after a week or two I went back to him frustrated by the lack of commitment. I'd watch disillusioned as my teammates pulled out of fifty-fifty challenges, half-hearted sprints and die-in-the-ditch tackles. They either weren't bothered or were thinking about the consequences. Maybe they knew something I didn't about avoiding getting hurt, but to me it didn't feel like the right way to play. I was all in or nothing. Disillusioned, I found myself moving away from team sports.

Mr Cowell was an ex-Commonwealth middle distance runner and had the measure of me. He could see I wasn't swinging the lead and trying to shirk. My fitness had dropped through my early rehab and I was determined to get it back. He agreed I could use the games lessons to improve my running. Although I'd let go of the dream of becoming a Royal Marine, I saw the selection criteria as my minimum fitness benchmark. I had to be Commando ready. I had no problem with motivation, exercise was already a compulsion and I'd get jittery if I couldn't get my daily fix.

Despite having competed internationally, Mr Cowell defied the typical beanpole runner's build. He was short, stocky and as fit as a mountain goat. There were five of us in sixth form who ran seriously; Keith, John, Jared, Katie and me. He took us under his wing. He entered us into the county cross country trials. We'd drive all over to various muddy courses listening to *The Stone Roses, James* and *Nirvana* on loop. I ran for the school and even on one occasion for Warwickshire at the Nationals outside Bristol, although at this level I was hopelessly outclassed. When Mr Cowell could, he'd run with us, coaching, giving tips and training advice.

'Remember, everyone always slows in the second half.'

We were breathless as he chatted away.

'It's the third quarter, that's the hardest. You've gone through the halfway point and your brain says you have that distance again.'

We were trying to keep up.

'The fourth quarter gets easier. You are nearly home. The third quarter, that's the time to push on. That is when everyone flags.'

We listened to the Oracle when he spoke,

'If you are fit, strong and well trained, most of your challenge is between your ears.'

We only raced once with Mr Cowell when he really opened the taps. He was in his mid-fifties and to underline his point, he left us all for dust as we started the second half. We'd been schooled, good runners push on in the third quarter.

During that next summer between my lower and upper sixth I won an inter-school competition in Warwickshire run by the local newspaper. The prize was a free three week Highland Rover Expedition with the Outward Bound Trust from Fort William in Scotland. As soon as school finished for the summer, I took the overnight sleeper train up. Over the next twenty one days we traced a massive 350 mile loop up Loch Ness by canoe and then trekked through the mountains getting re-supplied every four days. Outward Bound gave us barely enough food to survive and very little toilet roll. We had to grow up fast, take responsibility and fend for ourselves. I came home with a wispy beard and clothes so smelly that all attempts to wash out the stench proved futile. It was fantastic. My back felt strong and I could live my Royal Marine dream without all the killing.

I had one more year of A-levels but between revising and keeping fit, I wrote to all the Outward Bound Trust centres across the UK to see if I could get a job for the following summer. Eventually I hit gold. Although I didn't have the experience to be an instructor, the centre on Ullswater in the Lake District gave me a job in the kit room for £50 per week including bed and board. I had to finish my A-levels but then I was set for a continuation of my previous summer's adventure.

For the most part, this final year of school was relatively pain free. After my rugby spinal scare I tried my utmost to minimise my burden on the health service. I relied on ice and self-healing when I turned my ankles at cross country races and struggled for about a month on a tweaked hamstring brought on by a misjudged TaeKwonDo head kick.

Only one incident blotted my virtually clean slate at A&E. If I hadn't stood on broken glass with my bare foot, I would have managed to keep away from hospital for the entire year. This somewhat unfortunate incident hardly seems worth mentioning and was quickly resolved with a local anaesthetic and four stitches. I was getting a reputation for being disaster prone but shrugged these minor set-backs off and healed quickly. The limping didn't stop me revising, riding my bike and throwing my weights around. I could always find an outlet for my infinite energy. As soon as I finished my last exam Mum and Dad drove me to the Ullswater centre and dropped me with two bags and my trusty racer.

What could possibly go wrong?

Babushka, Babushka

Pete sat stoically, smiling, his sincere unflappable warmth radiating. I was struggling but I'd made it to the top of the ridge. He knew I wasn't my usual irrepressible self. We'd covered many miles together over the last two months matching one another stride for stride. With his jacket on against the buffeting wind and a genuine concern on his face, he suggested we call it a day.

'Do you want to head down and we can hitch a ride?'

Nineteen miles lay behind us and thirteen, the equivalent of a half marathon, still stretched ahead. I wasn't in great shape. It would be very easy to quit, let go of the bars and be back in the sports hall again.

I'd arrived in the Lake District eight weeks earlier full of anticipation about what lay ahead. During the previous summer on my Highland Rover Course, I'd embraced the values of the Outward Bound Trust, OBT. The three weeks of camping, walking, climbing, abseiling, canoeing and independent thinking had certainly helped me redefine my limits. I couldn't wait to be part of this inspiring organisation. From my research I knew the Trust had been founded during the height of the Second World War as an outdoor educational experience for young people. Forty five years on, they'd continued to take groups of school children with a mission to help them realise we are all capable of more than we think.

As soon as I arrived, I fell in love with the breathtaking location. On first impression it looked like paradise. The OBT centre on Ullswater is three quarters of the way up the lake, on the western shore and set in eighteen acres of gardens. With a rhododendron-lined winding driveway, a sweeping lawn down to a rocky beach and a four pillar door surround, it looks like a stately home. But as I crossed its threshold it quickly became clear outward appearances with both places and people can be deceiving.

At the twice weekly 'All Hands' meetings the centre's hierarchy quickly unfurled. The instructors acted as if they owned the place and sat at the front in the big comfy chairs. We, the support staff, shuffled in and stood at the back. The permanent team was small, with management principles stuck in colonial times. The organisation lived its founding principles on the hills with the visitors but not with its team. The front of house guest experience stood in stark contrast to the mood of the many despondent and demotivated staff. The previous year I had seen it through a pupil's eyes. Now I was on the teacher's side. For the first time in my life I was in the staff room alongside adults between classes dealing with the struggles of daily life.

My boss was a manager but still no happier than the rest. At first smiley and bubbly, like the centre's ground, he hid his darker side well. Outgoing and superficially effervescent, he did a mean *Van Morrison* at the local pub fuelled on a secret weakness for any strong spirit he could find. With a staccato wit, round tummy and mullet he fed his demon at night.

Reality hit hard and fast. I was eighteen years old and this was my first nine-to-five job. Caged in a cramped, sunless kit room, earning less than £1.50 per hour, the job was far from fulfilling. The company was unpredictable and the money wasn't enough to buy the *essentials* that I missed. To top up my weekly earnings, I got a part time evening job working tables at a local restaurant when they were short. With my moonlighting I was flush with cash compared to most. My couldn't-live-withouts were a twin cassette CD player and a growing collection of *The Doors*, *U2* and *Bob Marley* tapes. Luxuries, comforts and escape.

Not everyone was struggling with their lot. 'Pot Wash' John was the standout happy soul in our penitential social hierarchy. With an impenetrable Geordie lilt and his skin scrawled blue from self-applied ink, none of us understood much of what he said. He had an unapproachable aura, an unarticulated prisoner's frisson and edge. In all probability he saw a *parole* of washing pots here as highly preferable to where he'd been before. Beneath his jailhouse-tats he had an unshakeable stoicism, toothless smile and post-incarceration perspective that all of us lacked.

In this world of Russian Dolls, each painted layer was different from the next. Some light, some dark, coloured by lives of accumulated experience. Babushka camouflage, veneers of happiness, sharp wit or homemade body scrawls. It was my first taste of the real world and working with people who were struggling inside with self-created defensive facades. I'd come for adventure but found myself on the wrong side of the curtain in this self-development show.

In Pete I found a kindred spirit. I wanted to push myself, gain experience and enjoy the hills before university. He was probably a foot taller than me, Australian and, even when we trekked, never wore shoes. Three years older and a nomad, his personality was magnetic. On his world travels he'd ended up in Ullswater cleaning toilets and turning rooms. He read constantly, his conversation was engaging and his company addictive.

We were inseparable, instantly friends who enjoyed the healthy competition of stretching our limits. In the centre's hierarchy, we were support staff, anonymous, non-playing characters. When our jobs for the day were finished and I hadn't been rostered to a shift waiting tables, we had total freedom. We longed for space, fresh air and what was left of the light.

We would escape to the hills racing on our bikes to bag a mountain before dark. With small packs, bivvy bags and stoves we'd sleep high, wake early and hurtle back down to our locked steeds, spinning to get back before our morning clock ins. I was definitely in awe. We both had a deep aversion to conforming and accepting the staff's funk.

We'd already taken on most of the walking and biking challenges in the centre's *Instructor's Book*. We'd raced to the top of The Kirkstone Pass, Helvellyn and anything else that was timed. But none of these were as tough as what we had in mind, a thirty two mile hiking loop of the entire Ullswater Lake along the surrounding mountains and ridges. As far as we could see it had never been done before. We were anonymous in the prison hierarchy but this would put us forever in the centre's folklore. Convinced we were being true to the Outward Bound ideal of defying our perceived boundaries, we found ourselves nineteen miles deep, with thirteen miles ahead and me practically on my knees with exhaustion.

Hours earlier we'd both sat quietly over our breakfast; ten Weetabix and milk. It would be a big day, we needed the energy. Our plan wasn't complicated. The first leg hinged on gaining height on the trails that we knew before first light, then run-walking south along the ridges and western peaks to the Kirkstone Pass. We'd then regain height on the eastern ridges along the old Roman road heading to the top of Ullswater Lake and the small town of Pooley Bridge. Finally we'd have an easy yomp to the centre and our evening meal. It had sounded so simple as we'd planned it out from our hill top bivvy.

Before we even started I didn't feel great. I had a lump in my throat and swallowing was gravelly. But I put it down to the early hour. This would be our last adventure together. Summer was almost over and in a fortnight I'd be off to start university. The weather was perfect. We'd planned it for weeks, thought through our kit, food, route and navigation. I wasn't going to let Pete down because I felt a little groggy. I quietly reminded myself,

If you are fit, strong and well trained, most of your challenge is between your ears.

It was 3am when we set off. This was a serious endeavour and even Pete was wearing footwear. It had been dry for weeks, the trails were parched and we'd move quicker in our running shoes. Trudging from the centre, I figured I'd find my form as we went. As the darkness lifted, Pete broke trail, I fell in behind. Normally we were evenly paced and well matched. Today I was the passenger, drafting, placing my feet where he put his. Head down, locked in a battle inside. I believed I'd come good but was actually getting worse as the darkness melted away. However, the weather was on our side. It was turning into a glorious day as we crossed the lowlands of Matterdale Common and climbed to Great Dodd. We knew these trails well and blew over Stybarrow Dodd, Helvellyn, the beautifully named Dollywagon Pike and then Hart and Dove Crag.

The miles and cairns were passing but I was in a trance. Pete assured me we were making good progress. I wasn't finding my mojo and he'd patiently wait at the top of each steep drag as I plodded up, frustrated by my lack of vim. We crossed Red Screes and zipped down the winding Kilnshaw Chimney, hardly pausing at the top of the Kirkstone Pass.

We pushed on to the second phase. After the long dig up to Stony Cove Pike we would have all the big climbs behind us, but my resolve was slowly ebbing away. Gravity was getting stronger and Pete was soon a dot in the distance. I couldn't seem to kick start my system. I ate but the food had no effect. The wind, channelled by the hills, was strong and knocked me sideways. I was slipping away, stumbling, losing the fight. I couldn't figure it out and was struggling to stand. This wasn't me. Cursing, I drove on. It was the longest, hardest climb I had ever done. As I crested, there he sat in his jacket offering me a free pass.

'Do you want to head down and we can hitch a ride?'

He was happy to call it a day, get me home, live to fight another day. He was in great shape and could easily push on but knew I was having an uncharacteristic nightmare. If we turned now we'd be back at the Kirkstone Pass in thirty minutes. Being accomplished hitchers, we'd be in the warmth of the centre in two hours at the very maximum. It was very tempting as I stood level with him on the trail, the wind buffeted my pack. I was completely spent and could easily let my fingers slip from the bar.

I jolted from the dream.

I could hear the pounding of my heart.

A stillness closed in my mind. Sharp focus, clarity.

35

'No.'

An anger burned inside me. I was mad at myself. I wasn't ready to fail in front of Pete or face public humiliation at the centre. I wasn't going to turn back and admit defeat. We were going to loop Ullswater in a day. There was only one path and that was the way we had planned.

'Let's run!'

He looked at me perplexed, I suspect wondering how long I'd last.

I gritted my teeth and we ran. Instantly I felt better. Hardly stopping we yomped the ridge passed Rampsgill Head, Red Crag, Loadpot Hill and Barton Fell. For the first time that day I was vividly awake and felt in control. We were getting home, shifting, getting this thing done. We didn't relent on the pace until we reached the civilisation of Pooley Bridge at the north end of Lake Ullswater. From here we had a mere six miles back to the centre. As we finally padded down the access road to the Outward Bound Trust's pillared front door we felt elated.

We'd done it, pulled off a heroic feat and looped Ullswater Lake in a day. I'd gone somewhere hard and dark in my mind. We'd snatched victory from the jaws of defeat. Famished and tired, we grabbed some food and regaled the other staff with our adventures. I felt achy, light headed and my throat was very sore when I went to bed.

Two days later, I was in Penrith hospital, under observation, on a drip and diagnosed with acute glandular fever. It was the first time my endurance feats hospitalised me. I guess I still had some work to do on recognising the difference between when the problem was *between my ears* or rather a loud siren screaming for me to physically stop. It has never been a distinction that has come naturally. Again I'd failed to foresee the consequences of my actions and was experiencing first-hand how deep my single minded streak could take me.

As I lay in the hospital bed, I had a long time to reflect on my first taste of working life. It had been only eight weeks but had been the polar opposite of what I'd expected. What was very clear was that toiling for a pittance definitely wasn't for me. Perhaps more importantly I'd not enjoyed the uncomfortable contrast between the front of house show and the mood of the cast. I was witnessing first hand despondent adults, post education, with families and responsibilities, trying to cope successfully and unsuccessfully with the realities of poor reward and the daily grind.

My babushka veneers were pretty light, a wee red-headed bairn, a teenager with sports and outdoor gear. I'd been born free, somewhat closeted and only lived with respect and equality. Hospitalised many times but never touched with internal scars to camouflage and disguise. Neither Pete nor I had been ready to be dragged down by the negativity. We'd escaped, challenged ourselves, shaped and defined our own identities in the hills.

It had been a rich summer but not in the ways I'd expected. I was not quite nineteen and already sensed I had an unusually strong drive. But I hadn't yet joined the dots on what a potent fuel my search for stimulation and resistance to monotony could ignite. There was a lot to consider as I watched the tube drip into my arm.

However, my much more immediate concern was that this was my second A&E trip in a year. I had been doing so well! I was discharged and headed home two weeks earlier than planned to get recovered and ready to start university. Surely I couldn't get myself into any more trouble.

Lucky Linds

Once again I bounced back from my hospital stay and a fortnight later started at the University of Southampton.

With the ups and downs of the last two years, Mum and Dad didn't voice their concerns but probably wondered where my gung ho! *Now Get Out of That* attitude would lead me next. Oblivious to any peril, I was ready to fly the coop when they nervously dropped me off for Freshers Week.

As they drove away, it dawned on me that I had total independence. I was determined to make the most of the opportunity. The scaffolding that had enveloped my childhood development was gone. I was studying History and my weekly teaching contact time was minimal. There were no classroom walls and no one was checking whether I did the work, attended lectures or digested my reading lists. Much of my learning would be down to self-motivation and discipline. I was living with the perfect balance of freedom, stimulation and deadlines. I thrived on the variety, discovery and creativity. The risk of being unprepared, not handing in essays and found wanting in my weekly tutorials kept me zeroed on my goal.

Of course there were endless distractions for a busy mind. I threw myself into my studies but that wasn't enough to drain my inexhaustible battery. With my inherent love of being busy, I got involved with clubs, events and societies. I also demonstrated some incredibly poor emotional intelligence. One evening I gave Mum an extended fright when I called her from the hall's phone box feeling very excited.

'I'm off bungy jumping' I announced just before the last ten pence beeped in my ear.

I can now see, given my track record of unintentional self-harm, why she may have become a little anxious. Not thinking any more about it, I got a message from the accommodation administrator a week later asking me to call my very worried mother. I made sure to telephone home regularly from then on.

There was always something to do and I was having a ball. I made friends, bounced between lectures, tutorials and the library. I went to the gym, rode my bike and ran. I joined the canoe club and kept up my martial arts. I was catered for in my Halls of Residence and managed to sweet talk the kitchen staff into putting my evening meals aside whenever I was late. Even three weeks on crutches nursing a broken toe from a TaeKwonDo tournament couldn't dampen my enthusiasm for my busy, absorbing life. I didn't fancy a return home over the summer holidays and in my second term started to wonder how I could better last year's Lake District adventures.

Work in America.

They were handing out leaflets on the Student Union steps. Over lunch I found myself sitting in a lecture hall listening to AirPic's pitch from older students. Naturally, with my underdeveloped ability to see the downside, it sounded great. The programme was run through the British University North America Club, BUNAC. By the end of the hour I'd made a decision and was committed. What an opportunity. We'd get a temporary work visa, rent a shared house, hire cars and go door-to-door, selling aerial photos of people's homes. It all sounded totally legitimate.

An idyllic summer living in America stretched ahead. In my world everyone was honest and my naive mind couldn't see any catches. The elephant in the room, there was no salary. We'd only earn commission on what we sold. No sales, no money. My track record was far from a glowing testament towards possessing any clairvoyant gift. My recent bungee jumping was simply the latest reckless thing in nearly two decades of not looking before I leapt. I talked it through with

Dad and he thought it was a bad idea. But I was deaf to his wisdom and adamant I'd go. I was convinced, like a modern day Dick Whittington, I'd make my fortune in the States. I suspect he already knew I wouldn't but, hoped I might learn something from the experience.

Plans were set, I promised to call every week. As soon as my third term was done, I flew with Virgin Atlantic and couldn't wait to hit the streets. Skipping the official visa orientation, I caught a Greyhound bus two hours north of New York to the hotel for my door-to-door sales training. This was a long way from the boot room at the Ullswater Outward Bound centre. I was in deep but determined to prove I'd made the right decision.

Hard work trumps talent.

Things had to start going my way!

And sometimes being a reckless bungee jumper has its upsides.

'Who'd come to America to meet their wife?' I scoffed on my second day of the AirPic training when I'd been introduced to two managers who'd returned as a couple from a previous year's courtship. I was young, free and single, way too independent to get hitched.

A week later at the first regional sales meet, I wasn't so high minded in my disdain. She had long blonde hair, denim shorts, white Converse Chuck Taylors and slim tanned legs. Heads turned when she walked in the room. A stunner. Girls like this never even looked at me.

'I've locked my keys in my car,' she announced to the room.

Think! Think! Be the knight in shining armour!

'My Dad's a member of the AA,' it was a goofy line but it was the best I had. 'He's got international cover. I'll pretend it's my car and get some help.'

Trying to sound cool but a nervous mess inside, I was her saviour and at least until the recovery truck arrived she had to talk to me to be polite. Her name was Lindsey or as everyone called her, Linds. I was still nineteen and she was three

40

years older than me. What's more, she had recently graduated. She had the most incredible blue eyes and was way out of my league. I could hardly believe my luck, I probably had an hour tops in this heady place amongst the angels. But I knew I didn't have a chance and quickly accepted that this afternoon in the car park waiting for the American AA was the probable start and end of our short relationship. In all likelihood, I would be the only one even classifying it as a 'relationship'.

Like a lovestruck teenager, I thought about Linds all the following week. She was in another team about two hours north of us up the Hudson River. I'd see her at the next sales meeting and possibly have a chat at the company party on the beach in Connecticut in about ten days' time.

Incredibly my AA pick-up line worked. It was a whirlwind summer and beyond my wildest dreams. We found each other at the beach party and seemed to connect. We were inseparable and would talk most days on the phone. When we got together it was electric, fun and always unpredictable. We planned a big road trip once our twelve week AirPic tour was done. We camped in upstate New York not sleeping all night for fear of being attacked by bears. We rode mountain bikes in empty ski resorts, gazed in wonder from the bow of the *Spirit of Niagara* and listened to *Meat Loaf* on all night radio channels as we raced back to get our flight from JFK.

When we got back from America I had two more years of study. After a few months of long distance calls, Linds moved to Southampton, got a room and a job. I borrowed a tandem from my folks that we rode out to the New Forest, Salisbury and Stonehenge. The following summer we caught the ferry to Cherbourg and over three weeks headed south through France to the Alps. Perhaps she should have seen the red flags that, with hindsight, were fairly apparent in the early stages of our relationship,

'It's lucky we have the disc brake!'

41

Linds yelled over the wind as we raced down a mountain pass.

'We haven't. When I fixed the puncture, I couldn't figure out how to reconnect it,' I confessed as we swept through the next fast bend. 'We've been riding two days without it, just the rims.'

I took a whack to the ribs. She was clearly less oblivious to the potentially fatal consequences.

We were the best of friends, buddies, forever fooling around. Spontaneous, carefree, always there for each other. We'd go to fitness classes, circuits and Linds even got me to occasionally go to a nightclub. Secretly I preferred a few pints and a plate of cheesy, salsa nachos at *The Crown*.

***

It was 1995 when I finished my finals and moved in with Linds in Milton Keynes. By this time she had a proper, grown-up job on a graduate training scheme at the head office of a major high street bank. My own applications hadn't been quite so successful. Tesco had had the front and perhaps high minded pettiness to pen their rejection to me with, 'We require a higher calibre of graduate.'

But I reasoned that every cloud has a silver lining and things happen for a reason. If I'd secured a graduate training job I could have been placed anywhere around the country and we'd have been apart. I knew with Linds I'd found a keeper. I also relished a post-university life with no responsibilities, some money and none of the jeopardy of looming essays, assignments or exams. I got a job working in a call centre and now had freedom and disposable income.

Buzzing around in our first car with its cubby holes crammed full of dance and grunge tapes, I embodied the spirit of perpetual motion. By day, I took electricity metre readings until I was promoted to the noisy telesales floor. In the evening I taught circuits, step, boxercise and aqua aerobics. The extra money was great but the big benefit was that it gave me free access to various local gyms. I was always on the go. My default was a compulsion to move and continually occupy my mind. I flitted from one thing to the next. Movement and busyness brought focus and were a temporary respite from my constantly channel hopping internal radio dial.

It didn't take much to trigger my windsurfing obsession, merely a lone sailboarder buzzing back and forth across a sun kissed bay. His canvas tight, ripping along, skimming, barely touching the water. The speed, the grace, it looked the most wondrous thing. Instantly I became hooked, building a collection of boards and gear. I'd watch flags, leaves, trees, anything to tell me whether we were in for a blow. I was all in and it influenced my every thought in a sometimes unhealthy way. If it was breezy and social plans stopped me sailing, I'd get moody and sulky. It strained things but I couldn't seem to will myself to change. If I got my blast, all was quiet in my mind, the chattering and constant thought cycle were muted and still.

Our holidays were always guaranteed wind meccas; Greece, the Canaries, we even honeymooned on the Red Sea. For these weeks of the year I felt invincible but in the last days of our trips I'd ache inside. Like Peter Pan I longed to stay in Never-Never Land and craved the soaring, on tap exhilaration every day.

***

I'm not quite sure who came up with the affectionate moniker *Lucky Linds*. Its inception was definitely from my colleagues rather than Linds' friends. It was most certainly rooted in a deep sympathy for having to live with me. If my memory serves me right I think it was my first sales manager, the wonderfully named and equally glorious, Tony Tatton-Brown.

'How's the *Lucky Linds* after the weekend?'

And it stuck.

Lucky Linds.

I remember the moment she swept into the room in America like it was yesterday. She was out of my league. It's beyond me why she fell for me and why she has stuck with me throughout. I know who the lucky one *really* is. I'd met someone who cared for me, thought I was funny and made me laugh. Our childhoods couldn't have been more different but she is my soulmate.

Perhaps surreptitiously I'd found someone with boundless patience to make allowances for the adult-boy in me. In the coming years I'd prove very adept at continually testing this quality to its limit.

Tour De Trigs

Psycho Dave was a wild man. His real name is Dave Quinn. He earned his nickname on my stag-do after various antics left him with a bite mark matching my teeth on his belly. We also nearly drowned on his, when a white water rafting accident had us crawling underwater through a fallen tree. He was unpredictable, very funny and I liked him a lot.

We met when we were both doing telesales. We went to the gym in the mornings and worked together at night. He was instantly likeable, with a compelling, magnetic soul. When we added alcohol he went psycho, but even that was enormous fun. One time sitting in a pub while nonchalantly examining my work mobile phone he simply dropped it in the nearest pint. As I fished the dead thing out, he almost fell off his chair in peals of laughter. Chaos followed him everywhere and that made him very stimulating. Dave was fearless, ready to take on anything, but he talked of the Tour de Trigs in hushed, reverential tones with a post-traumatic, thousand mile stare.

'The Tour. Unless you were there, you wouldn't know.'

He'd riff endlessly of this mythical race. I'd looped Ullswater Lake in a day and I couldn't let go of his smack talk. We both knew we had to do the Tour. It sounded uncomfortable, but not impossible.

On paper it looked easy. The Tour de Trigs is a famous long distance winter walking race and always falls over the first weekend of December. It is a fifty mile orienteering challenge, bookended by a staggered start and a 24-hour cut off. The first group sets off at 10am on Saturday and needs to be back at the finish with a fully punched waypoint card by 9.59am on Sunday. The race HQ is at Bloxham School, south of Banbury and the route loops through north Oxfordshire, Warwickshire and Northamptonshire. This is farming country, tame and relatively flat. It is scarcely wilderness. Well at least it isn't in the summer. We were to find out how brutal it is in winter the hard way. It is organised by the region's scout groups with my old friends, St John Ambulance, drafted in for medical assistance.

Dave *had* to be 'bigging' this up.

I was four years out of university and we entered the December 1998 edition. Psycho set up some practice walks before the event to break in our boots, test gear and improve our night navigation. We'd normally finish at a pub and throughout October and November the evenings were mild. We were hardly able to comprehend Dave's hype. Invariably after a post-walk pint, the third member of the team, Declan and I felt hugely optimistic. Before we knew it the race was upon us.

'First of all we have a kit inspection.'

Dave, the wily veteran, directed us through the rigorous checks. We had to empty our packs showing the inspectors that we had the prerequisite warm layers, spare socks, waterproofs, food, medical kits, bivvy and sleeping bags, safety blankets, lights, spares and other sundries.

'Next the holding pen.'

We sat waiting for our call to the map room. Dave was clutching our 1:50,000 Ordnance Survey map in its waterproof case and pens for plotting the route. The mischief and mayhem that normally surrounded him were gone. He was business-like now, our group leader.

'When we are through, we'll be given our coordinate sheets. There are normally over a hundred waypoints we'll have to plot.'

We had our orienteering cards, white and shaped like a trigpoint, on string hanging from our necks.

'Team Fifty Two.'

We were called through.

'Here are your waypoints lads,' a bearded Scout master handed us our sheet.

'You have thirty minutes to get as much plotted as possible. When we call, you have to start.'

We found the nearest table and started marking the six digit OS coordinates with small crosses on our map. Never good with numbers, I found it was mind numbingly hard as we followed the faint blue horizontal and vertical lines. I was overdressed, hot and my brain jammed with concentration. It was like patting my head whilst rubbing my stomach. Fortunately Dave and Declan took charge and left me with the simple job of reading the long numbers slowly.

'Team Fifty Two. Time's up. Off you go.'

We were barely halfway through marking the route. Hustled out, we packed up and would have to finish our plotting later at a dry checkpoint. As soon as we left the hall the biting wind hit us, whipping through our layers. It instantly cooled the sweat patches after our furious indoor scribbling. With fifty miles ahead of us, Dave set the pace.

'We need to cover as much ground as we can in the daylight.'

With our start time and mapping it was now about 11.15am. We had less than five hours of daylight until sundown at 4pm. We then faced a likely fifteen hours of night navigation. The mercury was barely touching four degrees Celsius. With the wind chill, the benign temperatures of our practice walks had lulled Declan and I into a false sense of readiness for what lay ahead. The Tour was schooling us fast.

Unless you were there.

Dave was spot on with his navigation. The best I'd ever seen. We hit every mark and yomped for the first few hours. But as the afternoon wore on, the Tour took its first casualty when Declan's boots cut into his feet. At the eleven mile checkpoint he declared in his Irish brogue.

'I'm done boys. Yews push on without me.'

For safety, Dave and I couldn't leave as a pair so we hitched onto an intact team of three. We were now five and night would come before we reached the next checkpoint. Everything slowed when it got dark. The navigation was harder with the loss of easy sight points to a gap in the hedge, turn or stile. Every path had to be followed with a bearing, we couldn't afford to get disorientated. We clomped through ploughed fields, our boots thick and heavy with accumulated mud. It was tough. We clambered through ditches, squeezed through narrow, brambly gateways, over electric fences, slipping and sliding down wet pathways and ground up steep, short climbs. All we could do was push on. It was desolate and wild. We trudged through twinkling, quiet villages, past windmills, over blustery hilltops, with dark views and distant towns glowing on the horizon. The odd car would illuminate lost lanes and fields, the drivers warm inside, oblivious to our presence. We were between two worlds, out on the perimeter.

At about 5am the light started to imperceptibly change. Night turned to a darker shade of grey. Time was slipping through our fingers to the 24-hour cut off. We never thought of stopping, twenty miles to go, fifteen, then ten. Our legs were tired, feet numb and sore, toes wet and blistered. One foot in front of the next, it was relentless. All we could do was trudge to the next checkpoint. With glowing cheeks and beyond exhausted I'd unwittingly found a happy place. Finally, this was living my Commando dream. My mind was clear. My channel hopping radio dial was locked on one goal. All my worries, petty concerns were telescoped away. Suffering equalled pleasure. Here, in this non-conformist world, I'd found inner peace. I felt like me and I didn't want it to end.

Psycho Dave was right.

Unless you were there.

Eventually we clumped up the final climb back to Bloxham school. As we finished, we hugged, both too exhausted to speak. Over breakfast we both had the thousand mile stare. Soggy toast, beans and cooked tinned tomatoes, washed down with sugary lukewarm tea. Food had never tasted so good. Over half of the starters didn't finish. We'd hardly covered ourselves in glory but we crossed the line in under twenty three hours. The winning teams, who did the Tour de Trigs year after year and knew the limited route variations, had come in nearly eight hours earlier. Linds picked us up and deserved some conversation on the way home but my battery was finally drained, I was asleep before we'd passed the Bloxham village boundary.

What an adventure. I'd crossed a Rubicon, found a quiet place. Somehow I'd travelled through a day and the busy voice in my head had been silent. I'd lived purely in the moment, accelerated through time. In the bleakness of the Tour, I'd found mental stillness and physical exhaustion. Strangely this depleting tranquillity seemed preferable to the synaptic half thoughts and frustrations that perpetually darted and bubbled away. Unwittingly I was finding coping strategies for something running invisibly amok in my mind.

Back in the real world all the whirlwind of restless thoughts, worries, decisions and confused emotions accelerated into a cacophony again.

The Question

Psycho Dave was calling me on my work phone. He *never* called my work phone.

It was March 1999, four months on from the Tour.

I hesitated.

Why's he calling?

Of course I picked up.

'How do you fancy doing the London Marathon?'

'What?'

'It's five weeks away. My brother has a charity spot and he's had to pull out. Anyone that can raise £1,200 can have his place.'

For a nano-second I considered it. I had no doubt my Duracell battery had a long charge but was unsure I could run a marathon. I regularly jogged for forty minutes, was a gym bunny and was riding more and more on my road bike and turbo trainer. Due to inconsistent weather and unpredictable blows my obsession with windsurfing had morphed into frustration. Recently it agitated more than calmed me. I could control and predict the gym, being on two wheels or running and they settled me. What's more, these hobbies weren't so all-consuming or unreasonable which was better for my relationship with Linds. Time on tarmac had an endpoint and could be planned into a weekend's social schedule.

However, I *was* a long way from being a distance runner or an endurance athlete. I was fit, would exercise six days per week but my training was far from structured. I would do whatever I fancied. A marathon was surely beyond me. There was no way I was ready to cover 26.2 miles. But instinctively I sensed what happened next would be one of the most important decisions I ever made.

My thoughts stopped spinning. My eye caught the curly stretched cord of the phone, the computer, my fingers resting lightly on its keys. I could feel my suit trousers, my belt, the tightness of my collar and tie. The choking monotony of the day stretched ahead. Linds and I were both toiling and climbing our respective career ladders. We were growing up, no longer the carefree kids who had raced around America or cycled to the Alps. We had to earn, pay bills and couldn't simply cut free. I had accountability, was managing people and lived in a world I felt I couldn't control. I'd loved the freedom and independence of university and knew I wasn't afraid of hard work. But it was different now; occasionally creative, more often a dull, repetitive routine. I'd lost my autonomy and had responsibilities. Through the morning I'd sit working, silently listening to my thoughts, daydreams and subatomic neural butterflies that never settled in my mind.

At lunch time I'd leave work in search of a sandwich. Outside blinking in the sun, I'd feel the warmth on my face and see the wind in the trees. In the building I'd left a person that didn't feel like me. The suit, the tie, the boring meetings, the drudgery. I longed to move, escape and be free again. The Tour de Trigs had re-ignited my wanderlust and I wanted to return to the quiet place and mute the continuous snatches of worries, frustration and feeling trapped. My fingertips brushed lightly, clicking, undulating over my keyboard frets. I was playing by the rules, living in a dopamine desert, slowly dying inside.

Danger.

Exhilaration.

My heart accelerated.

'Go on then.' I replied, 'Why not?'

The rush of leaping with no thought of consequences. I felt a flutter, a clarity in my mind. I genuinely wasn't sure I could run a marathon and in an instant I was gripped. The 1999 London Marathon was a lifeline. In five weeks I had the opportunity to do something extraordinary. After a little back and forth with the charity, I was signed up. I had to raise £1,200 and then run 26.2 miles.

I felt invigorated, re-charged. The fog rolled back and my mind became laser focused.

Chasing The Dopamine Dragon

It was cold and misty at the 1999 London Marathon start on Blackheath Common. The queues for the portaloos were massive and I dreaded what I'd find when it was my turn in the green plastic box. Luckily, I needed to do nothing more than stand and try not to inhale the noxious fumes.

In the late 1990s to say you'd 'done' the London Marathon was the ultimate party brag. It was truly a marque endurance event with over 30,000 competitors. I'd never been involved with anything as big and universally recognised. The build-up had been intoxicating and I'd thought of little else for five weeks. Publicly I was styling it out but inside I couldn't escape my nagging worries. I had no idea how I would do and was beyond nervous. A decade earlier, I'd competed in school cross country races but they were only ever three to four miles. Now I faced 26.2. I was a complete novice, an endurance virgin who knew nothing about distance running, what to wear, fuelling or the ideal pace. What's more, I'd hardly had any time to properly prepare without risking getting injured or ill.

It was a cold grey morning and I was standing at the start of one of the world's largest mass participant city marathons. As we followed the crowds nervously to the predicted finish time pens, I was over-lubed with generous smears of Vaseline. I wasn't taking any chances with rubs or blisters.

What had I done?

My heart pounded in my chest. Huge surges of adrenaline washed over me. Every synapse tingling and alert. But despite the tsunami of nervous excitement coursing through me, I was clearly backing myself. Although I didn't realise it, something inside me wasn't worried about whether I'd finish and had made a decision to find out how fast I could run. Impulsively and with no thought of consequences, I decided to tuck myself in with the three and a half hour group.

What could possibly go wrong?

Rustling in a bin bag fashioned with head and arm holes, I jigged on the spot trying to settle my nerves, warm my legs and stave off the chill. As I looked about, everyone seemed as worried as me. With a long horn blast, we started to shuffle forwards. Twenty six point two miles stretched ahead.

Crammed like a hypnotic yo-yoing tube train, the pack was close. Running in such a large, tight group was new to me. There was the odd nudge, elbow, crossing of feet and apology. There was no angst, we were all fellow travellers, a long way from the podium and wanting to finish. My nerves quickly settled and so did the pace. The initial miles flew by easily. Before I knew it we were looping through Greenwich and around the Cutty Sark, carried by the crowd, the excitement and euphoria. The next landmark was the iconic Tower Bridge and famous London Keep. Within the blink of an eye we'd run ten miles.

This was a breeze.

As we headed out towards the Docklands passing through mile thirteen, the front runners flew by on the opposite carriageway at mile twenty two heading towards the finish. They were leading an international marathon and moving at an eye-watering speed. We were nine miles behind them and a long way off their race winning pace. Despite this minor dent to my ego, my spirits were rising as I went through the halfway point in just over an hour and a half.

Oh, I have so got this.

All of that was going to change! At mile fourteen, an unexpected gravitational heaviness gripped my stride. My naivety and lack of preparation weighed on my back like an overfilled rucksack. Alarming memories of my teenage twenty mile smash into 'the wall' experience swirled in my mind. I willed myself to go but I couldn't sustain my first half speed. Mr Cowell had coached, good runners always push in the second half. I was in the infamous third quarter and *everyone* was streaming past me like I'd dropped an anchor. The harder I tried, the slower and heavier my stride.

Panic.

I'd *seriously* misjudged my pace. By mile nineteen, my mind detached from my body, sensation ebbed away. It was like running in sticky tar, travelling backwards. I never thought of stopping but dreaded the long seven mile road stretching ahead. As I slogged through mile twenty two, where we'd seen the lead pack earlier, the tail-end runners at the back of the field were going through mile thirteen. I blinked,

Was that a Rhino?

On the other carriageway, I caught sight of two runners in huge grey horned costumes. I made a mental note never to run the marathon dressed as an endangered African species. I was a long way from owning the day. I was being humbled and schooled. I clearly had a lot to learn about endurance sports. The two miles along The Embankment took forever. Every time I looked up, Big Ben seemed just as far away as before. My peripheral sight blurred as my energy reserves hit empty. I was slipping into the dreaded letterbox vision. System shutdown. These were long miles. I willed myself to go faster but had nothing. Step by step I fought on. It took forever.

And then miraculously, as I skirted Parliament Square, I felt the vim course back into my tired muscles. For the first time I knew my marathon was nearly done. I opened my stride towards Buckingham Palace, past Victoria Fountain, on to The Mall and the finish. With a burst of speed I was over the line, in three hours and thirty four minutes. Despite my crushing second half, incredibly my final time wasn't a million miles from what I'd hoped for at the start. After five weeks preparation, I'd only gone and 'done' the London Marathon!

I felt indestructible. Well that was until I ran the following Wednesday, three days after my 26.2 mile jaunt. Despite feeling invincible, I'd obviously done some deep tissue damage. Within 300 metres I was limping back to the gym after a worrying twang in my knee.

Idiot.

Clearly I had to let my body heal and give my legs a rest. The next day I lowered myself in the pool, pulled down my brand new goggles and started swimming length after length. I'd not swum seriously for ten years. It felt good, like slipping on an old, comfortable pair of shoes, there was no dissonance or incongruity. Old memories flickered, circuit lights came to life; my teenage efforts, humiliation with Warwick Tri, time with Paul, indelible images from his well thumbed *220 Triathlon* magazines, pictures of the greats battling in the lava fields of Hawaii.

I was amazed it was still in circulation and bought that month's copy of *220*. In the 'up and coming' race section I saw and entered a short course sprint race in early September 1999 near Heathrow Airport, only an hour from home. After over a decade I was going to finally become a triathlete.

***

Of course, ten months on I'd plunged down an obsessive triathlon rabbit hole; training, buying gear and absorbing everything I could. Another friend, Neil, who I'd known for nearly five years, was the level headed one in our group. We'd regularly ride our road bikes together through the summer and were inseparable at spinning classes throughout winter.

'So where are you going with triathlon?'

Like I was going anywhere. But Neil did have a point, my commitment and all-consuming passions were already well known. Our house was filled with new tri-gear and I'd quickly assumed the identity of a triathlete.

'I'm going to do some sprint and Olympic distance races. But an Ironman, that would be insane.'

And when I said it, I genuinely believed it. But slowly something grew inside. I was reading armchair explorer books on Everest, K2, the polar regions and epic ocean races. As I sat there turning the pages my own life couldn't have stood in starker contrast. Nine-to-five, I was wearing a suit, cufflinked shirts, sometimes a tie. With a laptop, phone and my polished leather shoes, I was hiding behind an ill-fitting babushka veneer, burying the real me. A quiet discontent bubbled in my mind, like a supernova ready to explode. I was a short course triathlete, a gym bunny, living the suburban dream, slowly sedated by the insidious domestication of working life. This wasn't how I imagined it would be when I'd told my sixth form teacher, *I'd like to be a Royal Marine.* The only person I was kidding that I actually had *the strength of mind* to live the commando life was me.

Is this it?

The neural butterflies were doing warp speed laps in my mind. In the toughness of the Tour de Trigs and the London Marathon I'd been absorbed. In this newly discovered endurance world I'd stripped back the layers and found who I wanted to be. I'd discovered escape, distraction and an unlimited natural supply of the ultimate recreational drug, dopamine.

The confirmation email popped on my screen.

'Congratulations on your entry into Ironman Lake Placid 2001'.

Impulsive.

Stimulation seeking.

No thought of consequences.

I'd figure it out as I went.

I lay back and let the high voltage electrify my cells.

How To Eat An Elephant

I landed heavily on the road.

Head, shoulder, arm, hip.

A crumpled heap, my face grating on the tarmac.

For a split second everything stopped and then unbelievable, numbing pain.

I'd been hit by a car!

It was the perfect summer evening for a ride. Warm, not a breath of wind and I was nearly done, turning a big gear, less than a few minutes from the gym. The surface was smooth, the gradient slightly downhill and the bike was shifting. As I approached the roundabout I looked. All clear to the right. No need to slow, I pushed my pedals, maintaining my hurtling flight. I clocked the car, it was black and coming in hot from the left. I was sure it was braking, convinced they m*ust* have seen me. I had the right-of-way and thought no more about it.

But, as Neil said afterwards, 'Think like a motorbike. Unless you've made eye contact, they haven't seen you. In an accident you carry all the downside and have to be ready to stop. Assume you're invisible.'

Well when I magically appeared on this driver's bonnet, I must have given him the shock of his life.

Everything happened so quickly. There was no slow-motion reverie, where I had a zen-like perspective or out of body experience. Instead it was raw, violent and out of control. Metal against my ankle and calf, my back wheel suddenly weightless. Flying up, scooped skyward, the bike torn away, dragged under the car. I heard the screech of tyres, the scraping of parts on the road. In the next instance, with the vehicle braking hard, I was thrown forwards like a rag doll. Whilst in mid-air, hurtling toward the tarmac with a car inches behind me, the depth of my obsession became crystal clear as my single thought was,

Oh no! Ironman!

I smashed onto the road.

A split second of stillness and then the pain was beyond anything I'd experienced before.

Explosive.

Ironman!

I was lying, half-conscious in the middle of a fast and busy roundabout in Milton Keynes. I'd been hit by one car and knew there could be more coming. Instinctively I stood, limped to the central reservation and collapsed on the gravel. Helpless, foetal, I drifted in and out of awareness. My bleeding hand scrunched like a claw in front of my numb face. I couldn't feel my right side. I didn't dare imagine what damage had been done. As I came around there were feet and ankles, voices, asking my name, nearest and dearest's telephone numbers. I let go and put my trust in kind strangers. I closed my eyes and waited for the ambulance. My one recurring thought.

Ironman Lake Placid is three weeks away.

***

For the best part of a year I'd lived a life of extremes. I was in deep, really deep. I'd entered ten months earlier and the shift in my thinking had been seismic. As soon as the confirmation email had appeared in my inbox I'd committed every fibre to the challenge. My every thought and action were driven by the reality *I've entered an Ironman!* The enormity of the distances haunted me. A 2.4 mile swim! Then 112 mile bike! Followed by a marathon! All in a day!! I'd never struggled to exercise, always fuelled by an insatiable restlessness inside. But with the 29th July 2001 locked in my calendar my motivation had been beyond anything I'd ever experienced before.

Of course my boundless enthusiasm couldn't overcome the fact I was clueless on how to prepare for this 140.6 mile race. Nobody I knew had done an Ironman and in 2001 the Internet was still in its embryonic development. We were in the technology dark ages, desktop computers were expensive and laptops were very rare. There weren't smartphones, blogs, forums, social media platforms or podcasts. I could read articles in *220 Triathlon* magazine but these were mainly focused on UK domestic sprint and Olympic distance triathlon races. There was no obvious reference material or expert I could turn to. I was on my own. Necessity would have to be my mother of invention and I needed to get *very* inventive.

My endurance experience to date did little to fill me with belief in any natural ability to succeed in such an enormous challenge. I'd survived the 1999 London Marathon but had fallen short of my expectations in the second half. Although I'd run it with five weeks' notice, it had humbled me. This time I had just under a year to get ready and had well and truly thrown myself in the deep end. I was harbouring no illusions that I could simply rock up to the start in my plimsolls and hope for the best. With almost guaranteed public humiliation if I stayed as I was, I did the only thing I knew how to do, I went all in.

Hard work trumps talent!

Miraculously as the reality of what I'd entered came crashing down on me, my mind cleared. I had a single purpose and the spinning radio dial and the chatter all vanished. The race would start on the 29th July 2001 with or without me. In the eye of this self-created storm all was calm. I had less than a year to get myself ready and become an Ironman.

The maths was simple. I looked at each of the disciplines and broke them down. If I was going to eat an elephant, I'd better do it one bite at a time. The 2.4 mile swim equates to 3,800 metres. In August 2000 when I started my build up to Lake Placid, that sounded a *very* long way. I regularly swam in a standard 25 metre pool and could do sixty lengths, about 1,500 metres, in under thirty minutes. Therefore to cover the Ironman distance I would have to swim 152 lengths continuously. Taking one bite at a time, I built up, gradually increasing my distance, toughening my body and mind.

The bike for an Ironman is 112 miles. I pulled out some paper and a calculator. If I could manage an average of 16 miles per hour it would take me seven hours. If I could achieve 18 mph I'd be round in six and a half. I rode in the evenings on the roads if it was light and on my turbo trainer in the depths of winter. Going out in most weather with the exception of icy conditions, I built up my cycling time at weekends starting with three hour blocks, then four, five and all the way up to six. I knew to have any chance of finishing I had to condition my engine and 'soft bits' and still have the reserves to run a marathon.

A marathon!

A 26.2 mile run after the longest swim and bike ride of my life was mind blowing. In 1999 I'd been beasted at the stand-alone London Marathon but I quickly started to rationalise what was to come. I knew I needed to structure my preparation so I took the plunge and joined Milton Keynes Run Club.

The first rule of Run Club… You do NOT talk about Run Club.

I'd chuckle to myself as I parked, nervous butterflies flitting inside. After a few weeks my body adapted and I found keeping up with the faster runners gave me speed and endurance. I'd simply turn my brain off and fall into lockstep. The group dynamic also gave me the motivation to run every two to three days to ensure I was ready for my next pounding. I felt a very different athlete from the teenage boy who'd been left behind by Warwick Tri.

By the time I entered Ironman Lake Placid in August 2000, I'd been training at a different level for over a year. It hadn't happened overnight but unwittingly I'd experienced a gradual incremental creep of what constituted normal. Unconsciously I was repeatedly stepping over and redefining invisible boundaries. From sheer necessity, I was doing things out of my comfort zone, once, twice, then they became routine, a habit. Before I knew it I'd forgotten the previous self-imposed limit.

But despite my rudimentary paper and pen maths, there was no escaping the truth that Ironman Lake Placid was the biggest thing I'd ever set out to do. For the previous ten months I'd drained what I thought was my infinite battery and gone to the extreme. I'd bathed in elation, exhaustion and totally immersed myself in this new Ironman life. I'd drawn on all my previous exercise experience and still made constant mistakes. I'd been smashed at the infamous duathlon Ballbuster on Box Hill, survived overtraining, bonks, open water and group swims, lurgies, niggles and injuries. Somehow existing at the limits of my abilities had proven the perfect antidote for my busy mind and fidgety restlessness. Amazingly my focus had been clearer, more vivid, brighter than ever before. The emptiness and aversion to domestication were gone. I felt comfortable in my identity and alive. My every action and thought focused on one day, the 29th July 2001.

What could possibly go wrong?

***

My mind slipped in and out of consciousness, waves of despair washed over me with the pain. Blue lights, a stretcher, strapped to a gurney again. Linds was working away and Neil and his heavily pregnant wife, Jackie, had rushed to my aid. Hours later I hobbled out of A&E cleared of any bone breakages. I had stitches over my black eye and cut nose. My shoulder, knees, elbows and hands were raw, scrubbed and bound. I was limping badly and couldn't straighten my right arm. I'd cracked my helmet and my race bike was squashed and twisted beyond repair.

In less than twenty days, we had flights to America booked, accommodation paid for and no chance of recovering my race entry fee. I was in deep and had three weeks before the start of Ironman Lake Placid 2001. I looked for the TV crew,

Now get out of that!

Fifty Thousand Volts

I woke the next morning and the pillow and sheets were covered in dry blood from my face and raw skin. Despite my cracked helmet taking most of the impact, my head was pounding.

The thought again,

Oh no, Ironman!

Everyone knew about it and I had put in so much to get myself ready. It was three weeks to the start and I was struggling to move around the house. I'd never taken a sick day before and wasn't going to start now. Limping in late in shorts and t-shirt, my boss took one look at my bloodied face and pained gait and told me to get home and heal. I felt terrible and clearly looked pretty beaten up. With the thought of sitting still, being alone and feeling sorry for myself, I didn't go home, I couldn't face it. Instead, after a stop at the police station, I met Jules and Ian, a couple of colleagues, for lunch.

We sat in the sun and laughed, mainly at my expense. With distraction, company and banter, my spirits began to lift. We talked about my options. The legal position was clear. The driver had taken full responsibility. I'd been crossing the roundabout, it was my lane and my right-of-way. He was approaching from the left and despite looking, admitted that he hadn't seen me. His black tyre marks and the witnesses had put his culpability beyond doubt. But to his credit he never tried to deny it, he was very shaken up and even called the hospital to check on me. His insurance company had confirmed they'd cover any medical treatment and replace my damaged materials with receipts.

'They'll also cover the costs for your flights, hotels and entry fee.' Jules reassured me as we finished our sandwiches, 'You shouldn't be out of pocket for missing the Ironman.'

Missing the Ironman!

Everything went quiet inside. The clatter of the pub, the smiles and chat all faded. I had the perfect excuse, a free-pass. Everything I'd been through, the ups and downs, hours of training, dedication, single-minded drive, all for nothing. I could see the movement of mouths, the shaping of muted sounds, but couldn't hear what was being said.

The Ironman was *all* that mattered. I'd felt this before in the Lake District with Pete; a spark, a charge, an angry energy coursed through me.

I wasn't going to quit.

No way!

I didn't want to be that person that simply gave up. This time I wasn't going to let my fingers slip. I had to fight and try. A hardness grew inside, an absolute focus. I couldn't live with the self-loathing and crushing emptiness of defeat. My grip tightened. I was resolute, the decision was made. My mind became clear and I could hear again. Looking at Jules, I smiled,

'I'm not missing the Ironman!'

The world lurched forwards again.

Take responsibility and own it.

I'd find a way.

But although I'd said it, I'm not sure either Jules or Ian believed me. They had to get back to work and as we stood my body complained and creaked. As I limped to the car, I'm not sure I was convinced by my own bravado either. Three weeks wasn't long. I'd been served up another massive plate of elephant and I didn't know where to start. My radio dial of worries span at warp speed. The challenge felt more overwhelming than it ever had before.

Luckily I didn't have to sit in the office for the afternoon with my throbbing head. Sensibly I recognised that exercise wasn't my escape so I decided to go and spend the insurance money and headed to my favourite bike shop, *Phil Corley*

Cycles, in Milton Keynes. Within two hours and yet more laughs from Nick and Phil at my expense, I was back in the triathlon business. Well I had a new bike and helmet and had replaced the countless other damaged essentials.

But despite this welcome shopping distraction, all this new shiny equipment wasn't going to get me around Ironman Lake Placid. Linds nearly fainted when she arrived home and saw me wincing in the shower. After another uncomfortable night I woke the next day feeling creakier still. I knew my skin would heal but I was beginning to get worried about my joints. I hobbled around all day and headed to the pool that evening reasoning the water would ease everything. I got out after a single 25 metre length. Wearing my goggles was impossible with my swollen and stitched eye, my arm wouldn't straighten and the chlorine zinged every cut and graze. My survivor euphoria had vanished. I couldn't exercise and was suffering serious dopamine cold turkey. A constant stream of worries whirled through my mind and I could feel a bleak darkness rise inside.

Maybe I should let go.

Loosen my grip from the bar.

Let my feet hit the floor.

As I tossed and turned brooding at night, I could see that nobody was going to argue with my excuse, I'd been hit by a car three weeks before the start. The insurance company would pick up my out of pocket expenses. I was wavering. The elephant in front of me seemed huge. I couldn't swim more than a length in the pool. There was no way I'd be ready to race and finish an Ironman in twenty days. I had a mountain to climb and as I stood at its base I felt very small. I was filled with a grey, confusing fog and rising despair.

My Ironman.

Another day passed and the stiffness in my arm wasn't getting any looser. It would move but I couldn't get it fully straight. I had a meeting in London and headed in wearing a suit and tie in the July heat. I winced on the tightly packed tube and my head throbbed. The effort exhausted me. I felt really low and back in the office I confided to Jules,

'I'm worried about my arm.'

She pointed out the obvious,

'Go to a physio.'

I hadn't even considered it as an option, possibly out of dread of what they'd do to straighten me out. After a few calls I was in the treatment room that evening. Roxanne was from New Zealand, tiny and instantly understood my plight. 'We can fix you up,' she declared in her Kiwi twang, 'sure you can do the Ironman.'

The clouds rolled back. Sunlight and hope streamed back in. If Roxanne, *an expert*, says I can heal, then I'll be alright. The next hour was one of the most painful of my life, but I walked out fully mobile, with a rehab plan and my self-belief restored. I now had eighteen days to the biggest trial of my life. For the last ten months I'd thought the challenge was to swim 2.4 miles, bike 112 and run a marathon. But when I was this close, it was simply to be fit and healthy enough to get to the start line.

I was twenty seven years old and it had been thirteen years since my sports hall humiliation. In that time I'd developed a mindset that seemed to consider no other option than to simply push on.

***

The next fortnight from seeing Roxanne to boarding the plane to Ironman Lake Placid was crazy. My new bike arrived at *Phil Corley Cycles* but I hadn't really had time for a long distance ride before I was packing it down for the flight. I swam one 2.4 mile effort in the pool to restore my confidence but in these two weeks I'd only done light, low effort sessions to simply tick over, rather than anything I would call training.

Something inside told me I was as ready as I could be. I didn't run at all. My knee tweak after the 1999 London Marathon made me cautious and I decided to give the deep inflammation in my joints time to settle. Unusually sensible after the crash, I decided anything I did in these last two weeks would potentially jeopardise my dreams. For perhaps the first time in my life I counted to ten rather than charging like a bull in a china shop.

With warm good luck messages from colleagues and friends, Linds and I flew from Heathrow midweek to Montreal in Canada. The race was on Sunday and there was a six hour time zone shift. The town of Lake Placid is in upstate New York in the north east corner of the United States. It's a few hours' drive south of the Canadian border, surrounded by high mountains, deep ravines and forests. It's ski country and pulling off the interstate we followed the eleven mile ribbon road from the valley floor in Wilmington to the main town of Lake Placid. I'd been plugged into the mains since my decision with Jules and Ian over lunch. As we wound up the ravine I could feel the steady charge of energy really ratchet up. My nerves were on fire and I was brimming with adrenaline.

Linds and I found our bearings and went straight to the registration tent in the Ironman Village. After the necessary ID checks, I was given my transition bags, numbers, race pack and schedule. The competitor's band was clipped to my wrist. I was officially in Ironman Lake Placid 2001. Never one to read instruction manuals, uncharacteristically on this occasion I absorbed all the briefing material avidly. The first rule of the run section leapt out at me,

'No forms of locomotion other than running, walking and crawling are permitted.'

The information pack and mandatory race meeting explained what constituted drafting, the locations, distribution and content of feed stations and the multitude

68

of ways to get penalised or disqualified. I tried to absorb it all. With so much at stake I wasn't taking any chances.

Everything about these days and the proximity of the Ironman was designed to up the voltage coursing through me. This was bigger than anything I'd ever done before. Everyone was tanned, lean, athletic and I felt a complete impostor. I didn't look or feel like an Ironman. The players seemed to be training constantly, running up and down the main street and looked incredible. I'd planned to do nothing but have a practice swim and go for a quick test ride on my bike to ensure it hadn't been damaged on the flight. Seeing the activity of the other competitors, I was convinced I must have got this wrong and waves of self-doubt swept over me.

With Roxanne's help I'd got my arm mobility back but no amount of rehab could heal the broken skin. My final effort before the race was a single 1.2 mile loop of the swim course. In my wetsuit, the remaining scabs softened and were dissolved away leaving pink, fresh skin. My reserves were definitely brimming full. I'd made a decision that being healthy at the start line was my only priority and would likely give me my best chance of finishing.

Paranoid, I'd dreamt many times of not having my goggles at the start, forgetting my helmet or bike shoes as I got to T1 or trainers at T2. In our accommodation I went over and over my pre-race checklist with Linds. I meticulously counted each item I needed for the blue, swim-to-bike bag and then my red, bike-to-run bag. As we loaded the car I was sure I had everything. In the Ironman Village, I dropped my bags in the allocated zones and my numbered bike in the huge transition area. I let the air out from my tyres so they wouldn't blow in the heat and then worried endlessly I'd forget to re-inflate them before the race on Sunday. To speed up the finding of my bike in the fury of T1, I counted the racks from the change tent and walked the exits and entrances of each transition to ensure I had my bearings. I was running out of things to do before my day of reckoning. We had an evening meal planned but I'd lost my appetite. Like a condemned man, all I could do now was wait.

Tomorrow it would be race day and the previous year had been insane. I'd driven relentlessly with my foot hard to the floor, block shifting through gears in my brain. I was on the verge of doing something I'd said to Neil would be impossible. Of course, with pre-race tri-mares, I didn't sleep much. I woke before my alarm and crept quietly about so as not to disturb Linds but she was almost as excited as me. I brewed tea, had something to eat and we listened to some tunes, my choices not hers; *Marilyn Manson's* rasping *Sweet Dreams*, *Ozzy Osborne's* obvious *Ironman* and my teenage turbo trainer favourite *Paranoid*. Time was accelerating.

We drove to the start. I went through the final transition checks, re-inflated my tyres, jogged and warmed up. With thirty minutes to the start, I applied some final lube on the areas most vulnerable to friction and pulled on my wetsuit. I kissed Linds and headed through to the swim entry point. A low mist was hovering as I trod water with eighteen hundred grim-faced racers saying their silent prayers. The third edition of Ironman Lake Placid would start in five minutes.

Fifty thousand volts coursed through me.

Thug-Thinking

'*O'er - the - land - of - the - Ffffrrreeeeee,*'

A pin could have dropped. Frozen in time. Absolute silence held by a lone, female, gospel voice.

'*And - the - home - of - the -*'

Stillness, not a breath of wind. The call to arms. Vulnerable, raw, spine-tingling,

'*Braa - veee.*'

A pause of reverie before the answering rapturous applause.

I was in the warmth of Mirror Lake, now seconds away from the start cannon. The clear water lapped under my chin and I tensed ready to plunge head forwards. I waited and then,

BOOM!

The shock wave jolted through me.

The water erupted into white foam.

The roar of adrenaline as my heart leapt from calm to near cardiac arrest.

Fight.

Flight.

Survive!

I'd tried to position myself out of the pack but so had hundreds of others. There was no escape, everybody was in a horizontal aqua fight. Arms, legs, black neoprene bodies. My mind went blank, clear. I was experiencing absolute freedom. There was only now.

Swim.

Breathe.

It will settle down.

I coached myself, trying to calm my exploding heart and bring my breath under control. It was mayhem, I was surrounded by carnage. But this wasn't the time or the place for self-pity. I'd paid my entry fee and had no one to blame but myself. If this is what it took to be an Ironman, so be it. Suck it up. Lean in. I'd got myself into this mess, take responsibility, I'd be the only one to get me out.

I got smashed in the face, across the back of the head, pushed down through the shoulders, even swum over. I'd roll for a breath and take in liquid air. With the missed oxygen and close to hyperventilation, my heart jacked. Panic. My lungs burned, ached to inhale, were on the edge of enduro-asphyxiation. We passed orange markers and the buoys slipped slowly to our left as we circled the large rectangle 1.2 mile loop anti-clockwise. Safety divers' bubbles expanded, ballooning from the invisible deep.

Swim.

Stroke.

Breathe.

It will settle down.

It HAS to settle down.

Helicopters beat the air above with film crews hanging out of the doors. The whomp, whomp of their blades in Dolby surround sound. The mayhem and carnage didn't calm down until the top of the course. A five hundred metre face down fight. Coloured goggles, mirrored, tinted, sometimes clear showing wild dilated eyes, animal fear. It wasn't only me on the anaerobic edge.

We turned at the top of the course and the space seemed to open. Everyone was close but the aggressive intensity eased. With a short two hundred metre stretch we turned left again for town. The halfway point was only five hundred metres ahead. Buoy after buoy, divers' bubbles, herded by the safety canoes and I was finding my rhythm. I had some space, the fury settled marginally. I was swimming, it was no longer a fight. The course markers to my left, water-front town houses to the right. Steadily the first lap dropped behind. I coached myself,

Follow feet.

Keep a swimmer to the right.

Not too close, use their pace.

Let's get this done.

Every twentieth stroke, I'd look up to check I was on the right course. The beach drew nearer with every glance. The thump-thump of the TV helicopters was gone. The leaders were clearly already a long way ahead. Then, almost unexpectedly, the bottom loomed, steep to shallow and there was the exit ramp. Grabbed by strong arms I stood, helped up the carpeted slope. The noise, deep crowds, wild faces, a constant roar. I turned sharply ninety degrees to my left, wading back in to repeat the 1.2 mile loop. Up to my waist and diving forwards, I had space now, open water in front and to the sides.

I'd broken each of the three disciplines, the swim, the bike and the run, into their respective four quarters. Watched by invisible divers bubbling in the depths, I started the third quarter of the swim but with 112 miles on the bike and a marathon ahead, it was way too early to start pushing. But knowing this quarter was always the hardest, somehow made it easier. Since the start cannon, my life had become incredibly simple and one dimensional. The voice in my head focused on a single job, constantly running systems checks,

Get to the next buoy.

Stay with the feet in front.

Not too close that I'm annoying but near enough to get the benefit of their draft.

The course was passing behind. I covered the five hundred metres to the top, turned left for two hundred and left again. I was definitely in the fourth quarter of the swim and I could feel a lightness within me. My brain and self-coaching projected forwards to what lay ahead. The exit ramp, the long run to transition.

Keep my goggles on my head so both my hands are free. Unzip my wetsuit and start tugging down as I jog. Down the blue carpet, look for Linds. Soak up the roar of the crowd. Images. Flashes. Water in the ears, dulling the cheering, bells, fist pumping energy. And then I was there. The fourth quarter had flown by. I was in the transition tent, jacked on the day.

Settle down.

Get your bag.

Finding somewhere to sit, I pulled my wetsuit completely down. Keeping my feet off the ground I checked they were clean. Socks on, then shoes, helmet clipped under the chin, glasses wedged in the vents, number belt fastened round the waist. I stood stuffing my swim gear in the bag and gave it to a volunteer.

Go!

To the bike.

Simple instruction, a one dimensional, carefree life. This wasn't chess, some complex game of strategy, but instead thug-thinking, worthy of my neanderthal brain. I ran blinking into the sun and a sea of bikes. About half the racks were already empty which told me all I needed to know about my swim. A long way from world class but respectable enough. Maybe I wasn't the big fraud I thought. I found my steed and pushed it, following the stream of fellow racers to the exit. At the mount line I swung my leg over and clipped both feet in as I wobbled away.

One hundred and twelve miles and a marathon still lay ahead.

I'd finished the swim but was a *long* way from done.

Broken And Battered

I had water in my ear.

I wiggled my jaw, squeezed my nose and blew hard to break the seal. I pushed a finger in and gave it a vigorous wag. But nothing was shifting the deafening plug.

We'd roared out of town and sped along leaving Lake Placid and the Olympic Ski Park behind, flying on Route 73 towards Keene. The roads were as smooth as butter and as we descended from the ski resort plateau to the valley floor we were moving at warp speeds. The rollercoaster was fast and dangerous, tyre to rim close. With the muted cacophony of a two deep peloton, all the official warnings about ten metre drafting zones seemed to be out of the window. In this tight and dynamic snaking bunch everything was alien to me.

We were shifting and there was no way I could step off. Sirens wailed by, speeding to crashes ahead, signalling game over for some unfortunate soul. I was determined a mindless fall wouldn't end my day on either of the two 56 mile loops. With my skin pink and raw from the recent accident, my senses were being overloaded through my Oakleys and half useful ear. I sat vigilantly over my brakes, watching the wheel in front, on a hair trigger ready to react. Telescoped with concentration, before I knew it I was twenty miles deep into my first Ironman bike.

From Keene we cut left along Highway 9N passing beautiful rivers, gullies and crystal clear lakes. I glugged at the official energy drink. It was strong, sweet and already twisting my stomach. I swigged at some water to dilute its clawing strength but could already feel trouble brewing. I had to drink but instinctively sensed the race's disco juice was more poison than fuel.

The morning freshness had vanished as we pushed through thirty miles and on to the small town of Jay and the sharp climb to Wilmington. At a huge fire station we had a ten mile out-and-back in the valley to Black Brook. All the way to the U-turn I felt like a salmon swimming against the stream as an endless line of bikers passed me going the other way. It was crushing and the enormity of the challenge crept into my head. I still had three quarters of the 112 mile bike and a marathon to go.

Back at Wilmington and with the out-and-back done, the route veered right onto Route 86 and a long eleven mile climb back to transition and Lake Placid town. The sky was a clear vivid blue and the sun beat down baking the rocks and gullies that stretched to the colosseum of mountains arching above. This was big-country and I felt very small as the rugged landscape towered overhead. But this was no time to feel sorry for myself, I stood on my pedals and climbed. I'd come here to become an Ironman. The road seemed to wind towards the sky forever but finally the parched verges turned into houses, well-manicured lawns and golf courses. We skirted along Mirror Lake and I spotted Linds cheering in the crowd. After fifty six miles of suffering, this close brush with humanity and love brought a lump to my throat as I sped by. We looped past transition and onto the second lap.

As I passed the Olympic Ski Park suddenly my energy crashed. My feet felt like someone was driving nails in through the bottom of my shoes. My hands were sticky, my shoulders and back hurt, my stomach was twisted with the sickly energy drink and my legs felt empty. The euphoria and adrenaline of being in an Ironman race, the buzz that had given me wings, had vanished. What lay ahead seemed impossible. It was time for some positive self-talk again,

This is an Ironman!

Suck it up.

There is no other option.

Toughing it out, I lowered my shoulders and stretched my arms on the tri-bars to minimise the drag. This was the pointy end of the race and I was having to look deep inside to see whether I had the minerals to call myself an Ironman. With the blocking into quarters of each of the three disciplines, here I was in the third quarter again and being caught by the difficulties between my ears.

One bite at a time.

Don't think too far ahead.

Get through the next twenty miles.

Then the twenty after that.

The cheers of the locals sitting on their front lawns with refreshing sprinklers arching behind them carried us through Keene. I pushed along the rocky ravines of Highway 9N towards the turn at Jay and the sharp climb to Wilmington. On the long out-and-back to Black Brook baked in the windless, oven-like heat, I was deep in the fourth quarter. But somehow this time it didn't give me much of a lift.

As the road arched up the eleven mile climb back to Lake Placid I'd completely shrunk. The full weight and reality of the challenge of an Ironman was on top of me. Dwarfed by the enormity of it all, I couldn't find a part of me that wasn't sore. My feet were agony, my shoulders and back creaked and my hands sticky with the stomach twisting energy goo. Every other rider seemed to be moving at twice my speed. As I willed my steed forwards I remembered the teenage boy with a pocket full of Mars bars, who'd watched the men of Warwick Tri pull away.

As I climbed the long road back to my final transition at least the seal in my deaf ear had broken. The mountains stretched to the gigantic blue sky and I could hear a river running in its rocky bed, crickets revelling in the heat, the sun searing and crackling my skin. This second loop of the bike seemed way longer than the first, but again the barren landscape eventually turned to houses, golf courses and lush well-watered lawns. I passed Mirror Lake and Linds standing on her rock. With huge relief I free-wheeled into transition and dismounted.

Broken and battered, a marathon lay ahead.

Between The Ears

A volunteer took my bike at the dismount line and I'm ashamed to say it but I'd never been so glad to be rid of it. The last 112 miles had beaten me to a pulp.

I hobbled like an old man through transition to my bike-to-run bag and the change tent. It was cool inside and instinctively I made a beeline for a chair. It was a huge relief to take the weight off my feet. As I reached into my bag the sheer scale of what lay ahead bore down on me.

I have to run a friggin' marathon!

The run route was two 13.1 mile loops that headed south from T2 on Main Street. With no hills to speak of, the only real undulation on the marathon course was the descent past the black flagged Vietnam veterans' memorial towards Sentinel Road. Beyond this was the tiny airport and Olympic Ski Park on Cascade Road. From here we'd veer left onto Riverside Drive for an out-and-back. At the U-turn we'd retrace our steps back to town before a second, short dog-leg along Mirror Lake and Club Drive for the last turnaround of the lap at mile twelve. With a final mile returning to transition we'd have done our first 13.1 mile loop only to have to do it all again.

Automatically I unclipped my helmet, peeled off both shoes and my sweaty socks and unpacked my run gear. Carefully applying Vaseline between my toes, I squeezed into each clean sock, checking for creases, and then my trainers. With a sun hat pulled low and adjusting my smeared Oakleys, suddenly I had no reason to stay sitting there. Given how broken I felt only five minutes earlier, I had absolutely no idea what would happen next. I stood and headed for the exit. As I walked into the glaring sun I took a cup of energy drink and some water, sipping both. I felt truly battered.

Here we go.

Start to run.

My gait wasn't pretty but I willed myself forwards. Reassuringly everyone around me seemed to be going at the same pace. Compared with how I'd galloped away from Blackheath Common at the '99 London Marathon, I wouldn't describe what I was doing here as running. It was somewhere between a hobble and a jog. But as I descended past the veterans' memorial, the blood transferred from my cycling muscles to the ones I needed to run and slowly it seemed to be getting easier and more natural.

Get to the next feed station,

There you can have a walk and a drink.

This wasn't a place for thinkers. The marathon in its entirety seemed beyond comprehension but with my new elephant-eating-logic, running to the next feed station at just over a mile, I could cope with it.

One bite at a time.

This wasn't a game of strategy, just single minded, pig-headed grit. With the steady rhythm of feet slapping the road almost instinctively I fell into the pace of those moving around me. Unconsciously latching on to and being drawn by the will of someone else seemed easier than having to self-pace. Shoulder-to-shoulder, stride-for-stride, quite naturally within a few hundred metres it seemed churlish not to break the ice.

'Well this is fun.'

Perhaps it was my British accent but company was easy to find and the talking definitely eased the passing of the miles. My brain was so addled I can't remember any of the stories, names, or even what was said. But I had an overwhelming sense of struggling together, no longer being alone or closed in my mind. We weren't travelling fast, but we were certainly travelling together.

We got to the first turnaround at mile four, the end of Riverside Drive, in the blink of an eye. I was buoyant, in a good place, the pain and suffering of the bike long forgotten. Foolishly, in my head I did some maths and realised twenty two miles stretched ahead. I felt small again, momentarily broken by the reality of it all.

But then I remembered, I'd already swum 2.4 miles, cycled 112 miles and, although I wasn't setting the world on fire, I was still standing and moving slowly forwards in an Ironman marathon. Twelve months ago I'd thought this was beyond me. Three weeks ago I'd been hit by a car.

You're doing good!

Don't think.

With the padding of trainers on tarmac and encouragement and cheers from the crowd, I was living a mile at a time. I have snatches of memories; the smiles and warmth of the feed station volunteers, carried by their energy, hurting all over, running on fumes. But my mind was in a good place, single minded, focused on the job at hand. I was making progress and if I kept this up I would finish. I had to pinch myself; I was in a real life *friggin'* Ironman.

Linds was standing on her rock patiently cheering me on as I came back into town. I had held onto a hardness, determination and drive all day and was so close to realising my impossible dream. My chin trembled and my eyes filled with tears as we high fived. On I ran up Club Drive to the U-turn at the top of Mirror Lake, pulling closed the door on my suffering once again. Returning I saw Linds again, passed T2 and the finish zone to begin my second loop. A half marathon lay ahead.

The third quarter!

When good runners are supposed to push.

But today my head wasn't in that game. I'd completed the first 13.1 mile loop in about two hours. That was respectable but the wheels of my chariot wobbled and I couldn't hold on to the reins. Gravity grabbed me, sucked me down and the energy drained out of my feet. Experience should have told me I'd done half and had never been closer to home. But instead I was crushed. The excuses came flooding into my mind; I was beaten up on the bike, I'd had a crash, had to curtail my training, hadn't got the miles in my legs. It was easy to find justification. Without words many around me also independently lost their internal struggles and we collectively slowed to a walk.

The truth was I'd never been in this particular situation before, it was way beyond my comfort zone. I was amazed I was still in the game and had never had to ask myself these questions before. I wasn't rehearsed, experienced or ready with answers. My brain was so fried I couldn't reason or think straight. I wasn't in a state to rationally weigh the pros and cons of any difficult decision. My mind gave my body the easiest and safest option to survive. I was dismayed.

'I'm dying here.'

I confessed to the runner beside me.

'Don't worry buddy, everyone walks the second half of the marathon.'

I was relieved but these were dangerous words to hear. Something in my head let go. My pace sagged, the spring ebbed from my step. I was moving forwards but for now the fight had left me. Deep in my heart I'd come to Lake Placid with the sole intention of finishing. If this is what it took to get across the line of my first Ironman, so be it. I rolled the words back and forth in my mind, *Everyone walks the second half of the marathon.* I didn't think I was *everyone*, but today, in the company of fellow iron-athletes I could live with the label. We chatted, cajoling each other, exchanging stories, leaving some behind and being overtaken by others.

'I have got my energy all wrong, I'm running on fumes but I don't think I can drink any more Gatorade.'

'The chicken soup is delicious. Have you tried coke?'

Desperate for anything, I took the advice at the next feed station and they were right, the warm soup was incredible. The moment the savoury and salty broth hit my taste buds I felt revived again. I was nervous about drinking coke but although famously high in sugar it didn't twist my gut like the concentrated official energy drink. I am sure the caffeine gave me a welcome hit. I started to run again, albeit slowly and with none of my first half-marathon vim, but it was better than a walk.

As we passed the airport and ski jump and turned left onto Riverside Drive it was getting dark and starting to rain. I'd found my own terminal velocity and was feeling stronger. But it was humbling as runners of all shapes and sizes streamed by. I was in my late twenties, fit and strong, competing in an Ironman. For many it is the ultimate single day endurance test but clearly I had a lot to learn. In the last year I'd thought this would be my Everest, my highest peak. But as I headed to the eighteen mile turnaround point at the most southerly part of the marathon, it was dawning on me that I'd hardly reached base camp on my Ironman journey.

The skies really opened as I made the U-turn at the top of Riverside Drive and headed north for the last time. I thought of Linds waiting for my return. I had eight miles to go and when I went through six I'd be into the fourth quarter. I felt a renewed vigour surge through me as I thanked the volunteers. A weight lifted from me with the realisation this would be the last time I passed through here. I could feel my stride lengthen, the spring return and my pace quicken.

Nothing had changed physically from my passage moments before as I'd headed south with my back to Lake Placid. But now I was heading home and felt light again, full of hope. In either direction each step had been taking me closer to the finish. But strangely in my mind the turn and perception of facing towards the finish gave me a massive boost. I was learning first-hand the real determinant of whether this was hard or easy was more influenced by the ebb and flow of positive thoughts rather than the physical exertions below my neck. Mr Cowell's wisdom rang true,

If you are fit, strong and well trained, most of your challenge is between your ears.

As I headed north for the final time my heart was full of joy. Fuelled on chicken soup and Coca-Cola, I hardly noticed the distance. As I made the turn to Mirror Lake, there was Linds standing on her rock. I was ready to let the softness in and tears flowed down my cheeks as we hugged. I ran to the final turnaround and felt weightless as I lengthened my stride along Club Drive to the stadium. With the rain pouring down, all the pain and suffering of the last 140.6 miles were forgotten. I sprinted down the finish straight with my arms and legs pumping. I was huge again, seven feet tall and invincible.

It is a moment I will never forget. Pure, absolute joy. All the veneers were stripped away. I'd never felt more like me, the person I truly was deep inside my babushka doll.

I broke the tape in 12:34:39 but really the time was irrelevant.

In the previous twelve months I'd created a life that was bigger than the one I'd lived before. I was no longer turning the pages of other peoples' books but instead etching vivid stories into my own.

I was an Ironman.

Knobbly Tyres

'Well it looks like you have ruptured your hip bursa.'

That didn't sound good. It didn't look good either; like a balloon, purple, yellow, black and bruised. I was about to get a crash course in physiotherapy.

'The bursa are protective sacks around major joints like an airbag in a car. They'll take the impact, rather than the bone.'

'Can I still train?'

Claire, my new physio, paused and looked me directly in the eye.

'Stuart,' she smiled knowingly, 'what would you do if I told you you couldn't?'

She had me there.

It was the winter of 2002 and I had finished Ironman Lake Placid eighteen months earlier. After crossing the line I hadn't stayed content for long. In the days and weeks following the race I was hit by a melancholy the likes of which I'd never experienced before. I should have felt happy but instead was full to the brim with emptiness, completely submerged in a confusing fog of post-race blues. Caught behind a pane of glass, the world seemed muted and I struggled to connect. Once we returned to the UK and work, the journey kept rolling on and I didn't have the same absorbing focus and purpose. I felt the creep of domestication doing all it could to shrink me again. With the objective and jeopardy of the Ironman challenge, I'd found an outlet for my boundless energy and a play-area for my restless mind. But with no big scary goal for my insatiable need for stimulation, the negative neural butterflies started flitting away.

The problem was that the distractions that had quickened my pulse before Lake Placid, now hardly touched the sides. From perceiving one Ironman as the biggest challenge of my life in 2001, the next summer I'd bagged two; Ironman Lanzarote and Ironman Switzerland within ten weeks. Again my times hadn't set the world on fire but the stimulation roller coaster swept me forwards again and blew away the clouds. For 2003 I'd set my sights on Ironman France and The Longest Day, a non-WTC iron-distance triathlon in Wolverhampton. In only two years, I'd irreversibly shifted my comfort zone and raised the bar on my self-synthesised pharmaceutical regime. These big races gave me huge hits of adrenaline but a year has 365 days and even the training was becoming normalised. Unconsciously I was experiencing dose tolerance. I craved ongoing, daily distraction and the feel good high from variety, adventures and new projects.

This was why in December 2002, with my relentless quest for thrills and a near total blindness to consequences, I was back on a physio's couch and limping badly. I hadn't crashed on tarmac, this time I'd hit the deck on my mountain bike.

***

Off-road riding had floated in and out of my life for about fifteen years and this crash was exactly why it was episodic. I found road surfaces way more predictable than the twists, turns, loose tops and drops I encountered at speed on trails. My confidence would always outgrow my talent and I'd be off.

In the late 1980s I got my first mountain bike, a Carrera Krakatoa from Halfords. It had no suspension, was bombproof and I'd have a hoot rattling along local canal towpaths. But due to a flimsy lock at university it found a new, less honest owner. Without the money to buy a replacement, I settled for a skinny-tyred road bike for the next ten years.

But in the spring of 2002, I had a new job and was pretending to be a grown up. Someone had trusted me with a company car with a fancy six loader CD player, a laptop and a mobile phone. I was whizzing up and down the country in a suit and tie racking up miles. I had all the trappings of doing well, climbing the career ladder but really felt lost behind ill-fitting babushka veneers and a long way from being a carefree adventurer. Feeding the stereo with *Placebo, Tool, Limp Bizkit,* anything hard, I'd regularly drive 250 miles or more a day from our home in Bicester, Oxfordshire to Brighton in East Sussex. I'd dread the journey's stop-start unpredictability on the M25 and with sweet relief I'd peel off at junction 7 and take the rolling M23 past Gatwick and on to the South Downs.

They were breathtaking and I'd yearn to be on them as I flew by to my meetings. They promised fresh air, vistas, freedom and adventures. I'd known this range of hills for years and had walked sections of the South Downs Way, SDW, with Mum and Dad. I'd fought up the famously steep Ditchling Beacon before my extended stay with St John Ambulance on my solo, nutritionally naive London to Brighton Bike Ride. But I'd not really been on the ancient neolithic trail for a while. As the M23 cut through its impressive shoulders at Pyecombe I felt their incredibly strong call.

Slowly an idea grew in my mind. I checked my maps and found I could park at the top of Devil's Dyke or at Jack and Jill's Windmill. For my next round trip I packed my running kit and instead of driving straight home, I stopped for an invigorating ten miles out-and-back. With my mini disc player, epic views stretching south to the sea or north across the vast East Sussex plain, I felt free again and was released from the cage. I'd found a way to quieten my spinning mind and flood my system with feel good hormones. It also ensured I avoided the early evening rush hour's hold ups on the M25.

After a few runs I noticed a good number of mountain bikes bouncing along. As I drove home I figured it would be great to slide one in the back of the car for the next trip. The only problem was I didn't own a mountain bike. But if anything, the last two years had also taught me not to let minor equipment deficits get in the way of having fun. I walked out of *Phil Corley Cycles* in Milton Keynes with a new aluminium off road machine that weekend.

My adrenaline was off the chart as I opened the taps, blistering along paths, ripping descents, finding the line and flow. With perilous speeds, absolute concentration, no rules or thought of consequences. I had *Iron Maiden, Marilyn Manson, Opeth* in my ears, giving rhythm to my legs. My new steed transported me to another world and throughout the summer I rode every time I could. With no cars, the odd walker and breathtaking views, I was young, wild, the adventurer rather than the suited office drone. Soundtracked by *Anarchy in the UK* I felt like Sid Vicious with my middle finger in a defiant salute against corporate conformity.

Enduro-Punk.

Squeezing every minute of what remained of the day, I'd only pack my bike in the car as the sun slipped below the horizon. Slowly my dressing up box filled with mountain bike gear, long fingered gloves, a CamelBak reservoir, offroad shoes and two way double-sided pedals. I'd sit in long meetings, my head already in the hills, hardly able to contain my jittery excitement at the anticipation of the evening's blast.

***

'So I reckon it can be ridden in a day. End-to-end, what do you think?'

James is my oldest friend and like a brother. We'd met at primary school when we were both about seven. We'd practically grown up together, spending our summers alternating between each other's houses. As teenagers, he came on most of our summer holidays and we shared a passion for bikes. Like me, James knew the South Downs Way from our childhood.

'So what are you thinking?'

My cobbled together, do-it-yourself SDW challenge was simple. Basically one hundred miles off-road, Winchester to Eastbourne or vice versa, start-to-finish in a day. It would be on trails with about 4,000 metres of elevation. The equivalent of climbing Ben Nevis, Britain's highest mountain, three times. Linds had even agreed to drop us at the start and pick us up at the end. It was on a plate.

'Why not?'

On paper it seemed easy but we went to school the hard way. Our first lesson was don't try riding the South Downs Way end-to-end in early December. We set off at first light in the cold and wet. We started from Winchester and quickly realised neither of us knew the route this far west. Our progress was slow with wrong turns, map checks and double backs to find direction arrows. As the morning progressed the sun rose to its winter height and the temperature stayed in low single figures Celsius. It was a long way from the warm, idyllic rides I'd enjoyed all summer north of Brighton.

We rolled along ridges swerving deep puddles and skittered down slippery tracks with precarious ruts. It was filthy, we were head-to-toe covered with a grey, chalky, toothpaste goo that our tyres roostered everywhere. From the start we were soaked and in these winter conditions the moment we stopped the chill crept through our layers. The grinding ups would just about warm our cores but we found the long chilling descents instantly stripped the heat away. Balance and concentration alone were no defence against the whipping December air through sodden clothes. As the day wore on Havant, Emsworth and Chichester slipped away in the distance to the south. We stopped periodically to eat from our packs and before we knew it the afternoon was almost gone. With a creeping realisation we saw the flaw in our plan. It'd be dark by 4pm and the light would fade when we were only halfway to Eastbourne.

'We've got maybe an hour of light left. Shall we call it a day at Amberley? We can stop for a beer and call the cavalry.'

We were drenched to the skin, filthy and cold. We hadn't achieved our goal but we'd had an adventure and learned a lot of the route we didn't know. We were also now both firmly of the opinion any end-to-end SDW challenge should be attempted on a dry, sunny, summer's day. Decision made, I called Linds and we set off from Bignor Hill with less than an hour to Amberley to find a good pub and await our rescue.

Without warning, I was on the deck.

It happened *very* fast.

The scraping of flint on my helmet, metal parts against rock.

My breath punched from me as I stopped in a crumpled heap.

A moment of silence then the high pitched screech of brakes behind, skidding tyres.

James and his bike were on top of me too.

It was the last descent and Amberley's welcoming glow flickered in the valley. The day was fading fast and we were cooking it, racing the dark. Leading, in the half-light, I hadn't seen the green, slick, wet, off-camber chalk. My front tyre barely touched it before the washout and I was on the floor in an instant. My helmet tried to carve a groove but the protruding sharp flint wouldn't yield. My head and hip took all the impact. With me as his crash mat, James had a softer landing. We picked ourselves up and gingerly freewheeled, half pedalled the last few miles. It was dark as we followed the footpath into Amberley looking bedraggled and feeling sore. I was too concussed for a pint so we piled straight into the car.

The South Downs Way had won, we'd been well and truly schooled. It was the winter of 2002 and I had to recover. My next test would be Ironman France the following summer.

Coach Linds

In 2003 I had a lot to learn about actually *racing* Ironman as opposed to merely *finishing*. My first lesson was to come from the most unexpected of quarters.

We were in Gérardmer on the northern shoulder of the French Alps. Ironman France was starting in less than fifteen minutes. We'd driven to France with Simon and his school mate Dave. I'd met Simon in 2000 when training for Lake Placid. He was a fellow triathlete and we quickly became the closest of friends. Dave has a Peter Pan soul, is constantly funny, unpredictable and hugely entertaining. The three of us would go on to have many adventures together.

This would be my fourth iron-distance race, but of the three I had already finished, none of my runs had set the world on fire. *Everyone walks the second half of the marathon!* was the poor advice I'd received from a fellow competitor in 2001. With this lodged in my brain, when the going got tough, usually around the thirteen mile mark, I'd descended into a mix of walking and running, happy to accept I was finishing.

Perhaps this is a little unfair, in Ironman Switzerland I'd almost run the entire marathon, but it wasn't graceful or fast. When combined with a good deal of vomiting, my split time was barely quicker than when I ran-walked the 26.2 miles. I was being owned by the day, surviving rather than thriving, finishing rather than racing. But this was about to change in Gérardmer. Coach Linds looked me square in the eye as we exchanged our final pre-race farewells,

'Just f'in run!'

Whether these words were actually *said*, something she vehemently denies, or simply what I *heard* from her pithy man-up pep talk, we will never know. But instantly their intent was etched in my mind. What is beyond dispute was that her patience had definitely been stretched beyond what most would consider as reasonable with my obsessive preparation through the autumn of 2002 and the following spring. I couldn't let the *Coach* down.

Just f'in run!

But executing this command and actually attacking an Ironman marathon is easier said than done. My ability to deliver wouldn't have been possible without a friend and certified triathlon coach, Ian Mayhew, who I'd been working with since the previous autumn. Before starting on Ian's programme my training was very unscientific and consisted of doing whatever took my mood. But I'd watched fellow members of my tri club, *gearsandtears.com*, improve and didn't want to be left behind. Through Ian's structured plan I felt a progressive improvement in my speed, endurance and fitness. Here in the summer of 2003 at the start of Ironman France I was more prepared than I'd ever been before.

There was a lot at stake as Ian had picked Ironman France for the annual *gearsandtears.com* club championship and I was giving it full beans. The swim was incredible, in the crystal clear, calm mountain lake. The bike was brutal with little flat, lots of climbing and fast descents with sharp, dangerous bends. Tragically we found out later a fellow competitor fatally crashed on one of the twisty downs. We knew none of this as we raced.

Just f'in run!

And I did. With Coach Linds' race strategy and Ian's structured programme I felt a different athlete than I had twelve months earlier. As I left T2, it took the first mile for the familiar post-bike stiffness and jelly legs to drop away. But from the first feed station onwards I positively launched myself forwards. Gone was the painful shuffle, I felt incredible. I'd developed the engine and conditioning to *actually* race 26.2 miles. My plan was still to walk the feed stations and Ian had told me this was okay to ensure I took a proper drink rather than a soak from a bobbing cup. After my run-vomiting in Zurich in 2002, I couldn't face the official energy drink in the close heat of France, so I took a cup of water and coke, mixed them together to flatten the fizz. As soon as the cup was gone, it was time to head for the next feed station.

Never walk with an empty cup.

The marathon was simple as I broke it down in my mind. My inner voice looped,

Four 6 mile loops.

You do that every week.

It's just a training run.

Admittedly I didn't do four of them back to back in training but my mind games worked and the maths was easy with my *four-quarter-block-strategy*. As I got to the third quarter, past the half marathon, thirteen miles stretching ahead, I knew this was the danger zone, where I had previously collapsed into a walk. If I could keep running in that third six miles the last lap would be easier. As I came through transition I saw Coach Linds and she gave me time checks on the *gearsandtears.com* racers. To my utter amazement I was in the lead, ahead of my fellow club members. This was a huge lift.

For the first time ever, I was bossing the distance. I vomited a couple of times but the final lap was a breeze. I was elated as I crossed the line. It was the first time I'd gone under twelve hours, with a new personal best of 11:53:52. It had been a tough, mountainous bike course and I'd made the time saving on the marathon. I was in no doubt that I'd got huge value from a structured and tailored programme with a certified coach. Most importantly I'd also executed Coach Linds' instructions.

***

Ironman France was my fourth Ironman and I'd set my sights on another full distance race that same summer. I was racking up the finishes but I still had a lot to learn. Frustratingly I wasn't getting my feeding right and suffered nutritional issues on the bike and run. I seemed to be able to handle the vomiting and it looked impressive. I hardly missed a beat as I spewed mid-stride but it wasn't optimal, the pre-hurl bloated stomach was uncomfortable and had to be slowing me.

Remember this was 2003 and the early days of the Internet. The cornucopia of online advice, blogs, podcasts and resources we have now at our fingertips and take for granted, simply didn't exist. By chance, in the six weeks between Ironman France and The Longest Day, I met multiple Ironman finisher and local hero, Mark Kleanthous. He instantly knew the root cause of my intestinal issue,

'You're eating too much. Your body can't digest the volume you are putting in,' he explained, 'The rule of thumb is between ½ a gram and one gram of carbs per kilo of bodyweight per hour. Everyone is different. You need to experiment with what you can digest.'

He paused to let me absorb the numbers.

'Basically, if you eat more than these limits, it can't pass through your stomach. It backs up, you pile more in and boom! The only way to clear the blockage. You vomit.'

It made sense. I'd been stuffing what I could in, believing I couldn't overeat. Over the next few weeks I re-thought my race nutrition plan. I looked at the food labelling in more detail, noted the grams of carbs per serving. I calculated how much I should eat based on my new half-to-one-gram-of-carbs-per-kilo-per-hour rule.

The Longest Day was perfect. It was a flat course and the weather was fantastic. The temperature sat in the early twenties Celsius, it was like a training day. This was my fifth iron-distance race and with Ian Mayhew's structure, guidance and advice, it was starting to really feel like my world. I crossed the line with my arms in the air but was gutted with my finish time of eleven hours and

94

one minute. This was over fifty minutes faster than I'd raced at Ironman France forty days earlier. I'd smashed myself for the final hour and within sight of the finish line had watched 10.59.59 tick through on my watch. I hadn't broken eleven hours. For a moment I was devastated. Again the indiscernible creep of what constituted extraordinary. But as soon as my rational brain caught up with my thuggish, neanderthal logic, I was delighted. I'd gone faster than I'd ever imagined I could. After five full iron-distance races I was starting to feel like a proper Ironman.

But I wasn't the only one in Team Staples looking for a hugely rewarding, expensive, stamina sapping, challenge. Linds and I were about to embark on our greatest adventure yet.

Starting a family.

Ben

Ben was an early walker.

He was fast, his face full of concentration. With his mop of red hair, big brown eyes and podgy hands, he'd surf the furniture, skirting a room for stability. Quickly he built his confidence launching himself, half stumbling from one side to the other.

He was born in May 2004 and everything changed.

Linds was ready. I'm not sure I'd given it any real thought until it happened. Maybe, having kids is different for dads and mums or perhaps my utter unreadiness was simply me. For Linds, she'd had time to accept and process with a nine month gestation period and an increasingly big lump growing and wriggling around inside. With hindsight I am sure this gave her a certain edge in her level of preparedness.

In my mind there was *now* and then *never*. With a nine month pregnancy, despite the growing evidence of an imminent arrival, I'd put it into the *this-isn't-happening-now* category. As a result, I hardly gave it any thought until it *actually* happened. Of course, we'd gone for scans, decorated a room, bought clothes, a buggy, car seat and a huge supply of wipes and nappies. This was stuff. Beyond this I hadn't really contemplated the seismic event that was about to turn everything upside down.

Before the birth we went to National Childbirth Trust, NCT, classes to learn how to be good parents. I sat bemused looking at the other imminent mums and dads. The only thing I could see we had in common would be our kids would be the same age. My brain simply wouldn't engage. I was an adult-boy, Peter Pan. I'd never felt so out of my lane. With all their earnest middle-Englandness, this was a different world. The motherly NCT leader sat at the front, like a queen bee before her brood, the model of domestication. She rocked irritatingly on an inflatable Pilates ball with all the smug airs of someone who'd been pregnant all her adult life.

'This exercise is called "The Threes". I want you to write down how you think you'll feel three hours, three days and three weeks after the birth.'

Her voice cut through me. I wasn't in the mood for this and as ever when agitated, my brain was unable to control the gap between thoughts, words and actions.

'Elated. Tired. Resentful.' I blurted out.

She gave me a sideways glance labelling me a class troublemaker. I'm sure if she could have sent me to the corridor, she would. It's fair to say I didn't have a paternal bone in my body, I was struggling with my pending dad-identity. However Linds really wanted a family and I loved her. B-day really caught me by surprise. I woke on the 5th May to find Linds in the bath.

'It's started.'

I went into panic mode wishing I'd paid more attention at the NCT classes. I did what I do before many of my UK adventures and races, I made a lot of sandwiches. I was getting event-ready. Luckily Linds had paid more attention and read the books I'd left unopened. We set out for the hospital when the contractions got to a certain point. Convinced we didn't have enough provisions I stopped at a garage to get more supplies. In anticipation of the long day ahead, I picked up a copy of my favourite magazine *Evo*. Looking back, not my most sensitive move. When we arrived we were rushed into the birthing suite. Linds was having our baby and it wasn't hanging around. My recently purchased reading material lay untouched under my mountain of uneaten, tinfoil wrapped sarnies.

'He's a boy.'

At the moment Ben was born, an overwhelming sense of protective love swept over me. I wasn't ready but knew instantly Linds had made the right call, having children would enrich our lives. We were elated. Linds stayed at the hospital the first night. I made all the necessary calls choosing language that made me sound like a seasoned pro. I am sure I fooled no one as I assured family and friends, *mother and baby are doing well.*

All done, it was close to midnight and I found myself alone, standing in a silent house. This was the beginning of a new era. I did the only thing I knew to mark the occasion, I pulled on my running gear. The roads were traffic free and I floated on cloud nine. I was a dad, it was incredible. Back home I opened a beer and sat on the floor with my trusty CD player. Quickly downing the first, I opened a second listening to track after track of *Bruce Springsteen*. I fell asleep to *Racing in the Streets, The River, Reason to Believe.*

Me, Peter Pan, a dad! I was thirty years old but deep down only a big kid beneath the grown up veneer.

***

The next fortnight was a blur as my unprepared mind was accelerated through the nine month gestation period I'd missed. I mixed bottles, sterilised everything, changed nappies, swaddled, burped, took night, morning, anytime feeds. Reality came crashing down and I learned fast at 3am the house was *so* cold. The chill stripped me to the bone, time to layer up. Big eyes, mouth working away at the bottle teat. Trust, absolute dependence. Two weeks into our new routine, I confided in Linds,

'I keep expecting someone to knock on the door. A reassuring smile, an official from the hospital, arms outstretched. "You can give him back now."'

She looked at me.

'But I've realised they aren't coming are they?'

She laughed. I was adjusting, doing my share of the heavy lifting.

'What? Was he up again? I didn't hear the cry.' I feigned, 'You are obviously tuned into this parenting, a natural.'

Night-feed-roulette. Keep the eyes closed, don't move with the first salvo of cries. I was learning the game fast. But with a sharp nudge, an elbow, I'd be reminded it was my turn. To Ben's room, let him know I was on my way. Dress quickly; trousers, fleece, hoodie, socks, anything to protect against the pre-dawn arctic chill. Mix the night feed, on the sofa, snuggled on my chest, another twenty minutes of *The Last Samurai*. Empty bottle, get a burp, pray for no soiled nappy.

The zombie existence of sleep deprivation. At least I didn't have to be patronised at NCT classes anymore. I was determined to be a good dad. The phase of elation hadn't ended, but I was growing up. I felt a lifetime away from my first home in Scotland, *Two, four, six, eight. Who do we appreciate?* and the sing-song waits with Mum and Josie in my blue muppet pyjamas.

Iron-Dad

I didn't really have a plan. I simply wanted to push myself more and more.

The natural progression from Ironman and our playing on the South Downs Way was enduro-mountain bike racing. In 2003 James and some friends had competed in a team of four in the 24-hour non-stop race, Sleepless in the Saddle. I'd instantly been snared by the idea.

Hardly thinking through the complications of life with a family I'd entered the 2004 edition of Sleepless in the Saddle. I didn't fancy riding in a team of either four or as a pair but a solo effort sounded right up my street. But entry decisions are easy in early autumn, almost a year before a race. With three months of parenthood under my belt and staring down the barrel of actually riding my bike continuously for a day, it had suddenly lost its appeal.

'Are you okay missing Sleepless?'

It was Saturday evening on the weekend of the race. The starter's gun had gone off at 2pm but we were sitting in the theatre in Stratford-upon-Avon. We were enjoying a rare evening out and Ben was with his grandparents. Since his birth he'd covered a lot of ground and we'd been completely naive to the impact of life, travelling and racing with a newborn.

At five weeks old he'd been piled into the car to head off to Weymouth for my season opener half-iron distance in Dorset. Ben's baby gear dwarfed the mountain of tri equipment I needed to take on the sea swim, lumpy rolling bike and beach front run. Everything about the weekend was a near disaster apart from the race. Our accommodation was double booked and we ended up sleeping on the owner's waterbed in the basement. With a grumpy baby in a travel cot and two huge washer dryers making a noise from the room next door, we didn't close our eyes once. It's fair to say the five and a half hours of the 1.2 mile

100

swim, 56 mile bike and the half marathon were the least taxing part of the weekend.

Gluttons for punishment we then boarded a flight to Ironman Austria three weeks later. It was madness and there were a lot of moving parts. Both sets of grandparents had joined us, Simon was racing, James was doing his first Ironman and he'd brought his support team of his girlfriend, Nic, and his dad, Bill. Added to this, the usual *gearsandtears.com* crew were there for the annual club championship. We were determined that having a family wouldn't stop us having adventures but we had definitely bitten off more than we could chew.

Against all odds, I executed the perfect race. I'd been coached by Ian for two years now and despite eight weeks of erratic sleep, felt in the best shape of my life. I'd raced the 2003 Abingdon Marathon in 3:12 and in the spring of 2004 the Silverstone Half Marathon in 1:24. Since working with Ian I was a different athlete and recovered quickly. Despite everything, I had a good race in Weymouth and then smashed Ironman Austria, crossing the line in 10:53:54. I'd broken the eleven hour barrier and possibly found my favourite Ironman.

As we sat in the theatre my mind wandered to Sleepless in the Saddle. I was glad not to be there. I didn't have the fight in me for a 24-hour solo mountain bike race. I was worn out and stretched. We had a three month old baby, I'd raced a half and a full Ironman and I was shelled. Deciding to swerve Sleepless was a good call, but I was angry with myself for my Did Not Start.

'DNS,' Ian Mayhew assured me, 'Did Nothing Stupid!'

And he was right. I was tired and over raced. I couldn't put myself in the right place. A week after Austria I'd bowed to the inevitable, realising I'd finally bitten off more than I could chew.

'I'm not going to do Sleepless.'

Linds looked relieved and we decided to have our first date night since Ben had been born. We needed to settle down as a family for a bit of normality. Life with a baby was joyous but the previous months of sleep deprivation, disruption of routine, planning and change of priorities had worn us thin.

Throughout the Saturday my mind was half in the race. I pictured the start, the fury of the Le Mans run, the Viking style hoard dashing for the bikes. I watched the hours tick through the afternoon and into the evening as we drove to the theatre. We'd booked late and had seats almost in the rafters. As I climbed the winding stairs, pushing against gravity, my legs screamed. They'd been stripped empty with a year of hard training and racing. As the curtain went up I'd have been five hours into Sleepless, nineteen hours stretching ahead. We got home at 11pm and I imagined the riders readying themselves for the night. I had the 3am feed and as Ben chugged on his bottle, I wondered how I'd feel, thirteen hours in, eleven hours to go. All through the Sunday morning my head was at Sleepless. At 12 noon I'd have two hours to go. I looked back on what I had done over the last twenty two hours away from the race, it was mind boggling to think I could have been continuously riding.

By August 2004 my perception of what was extraordinary had moved significantly. I'd come a long way since Lake Placid in 2001 but I wasn't yet ready to race solo for 24 hours. My mind and body weren't in the right place. I could race eleven to thirteen hours no problem but pushing beyond that, doubling that time, I wasn't sure I had the right stuff. It niggled.

Each autumn I'd seen a pattern emerging with club mates and fellow racers dropping away. There'd be 'grown-up' talk of *too many sacrifices, costs, family, commitments, being less selfish.* I'd finished six iron-distance races, had a stash of t-shirts, medals and a lifetime of potential bragging but the thought of quitting, hanging up my gear, never even crossed my mind. It didn't even compute.

This was my life. I didn't train and race because it was something I felt I should do. It was completely compulsive, I was obsessed. I didn't need to get motivated to exercise, I couldn't stop. Exercise shaped my every day, thought and action. It made me feel good, calmed my spinning brain and for relaxation it was virtually the only thing I wanted to do. I'd get anxious if I couldn't get my dopamine fix. I resented commitments that got in the way and they could totally crush my mood. Without exercise I'd spiral down and couldn't settle in the day until I was sure I could top up my buzz.

There was no way I was ready to retire. I'd lost touch with and completely forgotten my pre-Ironman life. But we made it work and we found time to be a family. In 2004 we'd had an incredible year with the arrival of Ben and managing to bag a sub eleven hour Ironman.

But somehow missing Sleepless left a tear in my universe.

It was an itch I had to scratch.

Ouch!

He stood at our front door, his eyes flicked beyond me. He looked like he'd seen a ghost. Three hours earlier his daughter had been on her first solo drive. He looked at me and then at Ben.

Ben was nearly two years old, standing behind me, his arm holding the door frame, his pink feet and toes gripping the carpet for balance. He wore a mini lumberjack shirt and one of his small zip up hoodies. His face was round and chubby, framed under a mop of vivid ginger hair. He looked adorable, the picture of innocence.

The possibilities of the conversation he could be having now. His shoulders dropped and face changed in an instant.

'I am so sorry for what happened. Are you okay? She's only just passed her test. She's really shaken up.'

He looked at Ben again.

'I'm so relieved nothing worse happened.'

***

The thought of having grit scrubbed from your knee is always worse than it actually is. I looked past the nurse's shoulder, fixing a spot on the opposite wall. I could feel a tugging, a pulling on the skin, over the raw, red, broken graze.

'The nerve ends are frazzled.'

She assured me.

'They're numb now but it will hurt later.'

Comforting words. My helmet had split, the protective padding cracked from the crown to the rear ratchet. It was held together by its plastic coating. At A&E

they x-rayed my shoulder. Thankfully it wasn't broken but was cut and locking up quickly. My glasses had smashed on impact and the nurse put two neat butterfly stitches in my eyebrow.

I'd been lucky and unlucky depending on how you looked at it. I heard the car coming. It was narrow, the road sweeping right. Too tight to pass a bike if something was coming the other way. She pulled in quickly, not quite past me, her rear, left wing caught my tri-bars. With a nudge I was gone, a millisecond beyond my balance point. My head hit first, then my shoulder, right hip and knee. No protection against the tarmac. I lay in a heap, slipping in and out of consciousness, my right side numb.

Linds arrived after the ambulance to the sight of blue lights and lots of high-viz. Thankfully nothing was broken and by the time the nurse was cleaning me up I was in better spirits. I limped out of A&E feeling beaten and battered. I'd be off to see Claire, my physio, again and hopefully the driver's insurance would pick up the tab. The skin healed fastest but my shoulder proved knotty and to this day remains crunchy. It still locks when I hold it in one position, especially on the bike and periodically I have to unclick it with a sickening grind and crunch.

In 2005 the truth was I was totally worn out and had definitely bitten off more than I could chew. Rather than back off following Ben's arrival in 2004, as I'd seen other *gearsandtears.com* club members do with the arrival of kids, I'd upped my efforts and gone all in. I couldn't put my finger on what was pushing my relentlessness to press on into my self-created hurricane. But over the summer of 2005 I did three Ironman races. We flew to Lanzarote in May, Switzerland in July and then drove to the first UK Ironman in Sherborne Dorset in early September. The creep of extraordinary. In each race I'd become progressively slower and none of my finish times were dazzling. I was bagging WTC medals and t-shirts but hardly smashing records.

We'd also had another tilt at the South Downs Way pushing out from Eastbourne at first light after kipping on a friend's floor. On this summer attempt we made it beyond the halfway point but pulled the pin with a third of the ride stretching ahead. We were learning the SDW route but the challenge of end-to-end in a day was proving a tough nut to crack.

And I was nowhere near ready to lift my foot off the gas in 2006. I kept pushing with a return to Ironman Austria. But two years on from my '04 PB, I couldn't find the top gear that had propelled me to sub eleven-hours. I finished with a distinct feeling I'd lost my edge and I crossed the line close to forty five minutes slower than my previous personal best. In the five years since 2001 I'd finished ten iron-distance races. I'd entered Ironman UK in September 2006 but had to miss it due to a lurgy I couldn't shake. The infinite battery that had powered me for years was depleted. My brain wanted to push but my body and health were letting me down. I was exhausted but this turned out to be the least of my worries. Much more troubling was a lump I'd developed on the left side of my lower abdomen.

'It's a hernia,' my doctor declared.

'A what?'

'A hernia. It's the most common injury for men between thirty and forty five,' he assured me. 'It happens when you get a small tear in your stomach wall and your intestine breaks through. It's very routine to fix.' The doctor paused,

'Have you been exerting yourself?'

I looked at him, unsure where to start.

I had my abdominal surgery in October 2006 and faced four weeks of no exercise, recovery and convalescence. A month earlier I had entered Quelle Challenge Roth, an iron-distance in Germany for the summer of 2007.

It would be my eleventh 140.6 mile triathlon race.

The World's Slowest Ironman

In my mind's eye I had visions of a Gillette advert,

The Best A Man Can Get.

Father and son, arm-in-arm, slow embrace, soft focus, crossing the line, breaking the tape. The reality couldn't have been further from the truth. It was late and he'd been complaining, swearing and grumbling all day. The sun had set a long time ago and we were shoulder-to-shoulder in the pitch black following discarded gel wrappers and sponges. We were trying to find our way back to the finish of the original European Long Course Championship in Roth. Not for the first time that day I was questioning the wisdom of my rather magnanimous offer the previous autumn post my hernia operation.

'Dad, I'm not going to be in the best of shape. Why don't we race Ironman Roth together?'

Roth wasn't an officially branded WTC Ironman and had lost its licence to call itself one in 2003. In 2007 it was Quelle Challenge Roth. But it is an iron-distance, boasts one of the biggest fields globally for the format, has huge local support and everyone, apart from the WTC, calls it an Ironman.

In December 2006 I was sore after my hernia operation and knew I wouldn't be race fit. Dad was turning sixty and wanted to race an Ironman. It would be his second attempt. His Ironman journey had all started when he'd come to see me race Ironman Austria in 2004. I'd forgotten to give him the 'health warning' that supporting an Ironman race can be quite a moving experience. Dad, with tears in his eyes at the finish, declared,

'I'll do an Ironman before I'm sixty.'

We'd both come a long way since our *headmaster-inspired-the-school-wants- to-expel-you* drive when I was fourteen. I'd got my head down, become fitter and stronger, achieved good academic results and been to university. I was getting on with life, had a job, was married and we'd started a family. In those twenty plus years, they'd done a lot too. I'll swerve Mum and Dad's story as it's several books in itself. But it involves selling up, sailing to Patagonia, writing a cruising guide, buying a farm in Chile in 1997, forestry, tourism and honey. I know, a lot to pack in with serious undertones of stimulation seeking behaviour and poor analysis of consequences. But they'd had many adventures and although they were thousands of miles away, we'd never been closer. Somehow quite naturally they had made the transition from parents to friends.

But in terms of Dad's iron-distance readiness in 2004, it's fair to say he'd enjoyed more wine and good food than lengths in the pool, miles on the bike and distance in his trainers. After watching the Ironman race in Klagenfurt in 2004 all this changed. And of course, not to be left behind, but with no ambition to do an Ironman, Mum also set about getting triathlon fit. They pulled out their bikes, got turbo trainers, swam and ran. When I next saw them, they looked transformed. They decided to build up sensibly towards their multi-sport dream. In 2005 they raced shorter course races in Zurich, the day before we raced Ironman Switzerland. They both finished and were triathletes.

Dad now turned his attention to his sixtieth birthday goal and entered the 2006 edition of Ironman Austria. The race didn't quite go to script. He was forced to pull out with gastric issues on the bike. He was trying hard but wasn't getting across the finish line. When I was fourteen, he'd believed in me and helped me out of a hole. It was my turn to return the favour.

'Dad, why don't we race it together? Father and son? It will be like the ads, *The Best a Man Can Get!*'

We made a pact and both got down to training. I was sore after the operation and my recovery had taken longer than the surgeon had told me. But by the late spring I could train consistently and felt my form returning. Dad's preparation didn't run quite so smoothly. He had persistent stomach trouble that was proving difficult to get to the bottom of. However, way more painfully he crashed his bike and broke his hip over the Christmas holidays. He had seven months to the race, but it was a big injury to get over for a man thirty years my senior and by now north of sixty.

***

Perhaps with a recently broken hip, he had grounds to be grumpy and sweary as we rolled through the German countryside. We did the swim in a respectable one hour and forty minutes, pushed through T1 and got going on the bike. Careful not to be booked for drafting by sitting in his slipstream, I hung back the mandatory ten metres. I came up alongside every now and again to check he was okay and then dropped back five bike lengths. As the field streamed by, the urge to race was almost overwhelming. But I tried to disconnect my ego and settled in for the day.

He was chuntering away and his stomach wasn't happy with the high strength energy food. As we passed the thirty mile marker he stopped to be sick. This wasn't looking good and about where he'd DNF'd the previous year in Austria. Secretly and selfishly, part of me yearned to leave him. I calculated I could still bag a decent finish. I felt in incredible shape. But I pushed these thoughts away. I knew this was a one-time gig and there would be no re-sit after this attempt. I had to keep believing in him,

'I puke in races all the time,' I lied. 'It's easier when you have cleared it out.'

Not the stirring speech he'd given me in the car all those years ago but I wasn't going to give him an easy way out. He looked at me, straightening up. Smiled, wiped his mouth clean and swung his leg over his bike. He'd always been a stubborn old goat. We were making progress but it was slow, his laboured

109

pedalling sound tracked by my clicking freehub. I was doing the maths and started to mildly panic. At our pace we were starting to face the very real possibility we'd miss the ten hour cut off to start the marathon. I'd never DNF'd an Ironman and hadn't contemplated being outside the cut offs. I held my breath and willed us forwards. We made it with fifteen minutes to spare. He was spaced out and at the end of his reserves, really on the rivet. Things were tight.

'We need a fast transition here. We have to get out onto the run course.'

We ran out to the cheers and relief of Mum, Linds, Ben and Nic. With the swim and the bike behind us, we were flying. Our impressive run lasted about 200 metres.

'I'm going to have to walk.'

He didn't look good. His stomach was distended, he was pale and his hands and arms were puffy. I was worried and definitely didn't want to kill him. We were in this together but I'd now watch him like a hawk.

'No problem, let's get this done.'

Despite all his grumpiness and chuntering through the day I couldn't have been prouder to be there with my biggest hero, the one I'd always looked up to. He'd had a huge influence on my life. He was a force of nature, a real life action man. He'd stood by me all those years earlier and I would stand by him now.

'We've got seven hours, we can walk a marathon in that time.'

As we walked, we chatted and his mood got better. His gut stayed uncomfortable and his hands and arms continued to swell. At a feed station we asked them to cut his competitor wrist band as it was starting to constrict the circulation. He didn't look good and was digging deeper and deeper.

'Dad,' I looked at him, half joking but very worried. 'We don't need to do this. Mum is going to be upset if you end up killing yourself!'

We pushed on. The light gradually faded as the late afternoon turned to night. We were on our own. Unlike all other iron-distance races the official finish cut off in Roth is fifteen hours and I'd calculated at our pace we'd be closer to the universally accepted seventeen. As the time slipped through our fingers, the organisers were packing up the course initially behind us and then ahead. They knew we were still out and were willing us to finish. We'd get to feed stations, the tables were there with food and drink but the volunteers had gone. We went through mile nineteen as it turned completely dark. An organisation van pulled up alongside us.

'We can give you a lift to the finish.'

Delirious, Dad started climbing in. I grabbed him.

'Come on. We are almost there. We're not doing this again.'

He looked at me. Nodded. We were going to get this done.

We picked our way through the now pitch black woods. We could see the fireworks marking the fifteen hour cut off and the official end of the race in the distance. The constant litter was our only guide in the darkness. Eventually we made it to the town's suburbs and followed the trail of gels and wrappers all the way to the finish.

As we got to the crowdless stadium and the grandstand I let him take a half step ahead of me. I was never going to win an Ironman but I can say I was the last finisher. The Quelle Challenger organisers are more relaxed than the WTC. They liked the father-son narrative and had left our finisher medals laid out on chairs by the line. We finished in sixteen hours and forty five minutes.

***

Six months later he was diagnosed with a twisted intestine and had an operation to remove a sizable portion to straighten out the kink. His heart stopped for a minute on the operating table. But he is an indestructible old goat and wasn't ready to climb into the van then either. I'll never forget the day I did an Ironman with my old man. My hero, the one I have looked up to and always sought approval from. He'd believed in me and I hope I'd proven his faith wasn't misplaced.

In 2007 when we picked our way through the woods following discarded wrappers and sponges, I was the age he was when I was born in Stirling Infirmary in 1973. I was looking at the future. He was looking at the past. I'd resisted growing *up* for so long. For the first time ever, I didn't want to grow *old*.

The Hurt Locker

The blue, near translucent tent liner billowed above my head. It was sunny outside, the poles bowed and flexed in the wind. I was on a camping mat, half-in half-out of a sleeping bag. My head was fuzzy, my throat dry. I felt empty, depleted, completely shelled.

As I lay there semi-conscious I became aware of another body, it was Hugo. Everyone else had cleared out. They'd left us in exhausted comas. All we had to do was pack our bags, dismantle our shelter and drive home. I felt hungover, parched, totally drained.

Slowly it came back.

I'd done it.

Five weeks after Roth, I'd ridden a solo 24-hour mountain bike race and for a fleeting moment I'd forgotten the anger boiling inside. I had a knot, a darkness, a hurt the likes of which I'd never known before. Black neural butterflies overwhelmed my every thought. The drive for white space, escape, distraction had gone nuclear, fired by an insatiable seething rage.

The world I knew had dropped away from below my feet. They'd bulldozed my Never-Never Land.

***

'We'd like to meet tomorrow.'

I'd been asked to drive to Bristol. It was the Friday morning after we'd got home from Roth. I didn't bother to wear a suit. I knew from how it was set up, what was coming. He didn't use words like 'fired' or 'sacked'. He'd soft soaped me with 'different direction', 'not fitting in' and 'team'. It was easier to expel than empathise.

My employer had merged with a competitor. The management had changed, and I had failed to read the room. Despite the veneer of a suit, fancy watch and company car, I was really still the noisy, boisterous kid in class, hand up, ready with the answer or a quip. For over a decade this energy had been my superpower, a gift, I was the nail that stood tall.

'Stuart, you say what everyone else in the room is thinking.'

However, every coin has two sides. At times the quick-fire-yin of my words were more of a social-hand-grenade-yang that rubbed some people up the wrong way. Throughout my working life my naive honesty, lack of filter and positive enthusiasm had helped me rise. But the wind had changed; creativity was seen as not following processes and taking undue risk. Candour and speaking out of turn was a challenge to authority. The new management wanted subservience, asking permission rather than forgiveness.

I *could* have bent the knee, accepted deference and domestication.

I didn't.

It was a short meeting. I'd suspected it was coming but as I walked back to my car I was numb and stunned. It broke me. I sat in the multi storey car park alone in disbelief. I held the steering wheel and cried. It had been cold, cruel, impersonal. I'd been on an upward trajectory since I was fourteen. With my boundless energy people had always believed in me. Until then I'd felt unstoppable, invincible and special. I had to support a family, pay the bills, get another job, explain what had happened, rationalise. All I could see ahead was public humiliation. I'd been rejected, told I wasn't needed. My self-belief was shattered. As I drove home I could feel the rage, the indignation, the hot fury rise inside. I didn't play any music. They'd be condemned songs, ones I could never listen to again. I wanted no association or memories.

114

The tree remembers what the axe forgets.

Fifteen years on, it is the most painful crash I have ever had. It killed my Peter Pan and haunts me to this day. The indescribable hurt and fury has never stopped raging inside.

But I also see that it was the best thing that ever happened to me. The fuse it lit projected me on a trajectory that took me on adventures beyond anything I had yet dreamed.

***

Instantly I knew I needed to be practical. I had to dust myself down, bluff it out and get another job. I pulled my CV together and started to pick myself up. I spoke to old colleagues, recruitment contacts, set up calls, interviews and first stage meetings. It wasn't easy. I had to explain why I was in the job market with a nonchalant bluff, hiding my emotions.

I hadn't had time to process the dramatic change in my upward trajectory and the anger continued to rage. Instinctively I put my mountain bike in the car and headed to my safe place, the South Downs. Between my calls and interviews I made four visits mid-week, parked and rode six hour blocks to learn every inch of the route. With a new iPod and *The Kings of Leon, The Strokes* and *Kasabian,* I lost myself, drenching my cells in mind medicine. With these lone beastings I ironed out the fuzzy navigation sections and perfected every twist and turn. I was determined something good would come from this and I set my sights on cracking the SDW end-to-end, solo, alpine style. Two weeks before Sleepless in the Saddle it was time to put it all together.

***

As Linds, Ben and I headed to Winchester with the tent, it was the first time in weeks I felt a lightness in my heart. With the buzz and anticipation of adventure perhaps the little boy inside hadn't completely died.

I woke at 4am and quietly got myself ready. At first light I rode the five miles to the start at the King Alfred's monument in the city centre. It was cold, fresh and I felt the thrill of absolute freedom. After my four six-hour blocks I was bike-hard like I'd never been before. Physically I'd transformed myself and felt incredible but it wasn't only in my muscles. I felt an inner hardness, raw anger and was ready to explode. This was my world, my true identity, where I could remove all my babushka veneers. I had food in my CamelBak, energy powder to top up my reservoir and spare tubes in case I punctured. The fizzing thrill of a challenge, doing something extraordinary. It was just me, my bike and over one hundred miles of off-road trail. I felt like Stu again.

The sun rose, warming the air as I climbed up beyond the familiar landmarks around Cheesefoot Head, over Beacon Hill and passed the watercress beds in Warnford. The climb over Winchester Hill was long but I knew the ridge and valley to Butser, the A3 and Queen Elizabeth Country Park. I was flying, link after link fell behind me. I punctured but with a quick repair lost none of my momentum.

The events of the previous three weeks rolled around, surged, replayed. On the downs there were smells, views, the heat of the sun. Painful conversations and images faded, grew dull and less urgent. I couldn't get them out of my head but here they felt different, distant, not so real or important. The next sections through Harting Beacon, Linch Down, Duncton and Bignor hills were where we had walked as kids. By early afternoon I was dropping down into Amberley Valley, gingerly taking the descent where James and I had crashed on our first ill-fated winter effort. With some food I fought the steep climb to Kithurst Hill. I was in the badlands now, Mr Cowell's infamous third quarter.

116

Get to Brighton, your old after work playground, I coached myself.

Devil's Dyke, Jack and Jill's, over Ditchling and the fast descents down Castle Hill and Breaking Bottom. I punctured again but knew I was beyond the hardest part of the day and could smell the stables. It was late afternoon as I crossed the railway and the A26 on to Firle Beacon and Alfriston. The last climbs were steep, up narrow tracks but then suddenly I was skirting Eastbourne Golf Club.

I took a photo of my bike leaning against the most easterly South Downs Way sign. Even with my two punctures, reservoir top ups and food stops, I'd ridden end-to-end in eleven hours and thirteen minutes. It had been a huge day, I'd executed it perfectly and was elated. I rode to the pier, bought fish and chips, smothered them in ketchup and waited for my extraction.

Ben was three and in his car seat as I peered in. I was grinning ear-to-ear, my face splattered in mud and dusty. He knew no different. I didn't want to be remembered as an office worker, a domesticated, suit wearing slave. This is what his Dad did. It was totally normal, with a bike, taking on mad adventures, being extraordinary. This was the life I wanted to show him.

I had two weeks to recover before Sleepless in the Saddle. My first solo 24-hour mountain bike race. I felt a fraction overcooked but knew my mind and body were ready.

***

The race officially started Saturday at 2pm. But it didn't really. Things got going eleven hours later at 1am Sunday morning. In a solo 24-hour challenge it's in the dark Witching Hours when the wheat is sorted from the chaff.

We'd all got up to the event venue on the Friday and pitched our tents in the solo area by the course. Nic and James had offered to be pit crew. Hugo and I were racing solo. I had two bikes in case of emergency mechanicals; a black carbon-fibre stealth machine and my original 2002 aluminium hard-tail for backup. I hoped I was being overly cautious. On the Saturday morning we'd tried to sleep late but it was impossible in the oven-like tent so we all sat around lazily chatting and eating bacon butties. Behind my public veneer, I was still hurting beyond words inside. I had my game face on for James and Nic but couldn't wait to escape into my private endorphin world. Fizzing, I bathed in the pre-race nerves and quietly charged my battery with pent up rage, absolutely intoxicated.

As the start grew nearer, an entire day of riding loomed ahead. I thought I'd be cool-headed as we lined up for the Le Mans style start. But as the horn sounded a volcano of energy exploded inside.

I've pinned a number on!

This is a race!

I tore off like a hare with the team riders determined to get my nose ahead of Hugo. My first two laps were too fast. I couldn't afford to burn matches so early and coached myself to slow. We solo riders had a small marker hanging from our seats and the majority of the field were understanding of our sub-supersonic pace. The lead teams of four were fast and fresh riders would blow by when there was room and even when there wasn't.

'On yer right!'

'Left!'

The course was a joy. At times technical, but dry, flowing and fast. Long climbs and swooping descents separated the trickier parts. Quickly I dropped into a steady rhythm. Race lines were worn, the surface bedded down and with familiarity the corners swept, the downs accelerated. The difference in perspective between solo and team riders was obvious. We were out lap after lap and could learn the course. They'd have a lap, foot to the floor and then have to sit out the next three.

My plan was to complete a lap and then as I passed the camping area, pull over, step over the course tape, wolf down a sandwich, top up my reservoir and take a five minute break on my folding chair. That was the plan. I hadn't accounted for the red mist of the race. For the first six laps my breaks were closer to two minutes. It wasn't sustainable and if I didn't slow my pace I'd pay later.

But suddenly disaster struck.

On lap seven my rear derailleur caught a tree stump and ripped the hanger clean through. In disbelief I stopped as my drive locked. With most of a lap to go and non-existent bike repair skills I was in real trouble.

Panic!

But perhaps my luck was turning and good things happen to good people. Incredibly, a nearby spectator was a mechanic. Within ten minutes he had me going on a jury rig, setting my chain up as a single speed. I'd had visions of running, pushing, freewheeling the downs for the rest of the lap and I was delighted I could ride. The course was a figure-of-eight and at the pinch point in the middle I shouted my predicament to James. In an instant he jumped into action. He readied my second bike and checked with the Shimano tent to see if they had spares. As I climbed on my old aluminium work horse for the next loop, James assured me he'd have me on my preferred bike within a lap. Good to his word, although out of pocket to the tune of a shiny new rear mech, I was back in the race.

With eight hours done, my times were consistently about forty five minutes per lap but I was only a third of the way into the twenty four. Fortunately as we rode into the evening, the race had settled down. My sweet and sickly energy food had quickly grown tedious, so Nic and James kept me supplied with savoury sandwiches, peanut butter, cheese, anything to put petrol in the tank. Nic was getting the results as I crossed the timing mat and giving me an update when I went through the middle of the figure-of-eight. There were close to 120 solo

119

riders and in this first third of the race I was sitting in the top thirty. At 9pm it started getting dark and the marshals told us lights would be mandatory on the next lap. I had a long way to go; a night of riding, the following morning and through to the afternoon lay ahead. I steeled myself for what was to come.

A lap at a time.

This isn't a place for thinkers.

Forward motion is everything.

My Ironman wisdom was helping me through.

As I neared the camp at the course's cross over I shouted across, passing the lights message to James. When I stopped and fed he quickly fitted them. As I rode away their thin beam bobbed ahead. As the evening darkened to night, the temperature dropped.

I was on the far side of the course when the sunset finally came. The horizon was a brilliant orange, purple and grey masterpiece. I was here in my bubble, racing solo, about to push through the night. I wouldn't have chosen to be anywhere else. No one could touch me. I truly felt the person I wanted to be, who I really was deep inside. I looked left again across the black valley and incredible sky. This would be a moment I'd never forget.

My mind was clear of everything. No worries or cares. Simple survival. Like a machine. The next turn, twist, descent, fast section. Systems checks. Self-motivation. As it got darker my speed dropped. My laps were taking fifty five minutes to an hour, I was either tiring or less sure of the trail.

'You're in 24th,' Nic called across as I passed the camp. I was going slower but climbing up the solo-field. When I stopped at the end of the lap I was 22nd.

'What's going on, I have definitely slowed, but my position is improving?'

'The dude over there has gone to bed.'

It was midnight. We weren't even at the halfway point. It was cooler, damp, pitch black without lights and fourteen hours stretched ahead. We were getting to the Witching Hour when resolves were broken. It filled me with hope. I stood up from my chair.

'Forward motion is everything.'

I grinned at Nic. By simply riding I was climbing the field. I jumped on my bike and pedalled into the darkness. I came through again at 1am.

'You're in 14th.'

Fourteenth! The race had really started. I couldn't believe it. I'd shot up the order and was ahead of many of the teams of four.

'Hugo's gone to bed.'

Famous for his near narcolepsy it wasn't a surprise but the news was a huge boost. Nic's updates and the feeding of the results were helping me massively. I was strung out. I'd been awake for seventeen hours and racing for eleven. Thirteen hours of suffering lay ahead.

Too much. Don't think. Ride the lap you're on.

I muttered to myself pushing into the dark.

Between 2am and 3am it was very cold and my reserves were stretched beyond anything I'd known before. I wanted to stop and sleep. A dampness hung in the air, crept through the layers and whipped away my heat. I alternated between jacket on and jacket off, wasting time, disorientated, hardly able to think. I was on the edge, running on fumes, my mind screaming for me to stop, shut down, rest.

Forward motion is everything.

If I stopped it would be over, I'd go crashing down the field. I felt a hardness, a seething rage, an anger rise inside me. It wasn't difficult to find, barely below the surface. This was everything. I had no other option but to drive myself on. When I came to our camp there was no movement, even my crew had gone to bed. They'd laid out sandwiches in a box, some chocolate and two flasks of coffee and chicken soup. The creamy hot liquid was delicious and filled me with renewed vim. I was truly solo and on my own. If Nic and James are in bed, so are my fellow competitors. As I finished my soup I grabbed one of the spare batteries, swung my leg over the bike and pushed on.

And then another miracle happened. At 3.30am maybe 4 the darkness slowly faded to grey. I could make out the trail and when clear of the trees and cover, no longer needed my lights. Slowly, imperceptibly, the night morphed to dawn and with the growing light miraculously my body started to wake up. I felt stronger, more alert, my energy returned and the compulsion to sleep grew less. I rode on, lap after lap, 5am passed and then 6, ensuring each break was no more than five minutes. I'd almost done the third quarter and had less than eight hours to ride. As I pulled into camp, my attempt at creeping must have disturbed Nic. I heard the tent zip ratchet open.

'Morning. How are you doing?'

'Good. Good. Glad it's morning.'

'Anything you want on the next lap?'

She was like an angel.

'I could murder some more chicken soup.'

I paused. I wanted to know but was also terrified it wouldn't be what I wanted to hear.

'And if you could get an update on the results?'

I knew it would be sorted and as I neared the pinch point on the figure-of-eight I braced myself for either the lift or the crushing news. She was ecstatic.

'Stu, Stu,' the familiar Southern Irish brogue, 'you're in 12th!'

With less than eight hours to go, hope surged in me. It was a new day and the race was on. But despite my raised spirits I could do nothing to pick up my lap times. Even if my mind had forgotten the last sixteen hours, they had taken their toll on my legs and body. My shoulders and neck were stiff, my backside was raw, my thumb blistered and taped from the gear shifting. My forearms were pumped and locked despite the ibuprofen I was knocking back. I stepped over the tape and slumped in my chair. I was ready for this to be over.

'Linds texted. She's on her way with Ben. She says "Morning" and she "Loves you".'

I wasn't ready for that. Big tears rolled down my cheeks. I was in a hard place. Stretched like never before, on fumes, driven by competitive rage and a determination to prove I had the right stuff. I wasn't ready to go to a soft place yet. Fearful the race could break me, I couldn't let it in. Nic was knocked back. We cried together.

The sun was warming up and I shed all the layers and weight I could. It was time to finish this off. As the heat rose, the 2pm finish edged ever closer.

'How you doing buddy?' a supporter asked as I struggled up a climb. I didn't have the words to answer as he summed it up, 'In the hurt locker?' I smiled.

For the last few laps Linds and Ben had made it. He wasn't yet four but was already used to this familiar picture. His old man, a wild animal, with a bike and mud splattered face. He sat on my lap as I took my five minute break. I couldn't have been happier. He was in his element too but I suspect more for the attention and the amount of unopened chocolate on offer.

The last lap was incredible, elation. I knew the course so well now, every climb, corner, technical clattering descent, its flow. My bike had been amazing, my preparation and training perfect. James and Nic had been the ideal pit crew; patient, attentive, completely selfless. I finished twelfth, unable to break into the top ten. This was the hard end of the field, the ones that didn't go to bed. I was delighted to be in their exalted company.

As I stood in the steaming shower, the hot water was delicious. Around my feet, 24-hours of grime, dirt and dust swirled in the porcelain base. The weather had been incredible and over the next few years I'd learn how rain could instantly and dramatically change the race. But that was all to come. I don't remember falling asleep. From my coma I didn't hear any of the camp being packed away. Disorientated, momentarily lost, I woke to see the blue billowing fabric above my head. I was parched, my head bleary, my tongue swollen and dry. And then it came back to me. I'd crossed a Rubicon.

I was a different athlete. Maybe a different person too.

Tom

He was adamant he'd found a better form of locomotion than walking and he was sticking with his invention.

Tom was a bum shuffler and for eighteen months he was very accomplished at it. The technique was entirely self-devised and he could cover ground at an eye-watering clip. With his legs bowed like a bullfrog, the soles of his feet in prayer, a double arm downward scoop and a full body whiplash, he'd flick himself forwards, literally taking off.

Momentum was everything with his shuffle. It obviously took immense levels of concentration. There was never a mid-thrust smile, instead an intense focused scowl. But when the target of his effort was acquired, a toy, a lost comforter, something to pull up on, his face would light with joy.

Tom was born in July 2008. Like Ben before, everyone said he looked like me. He had brown hair and big round eyes.

He had three white and blue striped teddies. They were eight inches tall, cotton and identical. Due to his attachment to them, the necessity of a trio and a constant cycle of washing averted any biohazard risk. He was inseparable from 'Teddy' and oblivious to the hygienic switch-outs. He'd sit unconsciously stroking their ears, tugging them between his index and middle finger, calmly watching the room from his high chair.

Linds and I were seasoned pros on the routine and cadence of life with a newborn. For baby number two, my *pre-departure-contractions-hospital-prep* game was way better. This time, for provisions and delivery suite sustenance, I only made sufficient sandwiches for the two of us. More significantly I'd developed a slither of emotional intelligence. Instinctively I knew an en route to the hospital divert would cost more than the face price of any purchased car magazine. Linds had handled Ben's arrival with aplomb, on this second occasion I was much better prepared.

We had a family. I had two boys. Linds technically had three.

Before bed, reading time was the best. The three of us would sit all cleaned, washed and smelling of baby soap in pyjamas. Ben snuggled by my side, Tom, barely one, chugging on a bottle, words meaningless to him. His comfort, the steady tone, rhythm, laughter, warmth of each other's closeness. The safety of togetherness. We had our favourites. In unison, Ben and I would repeat the chorus with appropriate intonation; 'A Gruffalo', long pause of wonder, 'What's a Gruffalo?'. We loved Julia Donaldson, Hairy Maclary and Dr Suess. It wasn't all wholesome books. We were avid TV watchers too. With Tom feeding and Ben in control of the remote, we'd repeatedly watch Bob the Builder, Dora the Explorer and Lazy Town on DVD and we'd never miss an episode of Steve Backshall's Deadly 60. These shows were slicker, better produced, more commercial than the programmes I remember watching growing up.

And our telly was way better too. In the 70s and early 80s we had a tiny black and white TV, tuned manually with a dial on the back and to improve reception it had a coat hanger for an aerial. If someone moved in the room everything was lost in snow. But despite the technology, the picture quality and the lack of control of content, sometimes there were some programming gems. Some of the children's shows were highbrow stuff, classics, subtly subversive and often profound. The Wombles, the Muppets and the sometimes creepy Worzel Gummidge could never be missed.

The absolute classic from my childhood was the double life of Mr Benn. The sartorial elegance of his bowler hat and black suit, belied the twilight existence of the most enigmatic Mr Benn. A model of suburban conformity, on the surface accepting his existence, stoic and quiet. But Mr Benn had a coping strategy and also led a mysterious babushka life. On his way to work he'd call into his local

126

fancy dress shop and duck behind the changing curtain, the divide between two worlds. He'd shed his smart identity and tumble into an adventure only to re-emerge adorned in bowler hat and suit. The dual existence of Mr Benn, searching for adventure and exhilaration.

But my bedtime reading with Ben and Tom was inconsistent and my life on the work side of the curtain felt far from safe. I'd got a job in South Wales and was working away more. I was out of my lane and not enjoying myself. On Monday I'd don my 'bowler hat' and could be away for a week in Cardiff living in hotels and company apartments. A bike in the boot, a bag full of training gear to help me escape the drudgery.

It was nearly ten years on since I'd crossed the finish line at Ironman Lake Placid. I'd raced and finished thirteen iron-distance events. During this decade I'd worked out how to cope with the rigours of the challenge; the 2.4 mile swim, the 112 bike and the 26.2 mile marathon. They were my safe space. More recently it was the other 364 days of the year I was struggling with. So many things were out of kilter and I was finding it harder to be the real me. My tried and tested method of slipping into my fancy dress shop for escape and disassociation wasn't working. Things were spinning faster, out of control and it wasn't fun anymore.

I was in a dark place.

Did Not Sleep

The sun was shining, warm on my skin. It was Sunday morning and the race was in full swing. Bikes flew by, clattering along, their riders battling to make or defend a place. I was on the wrong side of the course tape. Hidden behind my wraparound Oakleys, tears streamed down my cheeks. I wasn't in any physical pain but I couldn't believe what I had done.

We were at the 2009 Mountain Mayhem, the UK's other big 24-hour summer mountain bike race. With two Sleepless in the Saddle races and a Mayhem finish, I now had three 24-hour solo challenges successfully under my belt. I'd invested in a full suspension carbon bike and some decent lights. I'd built experience, knew when the difficult questions would be asked and had rehearsed my answers. I'd discovered what I thought was a tried and tested way to prepare. I wasn't a veteran but I felt a long way from a solo-virgin. It was now my thing.

But for some reason I hadn't felt ready. Stuff had gotten in the way and I hadn't done my four consecutive weekends of back-to-back six hour mountain bike beastings. I hadn't got bike-hard and this left an indiscernible chink in my armour. The race had started well. I knew the format, steady, lap-after-lap, take a five minute break. For the first ten hours the placing didn't matter. These loops were a warm up, stay in the game. Get to the Witching Hour, that's when the thing really began. But something in my head wasn't clicking. I wasn't in the groove or feeling it. Instead I was sluggish, heavy and slow. We had a few rain showers through the afternoon and the course got greasy. At eight hours I wasn't enjoying myself and at nine it was a grind. My resolve was wavering and the Witches were getting to me. At midnight I slumped in my chair. My five minute break turned to ten, I couldn't stand or will myself up. With fourteen crushing hours stretched ahead of me, I folded.

'I'm done. I'm coming to bed.'

Linds looked at me puzzled.

'I don't feel right.'

I crashed. Fell asleep, passed out. When I woke the next day, the devastating realisation of what I had done hit me. I'd given up, let go of the bars and fallen to the floor. I'd stepped off. The suffering of the previous night was nothing compared to this. Darkness consumed me as I walked up to the timing tent to tell the organisers I'd stopped. He checked my position.

'Oh that's a shame. You were sitting in twelfth at midnight.'

My funk got deeper. I'd let go of twelfth. I could have easily made the top ten. Alone I walked back to our camp, broken, tears silently streaming. I couldn't watch the race.

'I'm going out for some more.'

I rode the last six hours. Having gone to bed, I'd fallen short of my expectations. I felt like a fraud with my solo number. But I smashed myself in a raging fury. A pattern was emerging and I wasn't doing well. '*You've changed*' became the rather unhelpful refrain. I didn't think I had changed, but everything around me seemed to be changing. The last few years had spun out of control. I was constantly yo-yoing between being on form and being ill. My Did Not Starts were becoming more frequent and expensive. In the late 2000s, Ironman UK at Sherborne Castle was scheduled for early September. I'd missed two in a row in 2007 and 2008 due to the back-to-school lurgies. My immune system seemed shot and fragile. I was less confident of myself, unsure.

Wanting to avoid the gamble on the cost of flights and accommodation with the uncertainty of being healthy on race day, I'd moved away from overseas Ironman racing. Instead I turned my attention to lower key, non-WTC branded full distance races, The Big Woody in Chepstow on the Welsh border, the Forestman in the New Forest in Hampshire. I'd bagged 24-hour solo finishes and even ran a double marathon with the ultra-distance London to Brighton 56-miler. Usually I could see a Did Not Start coming.

From four weeks before the start I was gripped by pre-race paranoia, living cocooned and moving away from flu addled zombies. When sniffs entered the house I'd even sleep in a different room to isolate myself and avoid getting ill. If something did get me I'd be angry with frustration but at least had time to prepare and could find the headspace for acceptance and resignation.

There was no doubt the DNS's stung, but the Did Not Finish hurt *way* more. Mountain Mayhem caught me unawares, smashed me. It took me six months to recover. Not physically but mentally, it shattered my confidence. Whatever discomfort I thought I was going through in a race, it would be over in a matter of hours. The rigours of endurance challenges were nothing compared with soul searching and endless analysis of stepping off mid-event. I was being schooled again, learning the hard way to *never* ever give up.

Failure hurts way more than the suffering it takes to succeed.

Deep down I had a much bigger problem, but I couldn't seem to do anything about it. The insidiousness of insomnia had crept up on me. For over two years I'd been working in South Wales, staying in hotels and hadn't slept well. It had never been a problem but now I couldn't drop off. My head would spin endlessly with thoughts as soon as I closed my eyes. When I did eventually doze off, I'd wake a few hours later as my worries surfaced again, continually looping, cycling faster. It was dehumanising and I was exhausted. With no escape I felt like a big kid living in an adult world. I couldn't have been less happy and hated the cage I was in. Craving exhilaration and oblivion, I was in a very self-destructive place. My filter between thoughts, words and actions was stretched dangerously taut. Something was ready to explode inside.

And that's how I found myself on a snowy night in Cardiff, driving to a TaeKwonDo class for the mind medicine that had been so effective for me as a teenager. It had worked when I was fourteen, maybe it could save me now.

National TaeKwonDo Championship

It was a blur, I don't really remember feeling much. I took a few kicks to the head, he landed at least a couple of punches. It was November 2010 and I was getting my arse handed to me in the second round of the National TaeKwonDo Championship.

My memory is hazy but I am sure the hunk opposite me was about twice my height. Maybe I have misremembered some of the details. What was very apparent to me and all who watched was that he was stronger, faster, younger, more flexible and was definitely better at TaeKwonDo. I was also experiencing how fast three minutes passes when you're absolutely saturated in adrenaline. In the blink of an eye it was over. I felt nothing, my mind detached, my body senseless and numb. We were standing either side of the referee. My arm stayed by my side and his went up.

I don't think there was ever any doubt.

***

My first night back in a TaeKwonDo class had been electric. At thirty seven years old, there were some sideways glances from the late teen undergraduates and early twenties postgrads in the class. I suspect I cut a rather undignified, slightly younger shadow of their parents. But to my relief the instructor, Mr Matthews, a fifth dan black belt, couldn't have been more welcoming. Despite my loss of flexibility, much of what had been drilled in during my teens quickly came back as the dusty synapses slowly refired. The patterns and set moves were re-learned and obsessively I pored over books and watched teaching videos on YouTube. I'd been preparing for and racing Ironman for a decade so my fitness was above average but my flexibility was shocking. Naturally, with my addictive, dopamine hungry mind, it swept me away and I lived for TaeKwonDo through the late winter and spring of 2010.

Mr Matthews could see my commitment and despite my two decade hiatus, quickly re-instated me to my former grade of red belt. I'd been prepared to start again but now I found myself just two gradings away from being a first dan and achieving a coveted black belt. I couldn't wait for the next class and would sit at work buzzing for my evening fix. It was like cat-nip for my stimulation seeking brain.

Of course I tumbled down the rabbit hole. I bought a suit that I meticulously washed and ironed before each class. I had a gum shield fitted and at each training session would relish the sparring, diligently adjusting my box to ensure my crown jewels were safe. Suddenly the sepia, monotones of my life in Cardiff were overwhelmed with vivid colour. On Tuesdays and Thursdays I'd thrash myself with Mr Matthews. I felt young again, vital, alive.

But it took its toll. My late thirties brain was sending commands to a long lost teenage body. I blew my hamstring in my third week. My feet, unused to unsupported running and bouncing, started to constantly ache and developed into vicious plantar fasciitis. The skin on the soles had grown soft and I quickly developed terrible blisters. I was doing this twenty years too late and my body didn't like it. For the first time ever, I was feeling my age. Naturally, despite the injuries, I didn't stop. I donned running leggings under my suit to keep my hamstrings warm and adapted my sparring style to avoid high kicks that stretched them. I taped my feet for support and tried to protect the blistered skin as best I could.

It was self-destructive but I was having a blast. I'd finish the session red in the face, my suit so wet with sweat it was transparent. I was tingling, buzzing, electricity pulsed through me. I knew I wouldn't sleep well but didn't care. As I drove the few miles back to my hotel for the night, the stiffness would set in. I'd get sideways looks as I hobbled through reception, my bag heavy with sweat-soaked gear, the effort on my salty skin already dried crusty.

Like Mr Benn, I was soaring in the twilight between two worlds. In the day, living a life I hated, feeling trapped and uninspired. In the office, the hours would stretch ahead of me until I could close my laptop. I'd go to the gym most mornings or head out for a run. In the hotel there was a twenty metre pool and although not ideal I'd lap length-after-length. I kept my mountain bike in the car and through the winter with lights I'd ride out into the dark, wrapped up against the cold. Losing myself with *Ministry's Khyber Pass* on repeat, *Mumford and Sons* or *The Dropkick Murphy's* in my headphones. In this limbo life I couldn't see a future and was not really coping. I was away all week, existing but not living, keeping fit but not feeling healthy.

Work wasn't sustainable and came crashing to an end in May 2010. It was a short meeting and hadn't been altogether unexpected. Again they didn't use words like 'sacked' or 'fired'. The meeting was a relief and a massive weight lifted from my shoulders. I'd known from the start I should never have taken the job. I packed up the car and headed home. I'd find a way to make a living but not out of a suitcase, away from Linds, Ben and Tom. That wasn't for me.

***

And that's the backstory of how I found myself in Crawley at the National TaeKwonDo Championship in November 2010. I was too slow to see it, but I was in the wrong place at the wrong time. This wasn't the right adventure for me, and in the second round of the heavyweight, pre-black belt division this truth came crashing down on my head. It sounds impressive that I had enough talent to make it through the first round in the competition. The reality was my progress to the second stage was no reflection on my sparring skills. I was merely the oldest person in the division by a good fifteen years and with an odd number of competitors, they'd given me a 'bye'.

My luck didn't end here either. As I was just over seventy five kilograms at the time, this weight edged me into the heavyweight category! As I looked around at my fellow competitors, none of my potential opponents were as close to the threshold as me. Some of them were massive. David and Goliath I reassured myself as I fastened my head guard and clenched my gum shield.

The biggest one of them all turned out to be my gigantic opponent in the second round. I don't remember anything other than that he dispatched me effortlessly. He was twenty one and built like the proverbial outhouse. This Hercules was a black tag, the real deal when it came to TaeKwonDo National Champion readiness. I was a non-taxing inconvenience on his pathway to glory. Even the referee gave me a sympathetic pat on the shoulder, sharing a reassuring word as he led me from the ring. My consolation was that my second round nemesis went on to win the national championship for this division. But regardless of who I'd come up against that day, I'd have taken a beating.

With a two hour drive home from Crawley, I was in bits. This wasn't sustainable. I had to re-find myself. I desperately needed a break, something positive to hold and get obsessed with.

The Legacy Announcement

The text popped up from Nic,

'Have you heard about the Ironman Legacy Programme?'

Few people had ever heard of Andrew Messick before October 2011. After his announcement on the launch of the Kona Legacy Programme, if you did Ironman and always ticked the 'Qualify for Hawaii' box, but had accepted it was *never* going to happen, you now knew Andrew Messick.

He's American, wears glasses and looks in his mid-forties. He's bald on top and the hair clinging on the sides is grey and cropped close. He's one of us; a keen, self-professed Ironman Age Group enthusiast. He also happens to be the Chief Executive of the World Triathlon Corporation, known to most people as the WTC. The WTC is the owner of the Ironman brand, host and organiser of all the 'official' Ironman races globally.

In October 2011, Mr Messick changed everything for Ironman Age Groupers when he announced the Kona Legacy Programme. It was the equivalent of the creation of the Willy Wonka golden ticket for the average Age Grouper, giving us the chance to participate in the Ironman World Championship in Hawaii. With Andrew's announcement, any Age Grouper, basically a non-professional athlete, regardless of finish time, could now become eligible to claim one of the coveted and highly contested 'slots' at the Ironman World Championship held every October in Kona, Hawaii.

Prior to Andrew's launch of the Legacy Programme the only realistic way to qualify for Hawaii was to be good. This meant finishing in the top three to five in an Age Group in one of the twentyish WTC Ironman sanctioned and branded races. To secure one of these slots you had to be talented, in fact, very talented.

In my Age Group, the racers fast enough to qualify for Hawaii were finishing with the professionals, literally hours ahead of me.

Hawaii entry for an athlete like me was beyond reach. In 2011 a typical Ironman race would have some 2,500 starters. A race this size would carry perhaps fifty qualification slots across all male and female age groups. Even with a decade of Ironman racing behind me, I had zero chance of swimming the 2.4 miles in the crystal blue water of the Pacific, cycling the 112 miles on the famous Queen-K through the iconic lava fields and finally running 26.2 gruelling miles in the merciless sun.

From flicking through *220 Triathlon* magazines in my teenage years, I knew Ironman Hawaii to be the spiritual home of triathlon. Kona was where the Ironman greats had fought heroic battles to be crowned World Champion. I'd long accepted, I was never going to Hawaii, but Mr Messick changed all of that. His announcement seemed to speak directly to me. He was an Ironman and he wanted Age Groupers to experience the thrill of racing the Kona World Championship course once in their 'careers'. If I understood correctly, all I had to do to get to Hawaii was to meet three eligibility criteria:

One - complete *twelve* WTC officially sanctioned, branded, M-Dot full Ironman races.

Two - complete *three* consecutive years with Ironman finishes up to and including the year I would race Hawaii.

Three - have *never* raced Ironman Hawaii before.

Well I had the third in the bag before I had even started. The first two criteria could prove to be more challenging. But with these conditions then satisfied, I'd be eligible to apply for a slot at the World Championship. Andrew was explicit with the small print of the deal; it was a one-time ticket and there was no ambiguity. I would only get one shot. Once I took my place, I had to get across the line or live with my regrets forever.

By October 2011, I had finished fifteen iron-distance races but only had ten official WTC Ironman sanctioned medals and t-shirts. I calculated that within three years and as many consecutive Ironman finishes, I could be on a plane to Kona. For over a decade, I'd trained, prepared, finished, not started, crashed, fallen and been broken by DNFs. Over the next three years I would find out whether I had the experience, beans and grit to get to the start and then cross the finish of Ironman Hawaii.

Before I'd even read all the announcement, I committed myself to the Legacy Programme. Taking up the challenge was instinctive, it was that simple. I didn't mull it over, sleep on it or weigh the pros and cons. With no thought of consequences, I didn't even talk it over with Linds. The news was like a clarion call and in a heartbeat I was in.

Unwittingly I was climbing on a roller coaster, about to play one of the world's most expensive and stressful games of snakes and ladders. I was injured, broken and deep inside I had lost my self-confidence. I felt a long way from having the right stuff.

Eligibility Year 1
Ironman Lanzarote 2012

'Do you want to go and watch the start?'

It was May 2012 and we were in Lanzarote. This was the first official WTC Ironman of my three consecutive years of finishes in my Legacy Programme journey. Thankfully I hadn't needed to explain the significance of Andrew Messick's announcement to Linds. Preparing for the biggest sales pitch of my life I laid them out for her.

'So I'm *guaranteed* a place if I achieve the following criteria.' I paused to give her time to absorb each point. 'Although I have done fifteen iron-distance races, only ten of them were WTC sanctioned Ironman finishes.'

So far so good.

'I have to do twelve official M-dot Ironman races.'

'So two more to go?' she asked hopefully.

'Not quite. I also need to have three consecutive years of Ironman finishes up to the year I do Hawaii. Because I did Forestman last year, I am technically on square zero.' I was kicking myself. I'd finished Ironman Nice in 2010 but missed a year of official iron-distance racing. 'The WTC will *guarantee* me a place if I finish an Ironman a year for the next three years.'

I repeated 'guarantee' slowly for effect, sure it would only increase the persuasiveness of my pitch. I didn't confess that I hadn't done any maths or budgeting and it was simply an emotional decision but I think she knew that anyway. Every year I ticked the 'Qualify for Hawaii' option when I entered, but I was never going to qualify. Even at my fastest race at Ironman Austria in 2004 when I finished in 10:53:54, I was still a good two hours slower than the qualifiers in my age group. Until Andrew's announcement I had more chance of getting to the moon than qualifying for Ironman Hawaii. Linds knew this was a once in a lifetime opportunity and without hesitation she agreed.

But six months later things weren't quite going to script. I was a mess. My dalliance with TaeKwonDo had left me broken. The plantar fasciitis was a really horrible chronic injury that made even walking hurt. I'd also torn both hamstrings and they had repaired awkwardly leaving them as taut as tripwires. These two injuries left my running in a very poor state. But my underlying engine was strong. My hamstrings had slowed me at the 2011 Forestman but I'd put in a good performance in the solo category in my sixth 24-hour race. I'd finally squeezed into the top ten, bagging my highest position of joint seventh.

The truth was I had been drifting away from the WTC's official Ironman format of racing. No one could touch them for delivering the most professional and electric *You-are-an-Ironman* experience. But I'd got disillusioned by the mass starts, ever increasing entry fees, the cost of flights and accommodation. I saw them as very expensive t-shirt sellers. They had seemed more focused on the front of the race and we Age Groupers were the forgotten shmucks, funding the spectacle for the elite few.

With Andrew Messick's press release all that fell away. In the blink of an eye I was back. For me, the Legacy Programme sent a powerful message, they were focused on us Age Groupers again. I'd entered the first WTC sanction race I could get to. Arguably one of the world's toughest, Ironman Lanzarote in May 2012. I'd finished it twice before and thought a third success should be a piece of cake. My quest to get to Hawaii was on and critically I had Linds' blessing.

***

'And what are you going to do about the Transalp?'
Ah yes, the Transalp.

I'd met the Prentice Boys two years earlier at Sleepless. Unlike me, John and Stuart were players on the national endurance and 24-hour mountain bike race circuit. They rode as a pair and were good, normally finishing first or second in their category.

Riding competitively as a duo in a 24-hour race is hardcore. As a team of four over the entire day you are riding for roughly six hours, albeit flat out. As a pair the pace is not far off, and often faster than all but the quickest teams of four. But instead of six hours you're riding for twelve at the same all-out threshold. It's full beans for a lap, change over and then hardly enough time to feed while getting cold before you're out again as your partner comes roaring into transition. In a pair there is no time to sleep.

John and Stuart were good. Competing as a team of two wasn't for wimps or the faint hearted. It took a special kind of mindset and I held these brothers in awe. The teams of four were usually camped in a field adjacent to the race venue at 24-hour races but the pairs were allowed to pitch up next to the course with the solo riders. By luck I'd parked next to them a few years earlier.

'How do you fancy doing the Transalp with a mate of ours?'

Despite my solo races and the South Downs Way, I considered myself an outsider to the world of mountain biking and had never heard of it.

'What's the Transalp?'

'It's an eight stage, UCI sanctioned, mountain bike race covering over 600 kilometres. You start in southern Germany and ride through Austria, Switzerland and into Italy. It finishes on the shores of Lake Garda.'

It sounded incredible and I was flattered to have been asked but it would be a *big* step up. It only felt like yesterday I was pulling my aluminium hardtail out of the back of the car at Jack and Jill's Windmill before my drive home from Brighton.

'I'm not very good.'

'You're racing solo 24-hour races. You must be alright.'

I considered it for about a second.

'Alright then. Why not?'

I met Nick later that day, we all exchanged numbers and over the autumn and winter of 2011 our plans were firmed up. The 2012 Transalp project was well underway before Mr Messick threw Ironman Hawaii qualification wide open. Within the blink of an eye I'd entered Ironman Lanzarote and the Transalp in 2012. I figured I could do both.

However, my debut on the Legacy Programme was less than auspicious.

***

'So do you want to go over and see the start?'

I didn't want to be anywhere near the start. It had come on initially as a dry throat three weeks earlier. I was back from a wet and cold, *get-to-know-you-better* Sunday ride with Nick, my Transalp partner, and within days I had a head cold. With less than a month to 'Grotty', as Ironman Lanzarote is affectionately known, this would be my first eligibility race. I'd thought nothing of it. But I wasn't sleeping well. Gripped by long term insomnia my cough magnified as I struggled to fall asleep night after night and then woke at 3am tossing and turning with an endless stream of worries. Without the bliss of restful recovery, it crept down my thorax and into my lungs.

As soon as I'd felt the tickle, I'd stopped training. I did nothing to aggravate it but my body couldn't push it out. I prayed it would clear. I knew, if I could get to the start line without the cold, I had a good chance of finishing. It wouldn't be pretty but I'd get around. The race was on Sunday, we were flying on Thursday. With it showing no signs of shifting, I'd lost all hope and didn't even travel with my bike. Something inside told me if I got lucky in the warmth of Lanzarote maybe I'd be able to hire one, pull out a heroic last minute recovery.

As we went to bed the night before the start it was clinging on, gooey and thick. I was hacking and it was clogging up and pulling at my lungs. There was no way I was racing. I didn't want to be anywhere near the event. On Sunday we played tennis, sat in the sun and slowly recovered.

Eligibility Race #1 - Did Not Start. On my road to Ironman Hawaii, I was an entry fee, flights and accommodation down and no closer.

Actually I was now two entry fees deep in my first year of eligibility. Ironman Wales 2012 still had places. In despair, I'd entered on the Tuesday night before we left for 'Grotty', determined to bag the first of my three consecutive years of Ironman finishes.

Despite the disappointment of the DNS, Linds and I had a great holiday, our first 'normal' one in years where I'd not been obsessively training. We both needed the break. We met when I was nineteen and were approaching a significant milestone, we'd been together for almost twenty years. With Ben and Tom at home with grandparents, on our final night we went out for a romantic seafood dinner.

As ever my timing was immaculate.

'Sorry?' she exclaimed, 'You've entered Ironman Wales!!'

I'd lost the room.

The Boiler Room
Transalp 2012

'Where's Nick?'

'I don't know.'

John and Stuart glanced at each other. Trevor, Nick's dad and driver of our camper van, looked worried. I'd broken the cardinal sin, one that would get us disqualified. We were on the penultimate stage of the eight day 2012 Transalp. A single day away from our finisher medals on the shores of Lake Garda. I'd ridden away from my partner and guaranteed our disqualification.

After what we'd been through, I didn't care. I could feel nothing but white rage pulsing inside. I was ready to explode. I'd deliberately got Nick and I DQ'd. We faced a long and awkward evening, another day of the race and then a two day drive from Italy back home. The next seventy two hours would be very uncomfortable.

***

'That's not going to work,' Simon had observed six months earlier as we'd driven away from the first of four Winter Thetford Mountain Bike Races in the badlands of Norfolk.

'It'll be fine.'

As my closest friend, Simon knew me well. There was nothing wrong with Nick, we simply weren't compatible as partners. We also crossed paths when I was in a particularly vulnerable and fragile state. Critically, he was a racer and had talent. He knew how to handle a mountain bike, had skills, was good and fast. He nearly lapped me at Thetford. We were different athletes; he ran on octane while

144

I had a go-forever diesel engine. The previous summer we'd ridden the last lap of Sleepless together. I had twenty four hours in my legs and he had twelve from riding a single-speed bike in a pair. At the time we seemed well matched. Thetford proved we weren't.

We hadn't done much to bond as a team and had only picked up riding together on a rainy day around Leicester a month before my May Lanzarote DNS. That had been the last I'd seen of Nick until we were packing the camper van for the trip to the 2012 Craft Transalp. We had a two day journey across France and through Germany at fifty miles per hour in a five berth, cramped motorhome. The two teams were John and Stuart and then Nick and I. Trevor, Nick's dad, was the fifth traveller and would be driving between stages.

We'd start in Oberammergau in Germany and weave our way through Austria, Switzerland and the northern ranges of The Dolomites in Italy to Riva del Garda. Over eight stages we'd cover close to 620 kilometres and climb 21,000 metres, the equivalent of over two Mount Everests. We'd go over high mountains with grinding endless ups and very fast and technical descents. This was dangerous and it was critical we stuck within our teams. For safety we had to cross all the timing mats no more than thirty seconds apart or risk instant disqualification. This was a UCI, Union Cycliste Internationale, World Tour sanctioned event and would have the top pro mountain bike teams from around the world. It was a marque race in the off road cycling calendar and a long way from my rather amateurish bimbles on the South Downs Way with *Iron Maiden's Number of the Beast* sound tracking my post-work- avoid-the-rush-hour adventures.

The camper van was tight with the five of us, four mountain bikes plus a spare Nick insisted on bringing. On top of the cycling hardware was our gear, paraphernalia, food and bedding. We'd be together for the next twelve days. We'd breathe, eat, sleep, live and ride together. There was no social space, no breaks.

All niggles, annoyances, thoughtlessness, grievances and slights would be magnified. Inadvertently we'd set up a boiler room for strife.

The race was electric from the start. I'd never done anything like it before. With over five hundred riders, the peloton was tight as we rolled out of Oberammergau. Packed close, jostling for position, surging and abruptly slowing we weaved through the town centre. It was fast, furious and sketchy. With crossed wheels, there were inevitably some nasty crashes. The organisers kept the course wide and untechnical for the opening hour which spread things out. The first climb stretched the field further and started to test the bond between Nick and I. From the off I knew this was out of my comfort zone and beyond any riding I had done before. We were in the high mountains with long climbs and technical, loose surfaced descents. It would have been hard if I was on my own. But with hundreds of riders calling tight overtaking lines and buzzing by, it was dangerous and scary.

We were racing at eye-watering speeds on gravel fire tracks, through rock strewn gullies, twisting through narrow wooded paths. Nick wanted to go fast. I wanted to survive, not get hurt, stay upright and get to the finish. I didn't have the skills or experience to ride this at the speed he wanted. Afraid and out of my depth, I simply rode at my pace. At every feed station as he waited before the timing mat to ensure we weren't disqualified by crossing outside the mandatory thirty seconds, I could sense his frustration. He wanted to be in the mix, with the runners and racers. He couldn't hide his disappointment and as soon as I arrived, unimpressed and wordless, he'd clip in and pedal over the mat. Over the days we rode over snow-capped summits, flew through rock filled valleys, blasted flowing tracks across Germany, Austria, Switzerland and on to Italy.

Each stage was between fifty and eighty kilometres with the longest day over one hundred. We were learning fast, the short stages didn't mean recovery, they simply had more and steeper climbing crammed in. It could be bitterly cold on the tops and then oven-hot, with stuffy thermal waves baking the next valley. The landscape was spectacular, aqualine crystal ribbon lakes, breathtaking vistas, walls of jagged limestone. We climbed through long gullies with a twisting snake of racers riding, then pushing and finally carrying their bikes to the ridge. One by one they'd disappear over the crest on to the next heart-stopping descent.

This was in the deep end, sink or swim and my riding was improving fast as my confidence grew. After my DNS at 'Grotty' my self-belief was absolutely shattered. I was unsure of my immune system and felt like I was walking on eggshells, on a tightrope between bouts of illness. My sleep was still plagued by insomnia which I tried to keep from my fellow travellers. But despite my improvements, I wasn't the athlete Nick hoped I would be. Even John and Stu were blown away by the standard of racing at the sharp end of the field. They were winners on the UK national circuit but here they were only able to nudge into the top third of the field. They'd raced week in and out for years and, over and above being brothers who knew each other intimately, they were best mates and a team. Nick and I were two individuals who happened to be sharing the same number on our bikes. It had been a team of convenience, put together with no thought to compatibility.

Marry in haste, repent at leisure.

We weren't riding with the same objectives, had no cohesion and the resentment between us was building. Nick wanted to be in the mix, on a par with the Prentice boys. Much to his chagrin we were sitting firmly in the bottom quarter. Despite his clear frustration, I was on the rivet and simply happy being upright at the day's end. The pro teams were finishing in half the time it would take us to cover the stage. Nick would pore over the results each night determined we could improve our position, salvage some pride. I wasn't even looking at the summary sheet and was just relieved to be ahead of the broom wagon.

The pressure was building and off the bike there was no relief in our tiny camper van piled high with bikes, gear and the mounting mini grievances. Unreturned morning cups of tea, unwashed breakfast bowls, the unsolicited takeover of an unwatched charger, a lingering in bed, an unfilled kettle, all went on the silent irritation register. Overnight, between stages three and four a bout of dysentery swept through my system, weakening my already race sore body. The little things, thoughtless trivialities, meaningless ticks became magnified and drowned the importance and *esprit de corps* of our incredible adventure. I could hear my inner voice chuntering. My filter between thoughts, words and actions was hanging by a thread. We were riding towards disaster.

The crash happened on stage six. It was a massive day in the sweltering Italian Dolomites. We were going big, a hundred plus kilometres through the dramatically sharp limestone slabs between Livigno and Ponto de Legno. It was tough and both Nick and I were smoked. For the first time we were gelling, looking after each other, we were in survival mode. We were less than three kilometres from the finish and I was on second wheel, sitting in Nick's draft as we approached the final short climb to the finish.

I was too close, it was my fault. Our tyres touched. I was down before I knew what was happening. Although we were on tarmac, my momentum took me sliding through the gravel verge. Head, then shoulder, my hip, thigh and knee.

I leapt to my feet, raging with adrenaline. Sun-stroke, mixed with concussion, dehydration and anger. It was a heady cocktail. I grabbed my bike and set off, mad with my injuries, seething. The gears wouldn't shift and I was stuck in the go-fast cog I'd been pushing as we crashed. The mist had descended and I muscled up the final rise waiting for Nick before the finish. As soon as we crossed the line my adrenaline faded. I felt woozy, sore and giddy. Hurting, battered, running on fumes, my shirt was torn, my helmet cracked, my arms and legs a filthy mix of dust, gravel, cuts and blood.

'Right, I'm off to get some food.'

And with that, my team mate, partner and wingman, was gone. I took myself to the medical tent. It was a busy day for the medics and I sat under the shading canvas with an ever growing line of bleeding riders. As they patched me up, my head let go. Big uncontrollable tears rolled down my face. I wasn't hurting, simply emotionally exhausted and deep down tired. The situational tension, the conditions we'd been living in, the maelstrom, the danger of the race and my poor sleep had pushed me to a breaking point.

With its big jagged mountains, rocky paths, blistering fast descents, stiflingly still baked valleys and windswept snow-capped peaks, this was a long way from the South Downs Way or even the closed circuit of Sleepless in the Saddle. We'd been racing for six days and together for eight. But it went deeper; the pressure of the Legacy Programme, my DNS in 'Grotty', my yo-yo immunity, insomnia, losing jobs and shattered pride. Things had wound tight, I was completely frayed and beaten up mentally.

'You okay?'

The medic asked.

'I'm just exhausted.'

He squeezed my good shoulder.

'Want a Coca-Cola? It's the best medicine.'

He was right. I savoured the cool restoring drink as he put me back together with antiseptic, gauze, warmth and humanity. My tears were our secret. John and Stuart's smiling faces appeared at the door.

'Hey buddy, we heard you crashed. You okay?'

It was great to see them.

'Yeah, getting there. Cracked my helmet, a few cuts and bruises but I'll be fine.'

'Nick wants to head to the campsite so we don't lose our pitch.'

149

'I need to get my bike fixed. It's not changing gear. I'll try and get a new helmet from one of the stands and follow down when I'm all done.'

It took two hours to get my bike repaired. With a new derailleur, brake lever and shifter I was back in the race. I ate at the finish and savoured the few hours of solitude away from the van. I had my phone and spoke to Linds and the boys and then looped my old favourites *Khyber Pass, Awolnation's Sail* and *Adele's Someone Like You*. Strange times! The final frayed thread of any team spirit gave way.

The next day, on the penultimate stage the string completely broke. I hadn't meant to, it simply happened. Nick's octane had run out. We'd ridden over forty hours of hard racing, covered the thick end of 550 kilometres, climbed close to 20,000 metres as we fought up the final long climb before the descent of stage seven to Madonna di Campiglio. There the two of us toiled, small specks on a huge mountain side, the hare and the tortoise. This was the place for a diesel engine and inexplicably he slowly drifted back from my wheel. I pushed harder, stretching the gap. I clenched my teeth.

That's how it feels!

Glancing back, Nick was now a dot.

Strong are you?

My rage exploded. It wasn't really Nick I was mad with, he merely gave me a focus for years of accumulated fury and frustration. My injuries fell away and the last seven day's exhaustion were gone. I accelerated. Briefly I paused at the summit, taking in the breathtaking panoramic views. I looked back and couldn't see him. Rocking on my pedals, I glanced down the rocky path towards the finish. I was balanced between two worlds. Foggy with mist, deafened by a roaring in my head, I hadn't planned this, I wasn't thinking straight. I hesitated for a split second but not long enough to unclip.

Then I plunged into the next valley and on towards the finish gantry in Madonna di Campiglio. Even as I made the last turns into the ski resort I thought

I'd stop and wait for him. I wouldn't pull the trigger and cross the line, do the unspeakable and get us disqualified. Conformity, compliance, self-subjugation and sacrifice. My filter between emotion and action was in tatters. Powerless to resist, I drove forwards and hit self-destruct. Stamping on the landmine, I crossed the line. Maybe I'd never had *the strength of mind* to be a Royal Marine Commando. The DQ timer started.

'Where's Nick?'

I shrugged. I'd committed the cardinal sin.

Thirty seconds went by.

I went to the food table, I was hungry.

Five minutes.

Slowly what I had done dawned on me. My fury retreated and now the rational me needed to pick up the pieces.

Ten minutes. No Nick.

We'd driven across Europe, lived together, ridden seven days. We only had stage eight, seventy five kilometres and 1,500 metres of climbing left to Riva de Garda.

Twenty minutes. He appeared on the final straight.

Show time.

Action stations.

I'd done a very bad thing and was cornered. My nerves were on fire, my sense jangled, my adrenaline beyond anything I'd known as I'd faced the herculean TaeKwonDo champion. I had no idea what would happen. John, Stuart and Trevor retreated from the unfolding scene.

***

151

I'll spare you the details as fortunately it wasn't too dramatic. The disqualification didn't happen. We were so far down the field, the officials didn't even notice or turned a blind eye to the discrepancy in our finishing times. Between Nick and I, voices were raised, things were said, fair grievances voiced from both sides and the air was cleared. Within an hour we'd hugged and apologised. We were grown men, both nearly over forty with families. We were three quarters of the way down the field in a once in a lifetime adventure. We'd behaved like juveniles. We opened a bottle of wine, ate pizza, laughed at ourselves and how silly it had all got. We rode the final day together, as a team, crossing the line to free and very strong German Weissbier and a swim in Lake Garda.

We'd done it. Finished the 2012 Transalp.

The powerful wheat beer went quickly to my head, relieved it was all over, the pressure valve open. My cheeks glow when I think how I behaved, how badly I handled the situation and consider the countless, more mature ways we could have resolved our differences.

'So you want to ride again next year?'

I was arm-in-arm with Christoph. We'd met on the second day and ridden together throughout the race. He was a shaved-headed, bearded artisan baker from northern Germany, about my age and heavily tattooed. I couldn't have found anyone more different with whom to make a friend. We'd exchanged shirts before the final stage and rode in each other's team colours into Garda. Over the last week we'd got to know each other riding side by side. We'd had eight days of natural selection on whether we were compatible on speed and temperament to try this race again. We were a good fit. Critically we'd both been in teams that hadn't quite worked and now knew the race wasn't only on the bike. Fundamentally it was about looking out for each other, finding space, empathy, consideration and having vigilant emotional intelligence.

Despite the angst we'd experienced, as I stood in a fuzzy beer haze in Riva del Garda, I was a different rider. The last eight days had conjured up some of the richest adventures of my life. This was where I belonged, my safe place. At the finisher party I revelled in the energy and laughter of this circus of misfits. It dawned on me, I was with *my* people. I looked at Christoph and smiled.

'You bet!'

However, first I had unfinished business on my road to Kona. I had to bag my first eligibility race.

Ironman Wales was in six weeks.

Eligibility Year 1, Act II
Ironman Wales 2012

It was early Saturday evening. The multistorey car park in the centre of Tenby was rapidly emptying.

I was on the top floor overlooking the castle. It was 6pm and I'd just come out of the final race briefing. The start of Ironman Wales 2012 was roughly twelve hours away. With a meal, a good night and a hassle free start, I'd be on my way to finally bagging my eleventh official WTC Ironman finish and critically my first eligibility race for my three consecutive years for the Ironman Legacy Programme. The weather outlook was terrible but I was prepared with a rain jacket and warmer layers packed into my transition bags. Sunday was all about rolling a six and moving off square zero in this game of Legacy snakes and ladders. I had to get across the finish line.

I turned the key in the ignition.

The battery was completely dead.

Panic rose in me.

This couldn't be happening.

Give me a break!

I looked around. I didn't have jump leads and there were only a few cars left. I leapt into action.

'Sorry, my battery has gone completely flat. Do you have any jump leads?'

I was learning fast, triathletes carry bike pumps, tools, lots of energy food in their boots but no one, including me, thinks to bring jump leads. I had to change tack and figured the locals would be way more practical. There were some 1990's motoring classics up here; faded Escorts, beaten up Mondeos, old red Volvos. I was certain the flat battery eventuality would be a daily occurrence in these parts.

The local family I asked were walking towards an old Ford Sierra. Looking at its worn body work, I imagined they'd never leave home without some trusty leads. This had to be a shoe-in.

Incredibly they seemed oblivious to the fact an Ironman was happening in their town. This was quite astonishing given that when a WTC race takes over, it is really very hard to miss. Apart from the mass of skinny, tanned people in compression socks who definitely don't look like locals, pushing high value bikes around, wearing a variation of *event-t-shirt-chic*. Roads are blocked with the direction signs, M-dot logos are everywhere, as are the barriers and the disruption. Despite all the clues, I managed to find the only local family that was completely unaware a huge black, white and red endurance event had taken over Tenby.

'Excuse me, can you help?'

I explained my predicament about the battery.

'When've you got to be back 'luv?' the mum of the family asked.

'Back?'

I was confused. She pointed sympathetically at the champion-chip on my left ankle.

'It's okay 'luv, I've seen the ankle bracelet.'

It started to dawn on me.

'You on day release? What time you got to be back at the nick?'

It's a different crowd in Tenby with a non-conventional world view!

'Oh there's an Ironman here tomorrow,' I reassured with my poshest English tone, tapping my champion-chip. 'I haven't escaped from prison!'

To my absolute astonishment, given the guaranteed unreliability of their car, they didn't have jump leads. I had to wait over an hour as the sky turned grey and the day faded to dark for a recovery truck. I drove to my accommodation on full beam, my wipers at warp speed with a deep foreboding about tomorrow's race.

My insomnia was still haunting me and it was a battle I wasn't going to win. I was struggling to concentrate, was continually making avoidable mistakes and couldn't break my worry cycle. That night was no exception. Unsure whether my car would even start the next morning, my anxious butterflies spun with tri-mares. I eventually fell asleep a few hours before my alarm sounded.

***

The sand was cool on the beach, almost cold. I closed my eyes. I'd made it to the start. Ironman Wales' swim is in the sea in a cove overlooked by an amphitheatre of cliffs. With a zigzag path down the sheer face, the beach was packed with wetsuit clad racers and the steep walls lined with supporters.

I was there with a friend, Gareth Jones. Neither of us had known the other was racing. I like Gareth a lot, he is a kindred spirit and it was a special moment to share. I'd made the start and knew it was likely I'd finish. As the cannon got closer everything settled, simplified, became less complicated. Chatting casually to Gareth and staring across to Goskar Rock, an invisible warmth trickled down my left leg, around the back of my knee and calf before disappearing into the cold sand. Well as they say, *A wetsuit isn't 'your' wetsuit until you have christened it.* We were minutes from the start and jumped on the spot, trying to warm our muscles as much as we could.

The day lived up to its billing and over the next 12 and a half hours I learned the hard way that the hype about this M-dot race in South Wales is well deserved. At the briefing they'd intoned, *'There's Ironman. Then there's Ironman Wales!'* and it did everything it could to live up to its fierce reputation. The start was epic with the Welsh national anthem and *AC/DC* reverberating off the craggy coliseum. With jellyfish stings to face, hands and feet, a steep zig zag climb and a near mile

156

run from the beach to T1, we were certainly getting our money's worth from the entry fee.

On the bike the weather was on point with the forecast. It was biblical and I smugly pulled out my rain jacket a third of the way into the bike. I knew it wasn't a day for a tri-singlet and had started in two short-sleeved shirts, sleeves and gloves. There were many who weren't at all prepared, dressed as if we were racing in the Lanzarote sun. The clouds hung low all day and everything was a verdant green from the constant watering. It couldn't have felt further from the arid, hot lava fields of Hawaii.

This would be my sixteenth iron-distance race but Ironman Wales' bike route was the toughest I had ever done. The weather conditions didn't help but even without the wind and rain, the course alone was very challenging. There was absolutely no flat, we rolled along the sea cliffs and past beaches buffeted by gusts tearing across bleak and angry white capped waves. It was unforgiving and relentless, see-sawing between steep grinding climbs or rattling down bumpy, slippery descents that allowed no speed for the next inevitable up. Despite all my layers I was cold but wouldn't have traded any of the suffering. My stresses, worries, insomnia couldn't touch me here. I was finally in a WTC sanctioned Ironman moving one step closer to Kona.

Ironman Wales is a locals' race. Half the names on the flapping numbers of the male field were either Neil, David or Gareth and a good balance of the rest were Mark, Alun or Owen. There were dragon tattoos everywhere and incredible warmth and camaraderie amongst the sufferers with each torrential downpour. Getting to T2 and the run was a sweet relief but gave no end to the suffering.

The only flat was along the castle wall as we exited transition. Until now I'd held the view that the unwritten rule in course design for an Ironman marathon was it should be mainly flat. This horizontal profile etiquette hadn't made it down to the race organisers in South Wales. The route took a few twists and turns

157

through the main shopping and tourist area and then climbed forever to a turnaround on the outskirts of town. The downhill punished the legs just as much and, with a few dog-legs, took us back to Tenby.

On each loop the crowds got deeper and rowdier as the pubs filled, taps flowed and they cheered us on. It was electric, lifting and by lap four riotous. I felt like a rockstar as the energy carried us through the darkening streets. The hours of suffering fell away as I rounded onto the finish straight.

My time was quite respectable given my year and the atrocious conditions on the day. I crossed the line in 12:20:38. This was fifteen minutes faster than my first Lake Placid time and on a much harder course. I'd clearly learned a few things over these sixteen iron-distance races.

Critically I'd moved one square forwards in the Legacy Programme. I had my first of the required three consecutive years. This was also my eleventh official WTC race. Of all those races, Ironman Wales was the toughest one I had done to date and I'd loved it. The course was incredibly challenging but the support and encouragement transformed the race into a very special day.

***

As I drove home and reflected on my flat battery the realisation came to me, *If I want to see change, I have to make the changes.*

My stress in the car park was just another mishap in an increasingly frequent run of bad luck. Deep down I knew there was something wrong. It was eating me from the inside, forever unsure whether I'd triumph or fail. I'd never get to Hawaii sitting at this roulette wheel. The situation with my insomnia was not sustainable. It was destroying my health, happiness and depleting my internal battery. If I didn't get on top of it, I jeopardised my chances of realising my potential and dreams.

Initially my road to Kona had appeared quite simple but it wasn't proving to be at all straightforward. In ten months' time I had to be race-ready for Ironman Austria in Klagenfurt. On my compass, I needed to get the needle back facing north.

It was time to make some changes.

Eligibility Year 2
Racing For Afghanistan
Ironman Austria 2013

'Alright Afghanistan?'

Another rider flew by me. I was no longer seeing the funny side.

'Go Afghanistan!'

We were at the 2013 edition of Ironman Austria in Klagenfurt. This was the town of my glory days and my triumphant personal best, 10:53:54, nine years earlier. Ironman Austria is incredible; from the crystal clear mirror flat waters of the swim, the mountains, the views, smooth, super-fast roads and the blistering flat marathon. It is definitely my favourite WTC race. I was in year two of my Legacy Programme quest. I had to cross the line in this race.

My heart sank when I picked up my race number.

'2006'

The number wasn't the problem. What I'd forgotten was my sniggering amusement when I'd entered eleven months earlier.

Which country would you like to represent?

A strangely worded question, open to interpretation, I'd mused. The list was alphabetical and it wasn't asking for my nationality, instead the country I'd like to *represent*. Afghanistan had been having a tough time in the news for the last decade and Osama Bin Laden had run into Seal Team Six the previous August. With the question's ambiguity, I was sure the people of Afghanistan would appreciate me flying their flag for moral support. In the Ironman Austria 2013 race programme, I was the only person *representing* Afghanistan.

'Go Afghanistan!'

A year earlier it had seemed a good gag. Now, thirty miles into the bike, it didn't seem so funny. But it wasn't the Afghan flag on my number and stream of passing cyclists that had poured cold water on my sense of humour. It was more why they were overtaking and my helplessness to do anything about it.

One of the spokes in my expensive but fragile Zipp 404 rear wheel had given way. The pinging noise and wobble twenty five miles earlier were sickening. When I heard it, I pulled over to assess the damage. Over one hundred miles stretched ahead with a partially buckled wheel. My plan wasn't sophisticated; pray it would hold out and keep riding until it stopped working. I couldn't detach the broken spoke so I twisted it around those that remained and pushed on. Two miles later a second one snapped.

WTF!

The thick end of a lot of biking lay ahead and I was losing spokes close to the same rate as I was covering miles. This wasn't an Ironman where I could afford to DNF. The possibility of a repeat of Ironman Lanzarote loomed. Two years in a row, my heart sank. But the wheel still turned, so I twisted the second dangling spoke and rode on. Riders streamed by as I nursed my wobbly steed.

'Everything okay Afghanistan?'

No it wasn't. With every rotation my rear brake was rubbing against the rim of the wheel. I couldn't see how it would hold for the next hundred miles. My only hope was to find a mechanic.

I couldn't believe my bad luck. I was feeling in the best shape that I'd been in for a long time, was finally sleeping well and had enjoyed a perfect build-up to the race. I was in control. I'd come into the 2013 season with new hope. My flat car battery at Ironman Wales had been a trigger for change, something had flipped inside and I'd made huge progress with managing my sleep better and getting on top of my insomnia.

For five years, I'd forgotten what it was like to fall asleep normally and habitualised waking up in the wee small hours, tossing and turning. The insomnia was untenable, unsustainable and I didn't want to live with it anymore. I needed predictability in my health and a robust immune system. I couldn't keep preparing for Ironman and endurance races with a fifty-fifty on whether I'd even get to the start, let alone the finish. After Grotty, the stress and anxiety of the Transalp and Ironman Wales in 2012, I embraced my new mantra,

If I want to see change, I have to make the changes.

By chance and with some fairly superficial research I found a self-help sleep book called *Say Goodnight to Insomnia*. Quickly it made a difference and I diligently followed its six week programme through late September and October. I found out about sleep-hygiene and adjusting my behaviours; no caffeine after a certain time of the day, cutting screen time, minimising late evening exposure to blue light, body temperature, serotonin, my circadian rhythm and critically my routine and brain activity before going to bed.

The changes weren't immediate but I persisted and gradually my confidence grew in the programme. I kept a sleep diary and found I actually slept better than I thought. I could see certain patterns of behaviour and thinking that impacted how I fell and then critically stayed asleep through the night. I was starting to appreciate the constructive and destructive power of my mind. I'd taken for granted how it had helped me achieve extraordinary things, driving way beyond anything I thought was possible. I was also starting to see how in a perverse and misguided way it was also working against me.

With the help of *Say Goodnight to Insomnia* I took control again. I re-taught myself to fall asleep and developed ways to de-escalate the ceaselessly blaring *Chicken-Lickin-the-world-is-falling-on-my-head* klaxon. The cascade effect on my health and happiness was enormous. As the spring turned to summer I felt a different person. I was sleeping and eating well and my immune system improved.

I swerved colds and my training was rock solid and consistent. I hadn't felt heavy but had lost some weight and was starting to feel lighter, stronger, like an Ironman again.

The book helped enormously, but so too did the arrival of a black and white, English Springer Spaniel puppy. Jess became my new obsession and I threw myself into training her. Needing regular exercise regardless of the weather, the breaks gave me much needed calm headspace that didn't involve a self-beasting swim, bike or run. We'd go for family walks, chatting, laughing, exploring the area at a different pace. For the first time in years I was sleeping well and feeling settled. My preparation for and execution of Ironman Austria 2013 had been textbook until five miles into the bike.

'Mechanic?'

'At the next feed station,' I was told.

Mile after mile I pushed on expecting the wheel to give way entirely. My heart was in my mouth, braced for the next ping.

Keep riding.

See how far you can go.

At every feed station I was told the mechanic was at the next. With the entire field streaming past me it seemed I had more chance of finding rocking horse poo on this Ironman course than a mechanic. I'd given up on a stellar finish time. I only wanted to get to the end of the bike and tried not to contemplate the consequences if I couldn't.

Pushing on I lost hope of ever finding repair redemption and simply reverted to praying to the gods of triathlon and Lady Luck. I went through forty, fifty, and then sixty miles. I was over half way. The road was smooth, the sun rising, it was a classic Ironman Austria day. I was covering ground, seventy and then eighty miles fell behind. Every turn of the pedals felt like it could be my last. I ground up the usually uber-quick climbs and held my breath as I sped down the descents, hardly daring to think of the bloody, painful consequences if my wheel gave way. Dick from *gearsandtears.com* flew by at mile eighty five.

'Alright Afghanistan?'

He yelled, assured he'd scalped me. He went past me like I was standing still. Simon came alongside a few miles later. He was delighted to have caught me until he realised my plight. I was seething at my mechanical misfortune and wasn't prepared to lose sight of him. Throwing caution to the wind, I pushed my pedals harder. I was going down fighting. Keeping out of the draft zone, I used his speed to pace the last twenty miles. As we swept into the outskirts of town the relief washed over me. If disaster struck now I could walk the final miles and make the cut off. I pulled alongside Simon.

'What are you going to do now?' he asked.

The underlying tension of years of frustrations, DNFs, DNSs, illnesses and out of my control bad luck had ignited an absolute fury inside and I was ready to blow. Dick had unknowingly lit my fuse. *Alright Afghanistan,* he now had a huge target on his back.

'Run Dick down!'

He smiled knowingly, 'I thought you might say that.'

My mind had flipped. I'd been in survival mode for hours unsure whether I'd even get here. As I readied to dismount I could feel my resolve harden. It was time to race, climb into the red zone.

Just f'in run!

Dick was my target. The insolence to pass me with such swagger and bravado, this was my race, my place, my comfort zone. I went into fight mode. It was mid-afternoon, there wasn't a cloud in the sky or wisp of wind. *Scorchio,* nudging over thirty degrees Celsius. We had four laps of six miles. I was on a mission and sped through transition shoulder-to-shoulder with Simon. We exited together.

'What happened?'

Linds knew there was something wrong. Dick and Simon were experienced Ironman racers but both ten years my senior and from previous encounters I was the bookies favourite to have my nose firmly ahead by the end of the bike.

'Mechanical.'

I didn't have much time to exchange details.

'Can you work the splits with Dick?'

Linds knew the game, she could read my mind. I'd raced Ironman Austria twice before and posted my fastest ever time here in 2004. With my slow bike any new personal best was out of the question. But I knew I could run fast here. The marathon was on a figure-of-eight course with the transition and finish area at the pinch point in the middle. With the weather and profile, the contrast with Ironman Wales couldn't have been starker. The first loop headed along the picturesque lake side and circled back to the finish area. The second larger loop followed the canal into Klagenfurt and the infamous bell. On each pass we could ring the suspended gong and get a mighty roar from the beer fuelled crowds. It was a skip to sound it, but definitely worth the vertical spring.

Just f'in run!

There wasn't a breath of wind. I pulled my hat low, glasses under the brim. At each feed station I drank my coke and water, took two wet sponges and soaked my head and shoulders, careful to keep my feet dry and avoid soft skin and blisters. I had a small tube of factor fifty spf sunblock and periodically smeared it over my exposed reddening skin as I ran. As I passed Linds she gave me my split to Dick. It was a lot but I had time.

Everyone slows in the second half, I assured myself.

I simply had to make sure I slowed less and charged on. I knew I'd see him along the canal where both directions of runner shared the same path. When we passed it was all smiles, encouragement and high fives. But we both knew the game. I calculated our difference and there was still a big gap to make up. Accumulated iron-wisdom came back to me,

Ironman. It's just a six mile foot race.

It is true. Posting a good time is all down to being in good shape to race the last quarter of the marathon. Slowing in the last six miles, walking, this was where he would bleed time.

'Five minutes.'

I got my split again as I blasted past Linds near the finish area. I had thirteen miles to go and had halved the original gap. But I was also suffering. The sun and temperature were unrelenting. Furious energy pulsed through me. I was on the rivet and revelling in it. I'd not be able to race like this in years. I was all in, everything on the table.

Alright Afghanistan?

My inner monster was still raging, when, at the top of the last lakeside loop, I caught him. I wanted to fly by but once I was level the fury subsided and we ran together, friends again. We'd both been doing this for over a decade. With *gearsandtears.com* we'd been to France and Switzerland and laughed over cake and hot tea after winter Monstermen. All my petty grievances were forgotten, brothers in arms, suffering together. After a brief chat, I pushed on.

I crossed the line in 11:17:18. Despite my mechanical issues for over a hundred miles on the bike I was only twenty four minutes slower than my fastest ever time. It felt like I was back. I'd overcome my insomnia, taken responsibility and control and was finally on top of my TaeKwonDo injuries. Through training consistently and a renewed confidence in my immune system I was now in great shape. I had my second consecutive year of WTC Ironman finishes and my twelfth official finish. In terms of my Legacy Programme eligibility criteria, I had one more year to go.

As soon as entry for the 2014 Ironman Austria opened I nabbed my place, opting to *represent* the United Kingdom this time. With a fair wind I would be back in Klagenfurt in July 2014 and then in October Linds and I would be flying to Hawaii to race the Ironman World Championship. I had a lot on the table in the Legacy Programme casino, but felt I was finally holding a winning hand.

I was also falling headlong in love with Ironman again.

Eligibility Year 3
Racing With Friends
Ironman Austria 2014

The sound of metal against metal was sickening.

Something hit my shoulder hard and I was wrestling the bike to stay upright on the verge. It had all gone bad, very bad, very quickly. There were riders and bikes everywhere. I stopped, threw my bike on the grass and ran back. Simon was stretched out cold, on his back, in the middle of the road. He was unconscious. His glasses had been knocked off, his eyes flickered. My stomach twisted. I looked up and the madness ratcheted up. A vicar with a billowing black cowl was running towards me.

What the F!

This couldn't be happening. We were in the middle of the road. It was December, wet, cold, the temperature in the low single digits with a biting northerly wind. I knelt next to my best friend.

'Simon! Simon!'

I didn't know what to do. Quickly I had to get my head straight. We were north of Bicester on a single track road. We'd gone around a tight, blind left hand bend as Aylesbury Cycle Club had come the other way. We'd passed the front riders veering to our left but the tail-end riders in the group had turned wider in the lane, cutting the bend, assuming the road was clear. It wasn't. The last one caught Simon square on, head-to-head, man-on-man. A combined collision speed of near as damn-it forty miles per hour. I looked down at my friend, oblivious to the carnage around. His eyes opened. I breathed a sigh of relief.

He wasn't dead!

There was a huge lump on his face and something protruding from his left sternum.

'What happened? Where am I?'

'We've had a crash.'

I tried to keep my voice calm, waves of panic rising inside.

'Don't move, we're getting help.'

Simon looked bad with a huge swelling coming up around his eye.

'You have to keep still.'

I looked up at the *now-late-for-Sunday-service* vicar and he was calling an ambulance. People were coming out of their houses as the unhurt riders from Aylesbury Cycle Club were blocking the road in both directions to ensure the accident didn't get any worse.

'I can't feel anything.'

'Just stay still.'

I tried to keep my voice calm, fearing the absolute worst.

'I'm cold.'

'Don't move, it won't be long.'

I was being useless. Someone from a house brought a blanket to try and keep him warm. It helped but I knew the cold wet winter tarmac and the merciless northerly December wind would be stripping away all his core heat. I called Linds, quickly telling her where we were and what had happened and then got through to Sally, Simon's wife.

'Hi Sal, it's Stu.'

I could hear the distress breaking my voice. Her husband, my best friend, was stretched out in front of me, unable to move. His face smashed up, a huge lump on his chest and complaining he couldn't feel his hands and feet. He was shaking uncontrollably from the cold.

'We've had a crash. Simon's a bit beat up but an ambulance is on its way.'

I could feel the lump building in my throat, my chin trembled with panic. Sal was smart enough to know if Simon wasn't speaking to her now the situation was more serious than I was making out. They both needed me now, I had to hold this together.

'Everything is okay,' I lied, badly. 'I'll call you when I know more.'

The ambulance seemed to be taking forever. I talked, I assured him, stayed by his side, checked he was okay. I knew more than anything there was no way he could move.

'I'm cold.'

He was shaking violently, his body fighting the chill.

'It won't be long.'

Linds pulled up in the car. Her presence instantly settled me and I knew everything would be alright. She took in the whole scene, Simon stretched out under a pile of blankets, me kneeling by his side. Lots of busy people, stopping traffic but not getting close. It was very serious. Finally we heard the sirens. The paramedics leapt out, quickly they had a gurney and were putting his neck in a brace. He was off the ground and away from the cold, floating toward the ambulance, warmth and help.

'You can come with us too.'

I climbed in. Simon was answering their questions. Linds was calling Sal and we were on our way to Aylesbury Accident & Emergency. The paramedics were clearly worried about a spinal injury and had their lights and siren on. Simon's face was smashed, his left socket and eye bruised and bloodshot. The protruding lump on his chest looked terrible until his phone appeared from the breast pocket of his winter jacket and the bulge miraculously disappeared. The paramedic was taking details, pen hovering over the clipboard and patient admission survey.

'On a scale of one to ten, ten being the worst, how much does it hurt?'

Simon paused considering the scale.

'Five.'

I looked at him incredulously.

'FIVE!' I echoed.

The tension vanished.

'What do we need to do? Kick you in the nuts to get a ten?'

I always knew he was as hard as nails. I remembered how scared I had been at seventeen. Strapped to the gurney, immobile, my eyes darting back and forth, people looming in and out of my vision, my future in the balance, tottering between absolute darkness and hope. With a boxer's face he walked out of the hospital six hours later feeling battered, bruised and miraculously with no broken bones.

Of course we rode the next weekend.

***

Over the years Simon and I have accumulated months of elapsed time speeding along on two wheels. He probably knows me better than me and occasionally drops me a pearl of wisdom.

'Stu…'

He had my attention and a huge grin on his face. I smiled back ready for his insight. I knew I'd enjoy this. We were climbing away from Kendal and the Lake District, up towards where the backroads cross the M6. We were doing the Coast-to-Coast in a team of four, but there were only two of us on this climb and a big chunk of the ride lay ahead.

Two hours earlier we'd set off from the beach on the western edge of the Lake District and had already gone over the famous Hardknott and Wrynose Passes. We'd roared down the rough descents to Skelwith Bridge and through to Ambleside. Here our team of four had suffered its first casualty as the gregarious and ever funny Dave Pepper had failed to unclip at a set of lights and dominoed through some very aggrieved fellow riders. He got back on but struggled on the rolling section to Kendal and pulled the pin, deciding to stop.

The diminutive Phil Corley was our other team mate. I've known Phil for close to twenty five years and bought all my serious bikes from his shop in Milton Keynes. He is a legend and a veteran of the national cycling circuit. He is also close to two decades my senior, was in his late-sixties and as fit as a flea.

But I felt good, the hard climbs were behind us, we had two thirds of the 140 mile ride ahead and I wanted to open the taps. With a tailwind and a fast, smooth road surface snaking through the North Yorkshire Moors and Dales, we were on for a flyer. I'd finished eloquently articulating the arguments to Simon paraphrasing another Milton Keynes race legend and frenetic, indestructible force of nature, Mark 'Boothie' Booth.

'If you have pinned a number on, it's a race!'

Social norms no longer count, you're beyond reproach and reproval. I reasoned Phil wouldn't want to hold us up and I was ready to press the accelerator. Simon looked at me and smiled.

'Stu…'

He paused for dramatic effect. He had my attention.

'you…have ZERO emotional intelligence!'

We laughed like drains.

He was right. Once again I was failing the Arsehole Test!

For those less familiar with the A-hole Test, it's a universal truth of virtually all social situations that arseholes are like rats, there is always one close by. The test is simple, if you look around and you're not easily identifying who is the arse, well I think you can probably figure the rest for yourself. Curiously the donning of a cycling helmet seems to magnify the qualities that get you top marks. But then, I suspect if you ask those who know me, they'll confirm my susceptibility to excel in the A-hole Test isn't limited to when I'm dressed in my Middle Aged Man in Lycra, MAMIL resplendor.

We pulled over by the verge and waited a few minutes for Phil. The three of us had the most epic ride at full bore with the wind on our backs. Phil, the wily old fox, used all his racing skills to squeeze a split second on the line with a half wheel as we rolled across together. He couldn't help himself. Well he *had* pinned a number on. Overlooking the North Sea, we drank more Guinness than I could cope with and ate Whitby fish and chips.

***

On our adventures we've had some good and bad race accommodation. We've found horses munching our Weetabix whilst camping in the New Forest. We've survived tent flattening winds on wet and blowy Tours of Wessex and learned that staying in a Bed and Breakfast makes it a much more pleasant experience. We've slept on friends' floors before hitting the South Downs Way. We much prefer it when we get a bed rather than an unforgiving and draughty carpet for our bivvy mats. I've slept in the driver's seat of a VW Golf after Ironman UK. We tried a caravan for a few years as a race base but with all the hitching, storage, packing, unpacking and painfully slow drives it proved more trouble than it was worth.

But all the suffering on hard floors, flapping tent outers and garage forecourts come nowhere near to the terrible living quarter recommendation I made to Simon for the 2014 Transalp. But let's not get too far ahead of ourselves. I suspect it wasn't merely where we laid our heads that tested our strong friendship bond to the absolute limit.

***

The previous year, Christoph and I'd had a fantastic experience in the 2013 Transalp race. We'd watched the carefree nature of those in the official TA camp and we'd heard stories of how easy it made the event whilst we were crammed in our respective dysfunctional mobile homes. As we made our plans and coordinated our entry we were adamant this approach would de-stress the 2013 race.

The TA camp consisted of various sports halls, indoor basketball arenas, schools and military bases in each of the towns we would stop at over the seven stages of the race. Compared with the hassle of the camper vans of the previous year, it made the racing so much easier. Christoph and I were evenly matched on form, fitness and temperament. We'd witnessed first-hand that those you are still riding with on day three and beyond in a hard multi-day race, will tend to be the people who share your physiology and capability. But more importantly we'd got on. We chatted, laughed, liked and looked out for each other. We also knew the pitfalls, dangers, stresses of the Transalp and the fundamental ingredients of riding as a team. We wanted to be safe, enjoy ourselves and never once looked at our place in the field. This was an adventure not a race.

The weather was glorious and we quickly fell into the rhythm of the mountains. The contrast in my preparation couldn't have been greater from the previous year with the Prentice boys and Nick. I had trained consistently throughout the build-up, was sleeping well and had absolute confidence in my immune system. I'd taken responsibility, made changes and felt in control.

The grinding ascents, fast fire tracks, tight and rocky pathways were familiar. We were in our comfort zone, normalised. Each day we crossed the line arm-in-arm, grinning from ear-to-ear. A German bike magazine did a double page spread on us, perplexed why a clean shaven English boy was having such a good time with a bald headed, bearded, heavily tattooed German dude. Our friendship and joy at being in the race seemed to encapsulate the spirit of the Transalp.

***

But I hadn't forgotten my unwritten deal with Mr Messick and the WTC.

In February 2014 the entry for that year's Legacy Programme intake opened. I diligently listed my WTC races, bib numbers and finish times. With a successful race in Klagenfurt in July, I'd be racing in Kona in the October. I pressed submit and waited.

Excited, Linds and I continued to scan the web, earmarking travel options and where to stay. Two weeks later an email arrived from April Dickerson at the WTC headed 'Legacy Programme'. With my heart in my mouth I read it. And then read it again. I felt like I was being soft-soaped. Words like *'loyalty'*, *'devotion'* and *'determination'* stood out. I read it for a third time. *'Want to reward'*, *'commitment'* and *'promise.'*

Struggling to concentrate, I read it for the fourth time.

This wasn't sounding good. This was how the bank wrote to me with a price increase or overdraft charges. I had so much resting on this, the message wasn't sinking in.

'Although you have been selected… oversubscribed…'

WTF!

This wasn't cricket. A deal is a deal. I'd done my end of the bargain. Placed my bets. I was on course to finish my three consecutive years. I had my twelve finishes. April went on,

'I can guarantee you a slot in the __2015__ Ironman World Championship in Kai'ua-Kona, Hawaii.'

The magic words. My Willy Wonka golden ticket. In an instant all was forgiven. The road stretched further into the horizon, but if I maintained my eligibility, defended my wicket, I would definitely be going to Hawaii in 2015. I knew I could do it.

***

When we landed at the 2014 Ironman Austria in June, I was ready to race. After my near misses of the previous two years, I was taking no more risks. Suspecting the problems with my wheel and spokes were down to thoughtless airport baggage handling, I booked overland transport so there would be no opportunity for mechanical damage.

The swim was as beautiful as ever in the crystal clear Wörthersee. I felt incredibly good as I set out on the bike, confident my sled hadn't been bounced on any runway or squashed in a plane's hold. As I came into T2 I could see I was flying. I calculated that if I could run close to a four hour ten minute marathon my personal best, 10:53:54, was within reach. I wasn't racing Dick this time, instead the ghost of the younger me.

What a scalp!

Ahead of me lay 26.2 miles in thirty plus degree Celsius. I whipped the horse's flanks. The first half marathon fell away in one hour and fifty three minutes. I was on course to not just shave my previous PB, but to positively smash it. I could see ten hours and forty minutes on the finish gantry. What a legend! I was back. But Ironman is an unforgiving distance and *everyone slows in the second half of the marathon.* I willed myself forwards but it felt like treacle and gradually my mile splits stretched.

Open the throttle!

176

I roared at myself. I could hear the finish tannoy getting closer but the minutes and seconds to my personal best were accelerating away, slipping through my grasp. My watch was screaming the terrible truth. I was at the back of the Ironman Village, turn after turn. On the carpet, in the chute and sprinting. Glasses and hat off without breaking stride. Under the gantry, the finish ribbon and mat.

The time.

Ten hours.

Fifty three minutes.

Thirty eight seconds.

I had a new PB!

I was fifteen seconds faster over 140.6 miles. It had taken a decade, but I'd beaten the thirty something me. Relief, redemption, I was beyond elated. I found Linds and we hugged. We'd travelled alone this year and had no other friends on the course. This was our adventure, our bubble, just the two of us. I'd found fifteen seconds. A quarter of a minute. It meant the world to me. After all my ups and downs it was a resurrection.

I had three weeks to recover before Simon and I headed to Mittenwald in southern Germany and the start of the 2014 Transalp. My third and his first TA and the biggest test of our friendship.

Transalp 2014
Failing The Arsehole Test

On our weekend rides, I'd talked non-stop with Simon about my previous two Transalp races and eventually twisted his arm to join me for my third.

On reflection, I'd sold the highlights and seriously skimmed the perils. It wasn't deliberate, I'd simply forgotten how out of my depth and unprepared I was for my first. But competing at this level had become normalised for me. I had over 1,200 kilometres of racing, 42,000 metres of climbing and a hundred plus hours of riding in the high mountains stretching from southern Germany, through Austria, Switzerland and Italy. Unconsciously it had moved firmly into my comfort zone.

Simon and I have trained pretty much every weekend together for years, I took his fitness for granted. We paced together well over our Saturday rides. However, these weren't seven-stage, UCI sanctioned races stretched over heart-stopping descents, granny-ring-smallest-gear ascents, ripping fire tracks and slippery rock gardens. We'd never tested each other's compatibility over multiple days in these conditions. I was also ten years Simon's junior and without realising it, doing much more training. In a role reversal of my first 2012 TA, I was now the thoroughbred in our pair.

As we rolled from the start in 2014 from Mittenwald with five hundred other mountain bikers, I'd forgotten my first Transalp-virgin nerves. From the off the pace wound up, riders jostled for position, speeds surged, brakes shrieked, tyres bit. There were skids, crashes, riders hitting the deck. For Simon this was going to be a baptism of fire. But the stress had really started thirty six hours earlier and as a result we'd almost not made the start.

178

With careless baggage handlers at Heathrow, our bikes weren't loaded onto the plane. After a day of calls we met an airport employee in the late afternoon between Munich and Mittenwald to be reunited with our steeds. Totally stressed, we missed the evening pasta party as we concentrated on re-assembling them and getting ourselves race-ready. And as if this wasn't enough, Simon's mood slumped further after a night spent on the hard sport's hall floor on his punctured bivvy mat. Unimpressed by the communal sleeping of the TA camp, bleary eyed and unrested he was now in the same panic-inducing melee of a full-on UCI mountain bike race I'd felt three years earlier.

The weather on stage one was grey with the occasional shower. On the second day it turned biblical with fist sized rain drops punching us from the start in Mayrhofen. We were cold in the valley but freezing in the thinner air and biting winds up high. With a few bottleneck waits and long descents to strip away the last wisps of warmth, we were dangerously cold at the bottom. At the feed station we took space blankets and wrapped them under our jackets and helmets to make gold and silver cloaks and hoods. By the finish in Brixen I'd never spent a colder, harder day on a bike. But our misery wasn't over. We couldn't find a new sleeping mat for Simon and when we got to the sports hall for the night, the floor was soaking from a hundred dripping riders. Much to my relief the weather on stage three improved dramatically. This was finally the Transalp that Christoph and I had enjoyed in 2013.

'I'm starting to get this.'

We were stuffing in cake at a feed station. I'd been convinced Simon thought I'd sold him a pup and with his words I could feel the tension fall away.

***

179

I didn't see the crash but I heard it. Metal hitting rock, the dull thump as he connected forcefully with the ground. I stopped and turned. He was up, but swaying on his feet, his heels on the edge of a nasty drop. I ran back and grabbed him away from the fall. We were on the last descent, so close to finishing the day. He looked shaken, bent double.

'I can ride.'

We gingerly rode on, stopping frequently. He was in a bad way. We went to the medics as soon as we crossed the line. He'd dislocated his thumb and cracked a rib. Unusually for me I read the mood of the room and I didn't dare ask,

On a scale of one to ten, how much does it hurt?

He'd had a bad night and woke up having hardly slept. He looked awful but declared he would ride on. I wanted to finish with Simon. He is my best friend and we'd come to ride this adventure together. This wasn't the time for me to fail the Arsehole Test but sometimes I am naturally an arse. Of course I wasn't trying to be, but frequently with my innate, virtually non-existent emotional intelligence it comes quite naturally.

I'd chat to fellow riders and fall into their pace and before I knew it I'd be two to three hundred metres further up the trail, leaving Simon alone to struggle and suffer behind. On the descents I thought nothing of having a blast, letting rip. I knew how to ride these trails and realised this was likely my last Transalp for a while. I wanted to whoop, holler and enjoy the freedom. But I was doing all the things that had left me seething two years earlier as my poor friend struggled with painful injuries on his first Transalp. Germany, Austria and Switzerland fell behind as we wound our way up and down the steep, hard climbs of the Italian Dolomites. I chewed on a piece of melon, chirping away oblivious to my buddy's plight as he glared at me hunched over in pain.

'Do you want to do this together?'

I could feel the venom as he listed his grievances with me. In an instance I realised I was guilty as charged and what a thoughtless arse I'd been. I gave him a hug and apologised. That was all it took to clear the air. We rode on together as team mates and friends. It rocked me how dumb I'd been. Simon meant the world to me, we'd been through so much together.

He took my wheel as we rode towards our next climb. Tears welled in my eyes as it dawned on me, I'd been the one precariously balanced on the cliff edge. Simon had saved me.

It wasn't for the first time. I suspected it wouldn't be the last.

Eligibility Year 4

IronKids

Ironman Austria 2015

'It's all in your head.'

As I sat there, she repeated it for effect,

'It's *all* in your head. Your mind is powerful in good ways and bad. You are stressed. The stress is manifesting itself as IBS.'

I looked at Yvonne, a private dietician I'd found after despairing with the lack of solutions I was getting from the NHS. They'd done everything to me. I'd kept food diaries, cut gluten and dairy, followed a FODMAPS plan avoiding all fermentable carbohydrates. As well as losing a further four kilograms, it had only got worse. I'd had fingers jabbed where it felt quite unnatural, been tested for bowel cancer and even seen my appendix scar from the inside during a colonoscopy. I was struggling and the worry was making it worse.

People rarely write about the early pre-race start routine but without being too indelicate, for me it is the most important play of the day. To race well I have to execute a guaranteed, bombproof, pre-event ablution game to minimise my risks of being caught out with an urgent *in-flagrante-mid-race* evacuation, desperately searching for a portaloo. Therefore before the start I needed to ensure I'd emptied my tanks. Like a rooster at dawn, I had to be consistent 364 days a year to know that for the one day when it really counted, I'd be like clockwork. For six months I'd been off my game.

'IBS?' I asked, not quite keeping up.

'Oh, IBS. Irritable Bowel Syndrome.'

She paused to let it sink in.

'You don't have an intolerance to anything, lactose, gluten, fermentable sugars. All your reactions to food are happening too quickly for it to be physiological.'

She looked me square in the eye.

'It's in your mind.'

It all made sense. I'd seen with Ironman, conquering the South Downs Way, 24-hour solo mountain biking and up high in the Transalp, how far my mind could push my body. It lifted me from the mediocre and helped me achieve extraordinary things. But my synapses could also play tricks on me. It could be little things like pre-race dreams; getting to the start and having no goggles or forgetting a bike shoe in T1 or losing my trainers before the run. My head would play mini-disaster scenarios, subconsciously tapping me on the shoulder to highlight risks. I had checklists to ensure the forgotten kit nightmares never came true. But it could also play bigger, longer term, catastrophic war games in my mind. I'd experienced this before. The morphing of healthy thinking and analysis of risk into harmful cycles with my insomnia and the subsequent springboard into self-destructive, dissociative cul-de-sacs.

'Do you have anything to be stressed about?'

The last seven years unfurled in front of me. I guess I did have a few things to be stressed about. Since the meeting in Bristol and the situation in Cardiff falling apart, we'd been trying to run a family business full time. Slowly, it had unravelled and I'd held the bar, dangled for too long, hoping it would come good. Linds and I had invested a huge amount and depleted our savings to nothing, run our credit cards hot, trying to keep the plates spinning and stay in the game. For eighteen months I'd been moonlighting with side hustles but we'd run out of money. Six months before I was sitting in Yvonne's office we couldn't make the next mortgage payment. I'd had to let go of the bar, my feet hit the ground and I limped away from the business.

Did Not Finish.

It broke me like no other DNF before. I'd thrived on thinking of myself as an entrepreneur, working on my terms, shaping my future. It was creative and different every day. We were grafting hard and everything we did was for us. It felt important and had meaning. As it ended I was overwhelmed by a sense that I'd failed publicly once again and it had shattered my self-image. We both found jobs quickly and our finances started heading up again. But my heart wasn't in it. I was eating myself up inside.

'Yeah. I guess I have been stressed.'

But with some help from Yvonne, changes to my diet and awareness of the dark ball of tension inside, the complications of the IBS started to fade. I had to get back on an even keel. I was approaching year four of my Ironman Legacy Programme. This was the year I'd get my slot and be flying to race on the Big Island. With the failure of our involvement in the family business, Kona was more important than ever for my identity. For me it was *virtually* everything.

***

It was April 2nd 2015 and the email simply read,

'*As a 2015 Legacy Winner…*'

I hardly dared read on but of course couldn't stop.

'*You are cordially invited to compete at the 2015 Ironman World Championship.*'

My heart beat faster.

I'd made it. I'd got my place. I had to finish Ironman Austria in July but with that WTC medal, I'd be going to Kona in October to race the world's most famous triathlon!

'*This invitation is valid for 2015 only and may NOT be transferred to another year.*'

My Willy Wonka invite was a once in a lifetime ticket.

***

Ben was now ten and Tom was six. In their eyes all dads should be an Ironman, they knew no different. They'd only ever lived with a dad who got up early to train, dressed in lycra, took piles of gear on holiday, book-ended family walks, outings and visits to relatives with a bike or a run. They took the crashes, cuts and grazes and smashed helmets in their stride.

In 2010, I'd taken them both across the finish line at Ironman France in Nice when you could without being disqualified. But I didn't want to be a pushy parent, make them race, get caught in the *do-what-dad-does*. I wanted them to find their own way. I saw racing Ironman as my 'personality disorder', my way of dealing with my demons, gremlins and stresses. As Linds often jokingly reminded me,

'There's a fine line between hobby and mental illness.'

Ben played football and was obsessed with Chelsea FC. He'd started karate early and was on his way to getting a coveted black belt. His once chubby legs had stretched and he was now lithe and fit as a flea, healthy and active as a ten year old should be. He also made me laugh. Once he ran headlong into a low, face high fence with a sickening thunk. He took the sharp side of the triangular beam across the bridge of his nose and I found him prostrate and inconsolable on the floor. When I peered up his swollen and bloody nostrils I was convinced it was broken. As we drove to the hospital I assured him,

'If you're brave, I'll buy you a new DS game.'

There was a long pause from the back and then a small voice,

'What if I'm not brave?'

Tears of love welled up behind my Oakleys.

'You'll still get the game.'

Tom was four years younger and fearless in the way a junior sibling has to be. With big brown eyes and a mop of dark hair he was a mini version of Ben and me. He took everything in his stride, determined to keep up with the senior members of the family. They'd lived with my single-minded-enduro-home routine for years but neither of them had come to an Ironman since 2010. We'd done the maths and would have loved to take them to Hawaii but it fell during school term. With a now regular income we threw caution to the wind and instead decided to make a family trip of Ironman Austria, the final race before Kona.

'Do you think they'll be up for IronKids?' is what I should have asked before I ticked the entry box and filled in their details.

IronKids is a WTC Ironman weekend tradition. It is a mini-race for competitors' and the host town's children, seeded by age, typically the day before the main event. The distances vary from a one hundred metres swim and a five hundred metre run to sometimes double or triple that for the older youngsters.

Thankfully Ben was game when we told him there was a t-shirt and a medal in it. If Ben was in, well Tom blithely followed. What I hadn't realised was that the whole weekend would now be about IronKids. We played about on the beach waiting for the race to start and watched the other families get ready. Whilst our two made sandcastles and raced in and out of the shallows, some families were taking it very seriously, talking sternly to their kids and pointing at various parts of the course.

As the waves and age groups started we wandered over to suss out the format and proceedings. Judging by the shouting and bulging neck veins of some of the mums and dads they saw this as their offspring's big break into triathlon fame. We were here for the t-shirt and wanted neither of our two to feel any pressure. After watching a few races Ben looked at me seriously with a knotted brow.

'Dad, where do I go when I exit the swim?'

'Just follow the others,' I assured him.

'But what if I'm leading?'

He'd clearly set his sights higher than his old man. I didn't have the heart to tell him it wasn't a problem I had ever encountered.

We'd never been prouder of Ben as he was led down the pier to the start. Standing next to some of the boys in his field he barely came up to their shoulders. He had his game face on and gave it full beans. Luckily he didn't have to worry about getting lost and he placed well amongst the terrified children fleeing from their draconian parents' screams of,

'SSSSCCHH-NNEEEELLL!'

Tom looked truly tiny in the six year old field. Linds and I exchanged worried glances, wondering whether this was wise. But the WTC race organisation had things nailed. Each child in this age category had their own one-on-one chaperone shadowing them in the water all the way to the beach. Tom ran, imitating his brother's scowl, all the way to the finish. Both of them bossed the finish line chic and looked the business with their IronKids t-shirts and medals for the next three days. I think they took them off in bed but I couldn't be absolutely certain.

The Ironman the next day was a bit of an anticlimax after the IronKids. This was my fifth Ironman Austria, my third in three years, I knew the format. I felt a peace and calm descend over me as I stood on the cool sands of the beach. The swim course stretched ahead. Behind me two hot air balloon burners roared as they prepared to float into the clear blue sky. The familiar helicopters whooped overhead and a few drones darted this way and that. The two piers on either side of the mass start were deep with spectators. It was electric. This was WTC Ironman racing at its apex and I was in my happy place, all my worries and stresses fell away. The near collapse of our finances, the failure to stay in our start-up business, finding a job, not losing the house, keeping the boys fed, safe and happy. My IBS, the poking, prodding and penetration, none of that could touch me here.

Determined to destroy the second-hand value of my wetsuit, the last remnants of my morning coffee trickled inconspicuously down my left thigh, the back of my knee and calf and into the now not so pristine sand. If I finished today I would have my fourth year of consecutive races, my fourteenth WTC race and my nineteenth iron-distance finish. Critically I would guarantee my place on the start line of the World Championship. I felt serene and knew what to do. This was me, where I belonged.

Eleven hours twenty eight minutes later I crossed the line. The boys stood hands on hips, looking nonplussed in their IronKids t-shirts,

'Dad, what took you *so* long?'

My next race would be Ironman Hawaii.

Kona - So What?

Kona, Hawaii, the Ironman World Championship.

To line up in the water at Dig Me Out Beach in October is to be on the most coveted start line in world triathlon, perhaps in ultra endurance sport. It's a big deal. In fact it's a huge deal.

Hawaii is where it all started in February 1978. The foundation narrative has been repeated countless times. Legend has it, whilst stationed on one of the smaller Pacific Islands, Oahu, the fittest in the US military were having an alcohol fuelled debate following an awards ceremony. The argument raged as to who had the edge when it came to swimming, biking and running. Egged on by military bravado it was agreed the only way to settle things was to combine the three toughest events on the island; the 2.4 mile (3.86 kilometre) Waikiki Rough Water Swim, the 115 mile (185.07 kilometre) Around Oahu Bike Ride and then finish with the 26.2 mile (42.2 kilometre) Honolulu Marathon. With a flourish John Collins, a US Navy diver declared,

'Whoever finishes first will be crowned the 'Ironman'!'

Judy, his wife, who played a huge role in making the event happen, knowingly added that, 'storytelling would be the *fourth* event'. The date was agreed and the entry fee was set at a mere $3. The 115 mile bike ride was reduced by 3 miles to link to the start of the marathon, hence the 112 mile cycling distance of the current Ironman format. One can't help feeling Judy had a healthy understanding of the mindset of the Ironman competitor. On the inaugural event sheet she immortalised the phrase,

'Swim 2.4 miles. Bike 112 miles. Run 26.2 miles. Brag for the rest of your life!'

The first race was held on the 18th February 1978. Fifteen competitors, all American, started. The hot favourite to win was US Navy Seal John Dunbar who led until mile fifteen of the marathon. But despite its roots in the military, it was actually a local taxi driver and exercise fanatic, Gordon Haller, who triumphed, crossing the line in 11:46:58. Dunbar took second place thirty minutes later. Ironman Hawaii was born.

Despite its current fame, the 1978 Hawaii race can't claim to be the first triathlon. This honour is held in San Diego Bay where the first officially documented swim, bike and run event was held on the 25th September 1974. It is perhaps no coincidence that John and Judy Collins attended the second San Diego Bay triathlon in 1975. However, with its dramatic landscape and harsh conditions very soon Ironman Hawaii would dwarf all other swim-bike-run races.

The profile raising started with a 1979 *Sports Illustrated* article by Barry McDermott. He was in Hawaii to cover a golf competition but he instantly saw the story in this extreme race format. He described it as a 'legal way' the competitors 'could prove their toughness'. With this article Ironman Hawaii attracted competitors from the US mainland. However arguably it was the February 1982 coverage that proved to be the turning point for Ironman. Until then Hawaii was well known only in multi-sport circles and with those who had seen the *Sports Illustrated* piece. All this was about to change in the spring of 1982 when the TV network ABC filmed the race. The dramatic pictures of a twenty three year old, diminutive Julie Moss crawling across the line suddenly etched the drama and vividness of Ironman Hawaii into the consciousness of stunned viewers globally.

Despite a relentless will to win, or perhaps because of it, Julie's body shut down. The heat and conditions had broken her and a seemingly unassailable twenty minute lead evaporated. Her legs gave way and down she went. Within thirty yards of the line she started to crawl as Kathleen McCartney slipped by to take the February 1982 female crown. Still on her hands and knees, Julie finished 29 seconds later. This footage changed Ironman history forever and cemented

Hawaii's reputation as one of the most coveted, gruelling one-day endurance races on the global calendar. But it wasn't just the coverage of the '82 race that made Ironman Hawaii so iconic. Due to its very nature it could do nothing but serve up drama every year. The inspiring images of speedo-clad, tanned, smooth legged, muscled triathletes racing through the lava fields embodied the very essence of the sport.

It was at this time in the late 1980s that Paul had loaned me his *220 Triathlon* magazines. Thousands of miles away in a village in Warwickshire I'd absorbed the incredible stories and pored over pictures of these heroes battling it out in the lava fields of the Queen-K. In 1989 Dave Scott and Mark Allen's rivalry had culminated in the legendary 'Iron War', the epic, shoulder-to-shoulder endurance duel that cemented Hawaii's infamy.

The course was a colosseum for modern-day gladiators, the fields got deeper and the narrative got richer. Through the 1990s we saw the rise of challenger nations to take on the initial American dominance. The debates over whether Hawaii could be won on the bike or whether it was a pure runner's race shaped the sport internationally. The German biking machines, Thomas 'Hell on Wheels' Hellriegel, Norman Stadler and Faris Al Sultan, were prepared to lay everything down to settle the argument. The age of the Aussies came with Greg Welch, Chris McCormack and Craig Alexander. Hard racers, gracious in victory, articulate, raconteurs, weaving stories, feeding the imaginations of their hungry fans. Year on year getting faster, the world record squeezed again and again.

The women's races had no less drama. Twice champion in the early 1980s, Sylviane Puntous, beat her identical twin Patricia into second place on both occasions. The 'Queen of Kona' is undoubtedly the petite but hard as nails Paula Newby Fraser, with eight Ironman World Championship crowns. Poor old Erin Baker took the second step many times through Paula's reign although she was crowned champion twice. The closest challenger to Newby Fraser's throne is unquestionably a Swiss triathlete, the first European female winner and six times world champion Natascha Badmann. She should have taken a seventh crown in 2004 on Alii Drive when the eventual winner, Nina Kraft admitted to using the banned performance enhancing drug, EPO. By the late noughties, the women's crown had found itself on a new head with the rise of the unstoppable, well-spoken, warm, friendly and incredibly articulate Brit, Chrissie Wellington.

My absolute hero was Chris McCormack, known universally as Macca. He was seven months older than me, born in April 1973 but this is where our similarities end. As I came into triathlon in 1999 he was winning virtually every international race he started. Unbelievably he wasn't chosen for the Australian 2000 Olympic team but went on to prove the Aussie selectors wrong by winning thirty three consecutive races. As I finished my first Ironman race in 2001 Macca was crowned 'Global Triathlete Of The Year' and 'Competitor Of The Year'. He made the move to long-distance racing in 2002. As I bagged my second and third races in Lanzarote and Switzerland, he won his debut long course race, Ironman Australia. He was unquestionably the hot favourite as he lined up that October 2002 for his first Ironman World Championship in Kona, confidently declaring,

'I'm here to win!'

He DNF'd.

The next year he toughed it out, but starting the run with a seemingly invincible lead, came 59th. Macca was unbeatable everywhere apart from Kona. From 2002 to 2007 he triumphed in every other Ironman race he entered, usually setting a new course or world record but Kona was his banana skin. He eventually won on the Big Island in 2008. It took him six attempts.

***

192

We stepped off the plane at 8.30pm. The temperature and humidity hit me like a blast furnace door being opened. The heat was unbelievable and descending to the tarmac the heavy, close wall was overwhelming. Although dark on the runway, it was still thirty plus Celsius. I couldn't even begin to imagine what it would be like under the glaring sun in the lava fields. A sense of foreboding started rising inside me. I'd put such a huge amount into getting here. There would be no way I'd get a second chance, this was my only shot.

Perhaps Julie's collapse and Macca's record in Kona should have been warnings. Ironman Hawaii wouldn't be like any other race I'd ever done and there was no guarantee I'd get through it.

***

Unquestionably the exclusivity of Ironman Hawaii rests firstly in the fact it's the World Championship and secondly it's a race you have to *qualify* to participate in. To line up in Hawaii puts an athlete in a very special club. Even if you make it to Kona one year there is no guarantee it will ever happen again.

Active.com estimates that 80,000 to 100,000 Ironman competitors vie for the coveted 2,500 slots in Kona every year. But that number doesn't really get close to the number of people who have the dream. In 2014 the International Triathlon Union estimated there were up to 3.5 million athletes globally who regularly combined a swim, bike and run. To get to the start line of the Kona World Championship puts a competitor in very distinguished company and year on year entry has become harder.

Since 1982 the profile of Ironman Hawaii has continued on an upward trajectory. Somewhat unusually there were two races in Kona in '82. The original race took place in February but the organisers wanted to open it up to the North American multisport community who were emerging from winter and not

193

necessarily in form. Therefore it was decided to run a second edition of Ironman Hawaii in October. This move to the end of season has stood ever since. Although the field size then was modest compared to now, Hawaii's popularity was growing and in the ten months from Julie's crawl to the second '82 race the start list swelled from 580 to 850. The organisers faced the problem of over-subscription. From 1982 to 1983 the principle of 'qualification' rather than *first-come-first-serve* came into play. Over subsequent years the various ways to qualify have evolved.

The most obvious and easiest way to get to Kona is to be a world-class triathlete. It is straightforward if you're gifted, simply win as a professional or place high in your Age Group. For an Age Grouper, typically finishing in the top three in your cohort will guarantee you a slot. An earned entry to Kona is then awarded at the post-race ceremony. If you finish just outside the number of slots in your Age Group there could still be an opportunity to get to Hawaii through a system known as 'roll down'. This 'roll down' process means those who finish outside the top places can still pick up a slot if the faster Age Groupers in their category decide not to take theirs or have already qualified.

Over and above professional and able bodied Age Group qualification places that are won on athletic merit, there are also slots for disabled and physically impaired athletes based on the same principle of merit. Furthermore there are a few North American events that have special military categories for US service personnel as well as some 70.3 WTC half-Ironman races.

One rather toe-curling qualification route is the 'Ironman Executive Challenge'. This involves a VIP package where *chief-executive-types* compete at specific races and the winner of this somewhat smarmy division gets to race in Hawaii. There is something about this board-room-bore concept that parallels rich aristocrats big game hunting. The reader can probably guess where my sense of egalitarianism falls.

For years, the easiest entry path for the untalented athletic masses was the Lottery. It was launched in 1983 and over the years has courted a lot of controversy. Its flaw was in its set up. To actually get to Hawaii a Lottery player had to go through two layers. Initially they'd buy a $50 lottery ticket. If this ticket was then drawn, the 'winner' then had to pay an additional $850 for their place in the World Championship. These two tiers of payment made the WTC a lot of money and was augmented with a Passport Club, a Valentine Lottery and a VIP Package. In 2014 there were 12,000 Hawaii Lottery entrants, half of whom were also in the Passport Club and had played for multiple years. They were betting on being one of the lucky ones to be selected to buy one of the hundred slots. For the 2015 Lottery, the participants had grown to 14,000.

Six months before we left for Kona in 2015 the WTC paid the US federal government a near $2.8 million fine and announced it would cease to operate the Lottery. The investigator didn't like the fact a player was betting for the opportunity to 'buy' a slot and Ironman was found in breach of running a lottery that wasn't compliant with American gambling and gaming laws. But aside from the lawyers, I suspect no athlete who, like me, lacked the athletic prowess to ever place high enough in their Age Group and played the Lottery, ever begrudged the WTC or complained about their odds. At least the Legacy Programme kept the door open for us no-hopers. It hadn't been the cheapest or least-stressful way to get to the start line but it had enabled me to be there.

But fear not, there are still more expensive ways to qualify. With the growth of the Internet after the millennium, the WTC embraced online auctions. Unlike the Lottery, they weren't lining their pockets with these e-bids but instead raising money for good causes. In 2002 they put a number of slots online for charity with a minimum starting bid of $10,000. This first auction raised over $400,000 and their charity didn't end here. There are slots available for 'Represent Women for Tri' and the 'Ironman Foundation', two programmes that continue to raise large sums of money every year.

Perhaps the least well known way to nab one of twenty annual slots is to be a resident of Hawaii. The locals say that there are so few entrants that it's probable you'll get a place if you throw your name in over a couple of years. Aside from the stifling heat and humidity, taking up residence in Hawaii for over three years to become eligible didn't strike me as too onerous a way to race the Ironman World Championship.

The final way to get to Hawaii was through the 'Wild Card' scheme. This is where the WTC invites someone famous to race the Ironman. It's win-win. The well-known and often newsworthy person gets a place and the WTC enjoys lots of free coverage on social media. In 2015 the two wild cards went to Gordon Ramsay, the TV chef, and Sean Astin, who played Sam in *The Lord of the Rings*.

Initially, with everything I'd gone through to earn my place through the Legacy Programme, my feelings were mixed. I felt I'd paid my dues with DNS's, DNF's, crashes and mistakes to feel worthy of being on the start line. But the more I thought about it, both Gordon and Sean would have fought hard, at times felt completely at a loss and faced real jeopardy in their respective journeys to fame and fortune. To achieve all they had, both embodied the Ironman 'never give up' spirit and if their presence brought the media spotlight to Kona and helped the WTC to promote our sport, well they too were welcome to the circus.

Getting to the start line in Kona is not easy. As I made my final preparations for the 15th October 2015 I was in no doubt that this was a once in a lifetime, never to be repeated opportunity to call myself an Ironman Hawaii finisher.

***

The Big Island is the largest and most eastern of the Pacific archipelago. It is officially called Hawaii and was where the British naval explorer Captain James Cook ended up in a cannibal's pot in 1779. It's a volcanic island with mountainous cones dominating the skyline and their black, angry outpourings shaping the landscape. In terms of landmass, it is one of the smallest US states but towers from the ocean at 4,200 metres. Fortunately, the Ironman World Championship goes nowhere near these dizzy heights and is concentrated in the north west corner of the island. The nearest international airport is Kona and a few miles south, the town of Kailua-Kona hosts the race. Although famous around the world, the capital of the Big Island isn't in fact Kailua-Kona but instead Hilo on the opposite side of Hawaii.

But Kailua-Kona is the heart of the race. The 2.4 mile swim is a long rectangular clockwise course that starts and finishes in Kailua Bay at Dig Me Out Beach. The transition for both the bike and run takes over the entire pier. From exiting T1 the bike initially heads south along the Kuakini Highway for a short out-and-back. On the return northwards, Kailua-Kona falls behind after a sharp dig up Henry Street and a left onto the Queen-K Highway. The course then rolls due north to Hawi situated at the top of the Big Island. With a population of barely 1,000 people it shouldn't be as famous as it is, but it marks the most northerly point of Ironman Hawaii. The weather conditions and wind direction here often determine whether a world record breaking time will be set in any particular year.

Rather unimaginatively the bike heads north and then south on the same roads along the coast passing idyllic settlements with fantastic names such as Kukio, Puako and the Hapuna Beach Resort. It is rolling, barren and untechnical save for two junctions at Kawaihae and the one-eighty U-turn in Hawi. Turning south the route traces the coast in the opposite direction. In terms of visual stimulation the only difference is that the ocean is now on the right. When the bike returns to Kailua-Kona it passes the airport and the famous Natural Energy Lab. From here it shares the road with the fast runners already on the marathon course. On this final section there is no out and back on the Kuakini Highway. Instead it cuts right through the northern shopping malls on the outskirts and with a few twists arrives at the dismount line and T2.

Like the bike, the marathon initially passes south of the town for about three miles following the legendary Alii Drive to a turnaround at the Pahoehoe Beach Park. On the return weary athletes head up a sharp dig on Palani Drive and then north onto the most iconic battleground of the World Championship course, the Queen-K Highway. Back in the barren lava fields the endless line trudges north, beaten by the sun to the last turnaround of the day in front of the gates of the Natural Energy Lab. This is a renewable energy plant overlooking the Pacific. It's a few miles off the Queen-K and accessed by a descent along Makako Bay Drive passing the Wawaloli Beach Park. At the Natural Energy Lab the marathon U-turns south, retracing the same route along Makako Bay Drive and the Queen-K Highway to Kona. The final switches and turns are in the back streets of Kailua-Kona, zig-zagging Kuakini Road, Hualalai and the final five hundred metre straight along Alii Drive, past the Mokuaikaua Church and onto the finish. I wish I'd known all this before we arrived, diligently done my research on what was to come, but I hadn't. I figured I'd heed my advice to Ben in Austria,

Just follow the others.

And it was at the IronKids in Kona that I got perhaps the most prophetic advice from Dave Scott, six times Kona winner. I'd been in awe of Dave since I was fourteen and listened to him in countless interviews. Caught up in the Kona-mania, I couldn't resist saying hello as we milled through the crowd as the IronKids raced by. He couldn't have been friendlier and was funny and dry. He is the ultimate Hawaii raconteur and with his experience and years in Kona he

198

sized me up in a heartbeat. As I sweated in front of him with my pale October complexion, he laconically warned,

'With that 'Oxford-tan' you're gonna get nuked in the lava fields.'

I laughed but knew he wasn't joking. I was days away from the start of my twentieth Ironman. It was uncomfortably hot simply standing still. In this heat and humidity, I was way out of my lane.

***

Six months earlier he'd put his tool box down in our hall. Our heating wasn't working.

'Where's the boiler?'

As he turned I clocked the Ironman tattoo on his calf.

'You've done an Ironman?'

'Yeah,' he replied nonchalantly, he'd clearly had this conversation before, 'a 70.3. In fact I have done six of them.'

I frowned. 70.3 was the rebrand of the half-Ironman format.

'What about an Ironman?'

'Yeah, a 70.3.'

Why don't you get six half tattoos? was my silent thought. I didn't push it, less out of principle and more because of his size. Although I haven't got one, I do 'get' the M-dot tat. I'm not an ink person but if you have the right calf they kind of look cool. But I do think as a minimum you need to have actually finished a *full* Ironman to have one.

What's more, you should be in no doubt you are putting the logo of a very valuable corporation on your body. The Ironman franchise has moved on a lot since 1978, especially the commercial side. In fact, the WTC had changed massively since I first raced in 2001 in Ironman Lake Placid. When I went to

Ironman Lanzarote in 2002, competitors could still enter the day before the race. It felt like the frontier. But in 2011, before Andrew's Legacy Programme announcement, Ironman and the WTC from my perspective, as an average Age Grouper, oozed money, money, money. Through the noughties, I'd seen the fields getting bigger, the profile higher, it was turning into a marketing machine. The pioneering, disruptive, rebel spirit of 1978 had certainly taken a back seat. It was slick, professional, a business. With the number of races expanding and excellent retelling of the historic battles, the awareness of Ironman had grown beyond sight, as had the value of the M-dot brand.

The ownership of Ironman has passed from various parties since 1978 and by 2015 was now moving into stratospheric valuations. Two years after its inception John and Judy Collins moved away from Hawaii and following their departure a flow of rather exotic names entered into Ironman history. The Collins altruistically and perhaps naively passed on the stewardship and ownership of the brand without payment to Valerie Silk and her husband, Hank Grundman. Valerie and Hank moved the race from Oahu to the Big Island in 1981 and created the current World Championship course. From here the story becomes a little soap-opera-esque.

Their partnership didn't last long as the next year, Grundman and Silk started divorce proceedings. Hank, who allegedly had done little as far as running or developing the Ironman race, demanded his share of the equity. Valerie couldn't buy her ex-husband out but local attorney, Don Carlsmith, stepped in and agreed to settle on her behalf. He took a 49% share in the race for $145,000 on behalf of a wealthy Hawaiian couple, Blitz and Mary Fox who were Ironman enthusiasts. In 1989, Silk sold her share of the race to a businessman with perhaps the most exotic name of all the Ironman proprietors, Dr Pitt Gills. He was a Californian entrepreneur with interests in dentistry, orange groves and property development.

In the 1990s, Gills created the World Triathlon Corporation, the WTC. Under his stewardship, he appointed management and the Ironman brand went through an aggressive phase of commercialisation. Through the decade there was a rapid expansion in the number of Ironman races globally. As the fields grew, the WTC's execution of the format got even slicker and its reputation as the premier gold standard in mass start, ultra, one-day endurance racing was cemented. By 2008, the WTC hosted fifty three full and half-iron distance races. Its logo could be found on everything from watches, wetsuits, goggles, clothing, even cars, vans and all manner of swag.

Three decades on from 1978, when the private equity firm PEP, Providence Equity Partners, paid a rumoured $85 million dollars for the WTC in 2008, one suspects both John and Judy Collins looked on in disbelief with a smidgen of regret at their generous-gratis-gift to Valerie Silk.

Twelve weeks before we travelled to Kona in 2015, a Chinese corporation offered $650m to buy the WTC and Ironman franchise. Under Andrew Messick's stewardship the business had almost achieved an eightfold increase in value from its still eye-watering 2008 value. No wonder they had settled the Lottery fine without dispute.

By all means get your tattoo but recognise the WTC is a corporate monster.

Also finish a *full* Ironman before you get inked!

***

But with all this talk of money, I have no axe to grind with Andrew Messick and the WTC. In October 2011 Andrew changed everything for no-hope Age Groupers like me with the Legacy Programme. When I ticked the 'qualify' box on my entry forms, based on my athletic prowess and finish times, I'd been kidding myself. I'd never seriously thought I'd get to Hawaii before the announcement. Without the Legacy Programme I would never be standing in Kona preparing to race the most iconic triathlon there is.

Since arriving in Kona I'd felt like royalty. This was the Ironman World Championship and as we moved through the final preparations of registration, the Parade of Nations and the athletes briefing, I'd been constantly reminded of the uniqueness of where I was. I'd never experienced this at any other Ironman. Every stage was so special, a VIP greeting, a warm welcome and heartfelt congratulations. This wasn't a *this-is-what-we've-been-told-to-do* vibe. In our accommodation, in every shop and restaurant there was a deep sense of local pride. The best Ironman athletes from all over the world travel to race in their town. This was Kona's Olympic Games and it happens every year.

Despite the vaults of cash at the WTC, neither Andrew nor his team had lost sight of Hawaii's uniqueness for every athlete. And this is how we found ourselves on a beautiful seafront lawn behind transition for a specially organised Legacy Athlete Reception two days before the race. We were greeted by a veritable who's-who of Hawaii race history.

First in the reception line was the man I owed my Legacy place to, Andrew Messick himself. Next to Andrew stood Craig Alexander, three times Kona winner, the infamous Dave Scott and Mark Allen, between them sharing twelve Ironman World Championship titles. Perhaps the most glamorous was the 'Queen of Kona' herself, Paula Newby Fraser, eight times female Kona champion and winner overall of twenty six Ironman races. Sporting an aloha shirt was the 'Voice of Ironman' in the USA, Mike Reilly. It was a very cool event, there was no rush and we had time to chat to each of them individually. It was a privilege to meet and thank Andrew personally. Quite spontaneously and gregariously he shared the story about the demise of the Lottery with Linds and I. He was enthused about the positive impact of Ironman and Ironman Kona on the lives of all the people involved. He made a heartfelt speech to all the invitees wrapping up with the words,

'That's what Legacy Athletes are very good at. Finishing.'

And he was absolutely right. Ironman is more than a brand or even a tattoo, it's a lifestyle. You don't finish an Ironman, through the process of preparing you become one. I couldn't fault the WTC for the care, attentiveness and thoughtfulness towards this year's class of Legacy Athletes. I left the event even more caught up in the Kona dream. But one person's words stayed with me longer than those of Mr Messick. When I shook Dave Scott's hand, he'd looked at me again with a glint in his eye,

'How's that 'Oxford-tan'?'

Gobsmacked and flattered he'd remembered me from the previous day, I tried to be nonchalant and shared my strategy on not getting 'nuked' by the heat and sun. He looked at me straight, the playful Dave gone,

'There's an Age Grouper saying out here, "You gotta pee by Hawi." Keep yourself so hydrated that you need to pee by Hawi.'

He'd won Kona six times. Dave Scott is Mr Hawaii. He shook my hand firmly and wished me the best of luck as I tattooed his advice in my mind,

You gotta pee by Hawi.

Dig Me Out Beach

I was wide awake at 2.30am. The morning of the race had finally arrived.

I felt refreshed and reinvigorated. Something very powerful was coursing through me. I'd finally run out of sleeps. It was here. The big day.

With my old iPod on I worked through *AC/DC's Thunderstruck, Mumford & Sons* and my Ironman favourite the *Old Crow Medicine Show*. With three cups of tea, porridge oats and honey, my pre-race-get-light routine worked like clockwork. Despite the early hour, Linds was as wide awake as me. As I brewed her tea and applied my sun cream I noticed, perhaps for the first time, the words on my orange wristband,

KONA ATHLETE

For a split second the thought of what it would feel like to finish flashed through my head. The emotion, the relief to be done. My eyes welled with tears. Getting to this point had taken so much. Telling myself to get a grip, I pushed these thoughts to one side. I had a long way to go in a very hard place before I could savour the finishing moment for real.

Outside it was dark, but from our hillside accommodation, we could see the lights of Kona town glowing below. The overwhelming thoughts kept bubbling up. I was here, on the Big Island, about to race the world's most famous, iconic and perhaps most difficult single day triathlon. My Mount Everest.

We jumped in the car at 5am and were in town for 5.20am. Parking up, we walked the three quarters of a mile to the start. Things were buzzing. The Ironman World Championship would get under way with the professional men at 6.40am. At the back of the Ironman Village by the 'Athletes Only' sign I said my goodbyes to Linds and plunged past the point of no return into the body marking zone.

With my number 1403 and the M-dot logo transfers on both arms, a timing official fastened a champion-chip to my right ankle, activated and checked it. At the next station my weight was recorded for medical and safety reasons. Following the flow I went through to my bike, found a track pump and re-inflated the tyres. My most important priority was to hold my breath in one of the white roofed, green walled, universally hideous and heinously whiffy portaloos.

Looping back to drop off my white 'dry bag', I was now standing in nothing but my speedos, a watch on one wrist, athlete band on the other and a champion-chip on my ankle. Holding my blue Age Grouper swim cap and goggles I was race ready. Even without the sun fully out from behind the volcano it was already warm.

As the start got closer, waves of adrenaline swept through me, instinctively preparing my body for combat. Helicopters circled low overhead, dark silhouettes against the purple, grey and orange dawn, their rhythmic whomps deafened by the blood pumping in my ears. Sounds seemed unconsciously muted, likely deemed superfluous for survival in the battle ahead. Dreamlike, I was there yet simultaneously removed. Silently the safety canoes, surfers and paddle boarders slipped out from behind transition. As the light slowly turned from a morning dusk to a brilliantly bright glow, I swam back and forth from the private beach to warm my muscles and settle my nerves.

It was 6.40 am. A distant cannon sounded and the professional men were underway. It was time for the Age Group men to make our way to the start. As I filed through transition for the final time I was surrounded by ultra fit looking, lean, tanned racers all with swim speed-suits on. I could hardly believe it, I was here, at the start of the Ironman World Championship. Quietly, nervously, we moved down the ramp leading to Dig Me Out Beach. Kailua-Kona Bay and the endless Pacific Ocean stretched ahead. The excitement from the Ironman grandstand buzzed. Mike Reilly, the announcer was building the already noisy crowd into a fever pitch. The cool, wet sand squeezed through my toes, the gentle swell washed my ankles. Surrounded by swimmers in speed suits I was sure I'd missed the memo. Half joking, half questioning I asked someone next to me,

'Where are all the speedos?'

He laughed.

'You're obviously a swimmer.'

I smiled, bluffing it out. I was a nobody; an average Age Group athlete, greying fast, over forty, with regular aches and pains, from a little market town called Bicester outside Oxford in the UK. I trained maybe fifteen hours a week, balancing family, working life and keeping my spaniel exercised. I was sometimes a good and, I suspect, often a thoughtless, definitely selfish, dad and husband. Those hanging bars at school, my scrunched up rugby socks and Mars bar stuffed pockets with Warwick Tri felt a lifetime away.

Here I was, on the start line of the Ironman World Championship in Hawaii in my budgie smugglers, fooling someone into mistaking me for a player because I wasn't wearing a race suit. I'd never been good at detail. I was bumbling through and as ever simply hadn't done enough homework to know that I could have worn a speed suit. But then perhaps if I'd spent more time reading instruction manuals rather than diving straight in with no thought of consequences, I'd have ignored Psycho Dave's hype of the Tour de Trigs and offer of a place in the London Marathon. In life's sliding doors I may never have even taken my first steps into this endurance life.

We had five minutes to go as I waded out. A traditional Hawaiian spiritual leader said a prayer from the sea wall as I swam forwards, careful not to get in the melee of uber fast racers. This was the World Championship and I was hopelessly outclassed by those around me. Like prancing ponies before a derby the players were ready to go. Given I had one shot at this race, a DNF in the first hundred metres would result in a short and very expensive swim. I saw no point

206

in risking everything here, losing my goggles, my rhythm, sacrificing my day for a few seconds either way. I was playing a long game today and wasn't alone in my caution. Maybe five metres behind the main field, a sizable proportion of my fellow travellers were nervously looking around to ensure we weren't going to get caught in a cock fight.

Time was accelerating.

Mike Reilly, standing at the end of the pier, was calling back the over-eager racers at the front of the grid. Canoes and paddle boarders were whipping up and down like bronco riders keeping the stallions in their pen. The helicopters hovered overhead.

'One minute thirty!'

We'd been told there would be no count down from here. The cannon would sound and we'd be off. I knew in less than ninety seconds I would begin this race. The big question now was whether I could and would finish it!

With Mike Reilly trying to get the thoroughbreds to hold the line I felt ready.

I trod water and waited.

Kailua Bay

BOOM!

The cannon sounded.

I jumped, startled in the water.

I hadn't expected it to be so close, so loud and so soon.

I was jolted from my thoughts and reflexively pressed my watch timer.

We were off.

Carnage.

The fury of the start.

White water and foam.

Bodies closed in around me, arms crossed my back. I had placed myself towards what I thought was the back, looking to stay out of trouble and shouldn't have been surprised by how many of my fellow competitors had a similar strategy. Despite my caution, there was no way to avoid the madness. I could feel my heart jack to near cardiac arrest, my lungs struggling for air. Feeling panicky, I was having to give it full beans. I stopped breathing on both sides and reverted to my dominant and more natural right shoulder.

As the fury settled I became conscious of where I was. The temperature was bliss, as warm as a bath and just right for speedos. The water was crystal clear and the array of exotic fish were dazzling. As we swam the coral below morphed from hue to hue. Sea life was everywhere. The bottom dropped away to a deeper greeny blue, the rippled sand and volcanic rock contrasted like zebra stripes. In the previous few days I'd had two practice swims and been shocked by the rolling swell and the strength and pull of the current. But at this time in the morning the water was much calmer and there was hardly any wind.

An arm across the head, a whack to the face jolted me back. Before the race Linds and I had calculated I would take an hour and fifteen, perhaps even thirty minutes. Here in the thick of it, this wasn't a time for thinking. There was only one way to get through this. Take a breath, swim two strokes, take another. Reach, pull, cup the hands, recover, stretch ahead.

You're in an Ironman.

The World Championship!

You just have to finish!

The course buoys gradually fell away to the right as we moved face down towards the turn boat, anchored 1.2 miles straight ahead. I knew this place, I had been here before albeit in less spectacular settings. The deep water here was still a vivid clear blue. Far below hovering above the coral and sand, fish were lazily patrolling oblivious to the carnage above. I'd never swum a triathlon without a wetsuit before, but the warmth of the Pacific would have been stifling in neoprene. I latched on to peoples' feet, drafting when I could, letting them disrupt the solid water. Time slipped into another reality. Halfway up the first leg we passed a jet ski hire boat moored offshore with swaying fake palm trees. As it drifted past to our right, the distant turn boat came into view. Slowly, stroke by stroke, it got larger and larger on each of my sightings.

Reach, pull, reach, pull.

Stay with the feet ahead.

Keep out of trouble.

All the time we were flanked by canoes and paddle boards. The sky was now a glorious cobalt, the sun getting brighter and sending long fingers of light through the crystal blue salty waters. We were lifted slowly up and down with the gentle swell as waves rolled in from huge oceanic distances. I was swimming with purpose, feeling the water glide around me. I knew I had this, I could swim 2.4 miles. I was running my programme of simple, well worn, self-instructions.

209

We swam the length of the *Body Glove* sponsored tour boat that was anchored 1.2 miles from the start. It was flanked by the familiar orange buoys and teamed with safety boats. This was a privileged VIP view point and as my head rotated from side-to-side I could hear cheers from the spectators above. With the waves and the wind we passed its stern and then swam to the bow. The anchor chain stretched down into the aquatic abyss and a stream of bubbles betrayed invisible divers peering from the depths.

We had turned for home. I was halfway around the swim of the Ironman World Championship and sighted for the next buoy. Fearing the offshore current would be stronger swimming towards Kona, I could feel the water pull me as I tried to leave the boat behind. My concepts of pacing and time were completely shot but I sensed that I could be in for a long stint. To my relief, I wasn't alone and hadn't been spat completely out of the back. I seemed to be with the same swimmers now and in a large enough pack to tell me I was in the mix. It was then the awful thought struck me,

Could this all be a dream?

Is this real?

Am I really in my bed?

My mind had been playing with me for so long. The tri-mares of no goggles in transition, forgotten trainers and missed starts. It was all going so smoothly I couldn't help but think my brain was conjuring up the ultimate prank. It seemed so surreal, so out of body. I worried that my cruel anxiety riddled neurons were fooling me into believing I was here. I'd wake in a moment and find I wasn't here at all.

It couldn't be!

It was all too vivid; the bitter taste of the salt water, the knocks of elbows, arms crossing over me, random bodies colliding, the occasional roughness of the feet on fingertips. I focused hard on waking but nothing changed. The waves, the chop, the divers' bubbles were all so real. Over my hands the rays of sun lasered through the aqua blue. The tiny grains of sand floated before me in the dark Pacific roll. Shoals of tiny silver fish darted in and out of sight.

It is too lucid, technicolour, three-dimensional!

I willed myself to wake. It couldn't be a dream, everything was going to plan. I had to swim back to Kona, get my bike, ride 112 miles and then run a marathon in this searing Hawaiian heat. No, this was real alright.

Three quarters of the way back, I could make out the pier, transition and the large lime green Gatorade bottle where Mike Reilly had stood trying to bring order to the start line. The strong offshore current was pulling now and it seemed to take forever. I coached myself that this was in my mind, I had to simply swim.

I'd been surrounded by blue hats but one by one and then in a flurry, pink hats started to pass through. These were the lead Pro and Age Group women who had started fifteen minutes behind us. We'd been 'chicked'. This was the World Championship and these pink hats were worn by women who'd won their age groups and were the best in the world. I kept to the left of the course so my slow flaying wouldn't spoil their day.

The pier gradually drew closer. The waves were getting bigger, lifting and dropping us in their lazy rolls. I was definitely slower now, making less progress than I had on the way out.

Swim, reach and pull.

Stick with some feet.

Make it as easy as you can for yourself.

We passed over ownerless blue hats, floating eerily maybe two arm lengths down. They rippled like jelly fish with beams of light flickering around and through them. I could make out one or two numbers as they slowly passed behind. It was an eerie sight. Eventually I drew level with the pier and the large inflatable Gatorade bottle. I could hear the wild crowd and the PA system flashed in and out of audio with my rotating head. My thoughts went to transition and my autopilot played out the next phase of the race.

Feet touch down.

Stand and wade up the beach.

Click watch, remove goggles and hat.

Wash under showers.

Find transition bag.

Automatically I went through the familiar transition routine as I swam.

There was definitely a strong current here. I had a hundred metres to go, then fifty, the last twenty five. I swam on, pulling against the backdraft of the swell. I could see the sand below, too deep.

Keep swimming.

Closer.

Think about the transition sequence.

I could see people standing around me. My feet touched down. The roar and cheers were constant now as I waded up the steep short sandy beach to the steps. Lifting my goggles, I clicked the time. One hour and twenty seven minutes.

Wow, that was slow!

The thought flashed through my mind but I instantly dismissed any negativity. My only objective today was to finish. As I climbed the steps I took my goggles and hat fully off and had a quick rinse under the hanging hoses. Within a few paces of the showers were the blue swim-to-bike transition bag racks. I called my number,

'Fourteen-oh-three!'

I was directed down the right channel, calling again,

'Fourteen-oh-three!'

The volunteers honed me in on my bag. I ran into the change tent, pumped and ready to go. I found a space, sat, stripped down, reached into my bag, pulled out my cycle shorts. They snagged as I squeezed them over my still wet legs. I grabbed my cycle jersey and pulled it over my dripping shoulders. It clung to my skin but went on. As I looked down to zip it, I realised I hadn't looped the shoulder straps of my bibbed short's up.

Slow down.

You have all day.

My only mission was to get a finisher t-shirt and medal. Ian Mayhew's words rang in my ears,

The longer the race, the slower the transition.

Mentally calming myself, I took my shirt off, placed it on my bag and carefully pulled up my shoulder straps. Sitting back I put my shirt on for a second time, zipped it up, found my socks, checking my feet were clean, sand free and there were no wrinkles in the fabric. I fastened my shoes, put my glasses on my head. I plastered my arms with suncream and applied any excess to my legs, face, neck and ears. My helmet was with my bike. Suddenly I had no reason to be in the change tent anymore.

To get on the bike course I had to complete a circuit of the huge pier and T1. I tottered out on the carpet and followed the channel to the top of the transition area and then back down half the length again to where my bike was racked. I fastened my helmet, put my glasses in place and pulled the bike from the rack.

There was a stream of racers heading to the transition exit and the bike mount line. The more proficient bikers around me already had their shoes clipped in. With flying kicks, they semi leapt onto their bikes and wobbled away. Less cocksure, I stopped, swung a leg over and clipped in my right shoe. Pushing away, I clipped in my left. With roaring crowds three to four deep on either side, I followed the route out.

The temperature was already rocketing up and 112 miles stretched ahead.

213

Oppenheimer's Hell

I hardly dared believe it, I was on my bike. The swim and T1 were behind me. I was in the mix, maybe I wasn't as slow and out of my lane as I'd feared. Hope rose in me.

Of course, I didn't have a plan over and above trying to ride as fast as possible without blowing up. Despite all the new-fangled technology on offer I still rode with only my watch, guided by how I felt. I was *so* old school, a digital dinosaur. I didn't have a handlebar mounted GPS, power, cadence or even a heart rate monitor strap. Over the years I'd learned to push as hard as I could and felt I had a pretty good understanding of the red lines that shouldn't be crossed. For the most important race of my life, I hoped this well-worn strategy would get me through.

I was in a pack as we rode through Kona town, heading south along Kuakini Drive to the one-eighty degree turnaround. We'd then follow the same road north, take a sharp rise up Henry Street before heading north towards the top of the island. With over half the bike done, we'd then turn and re-trace our route for a fast downwind blast south and back to Kona. Simple. No dramas. As I followed the stream of riders along Kuakini Drive, I had it broken down in my mind as two three-hour training rides. The Ironman mind games, nothing could be easier, three hours out, three hours back.

Suddenly the line of riders ahead lurched left.

Brakes jammed on.

Instinctively I winced for impact whilst swerving to avoid a rider who swung out across the middle line. He'd dropped his chain and while trying to recover it, nearly took four of us out with an abrupt lane shift. I whistled by and took a deep breath. That was a life used up and a very close call.

My mouth was already dry, my tongue parched. I glugged some drink and nibbled my first crumbling energy bar. Bits stuck to my teeth and I washed the detritus down with a long slug of sweet drink. At the most southerly point on the course I swung around the dead-end and was hit by an incinerator hot blast as the route returned to Kona, the Queen-K and Hawi sixty miles further north.

Every cell crackled and sizzled in the heavy, close heat. My DNA hadn't evolved to live in conditions like this, let alone race. My ancestors were from a small Atlantic island off the north-western coast of Europe. They were Anglo-Saxons, Picts, maybe Vikings and we'd thrived in temperate climes for generations with the cold and a benign sun that would hide behind heavy clouds. I'm ginger with fair skin that easily burns and I could feel my spiralling double helix starting to melt. I was six miles in, it was barely 9 am and this definitely wasn't my world. With a deep foreboding I knew this would be the toughest test I'd ever faced on my bike.

As we came back into town, the crowds through Kona were deep and wild. The short climb up Henry Street to the Queen-K was electric. With a sharp left turn we were heading north to Hawi. Black violent lava fields opened to the horizon, there was no protection from the legendary Hawaiian thermo-nuclear blast. I'd entered Oppenheimer's Hell and as Dave Scott predicted, I was already getting nuked.

Three hours.

I coached myself.

It's a training ride with Simon and then you're turning for home.

Drink. Pedal. Eat.

The heat and humidity were oppressive and sweat poured on my crossbar. The Queen-K is one of the iconic names of Ironman Hawaii. It's the main trunk road between the south and north of the Big Island on the west coast. As we passed the turning to the Natural Energy Lab the field was starting to stretch with ten metre gaps forming. I could feel a strong wind pushing me from the front and side. I put my head down, lowered onto my tri bars and got down to the business of making myself as small as possible.

But despite some riders flying past, I was keeping up with most. I calculated my speed at approximately twenty miles per hour. At this pace I would be done in five hours thirty minutes. Maybe I wasn't as shabby as I thought. Despite being a Legacy Athlete, I was mixing it with the Age Groupers who had actually qualified.

Maybe I am a player.

Carried away with the moment I was forgetting my *I'm here to finish* objective and like Icarus I beat my wings harder and higher, pushing for the sun. With no thought of consequences I slackened the leash and started to race. This was a huge mistake but I fought on in the furnace. Reminding myself I had to drink, I continually slugged at my two bottles. I'd almost finished the first and the second was emptying as fast as it warmed in the cage. Ripping the top of a gel, I squeezed it dry. Settling back on my tri bars, I returned to my battle with the vicious wind.

It was here romance smacked into harsh reality and Ironman Hawaii revealed its teeth. The brutal landscape was cooking. Searing lava fields radiated to the right framed by black, chaotic rock freezes. To the left, out of reach, the cooling relief of the Pacific Ocean. But despite the hostile surroundings I was racing and calculated I had two hours to go to the turn at Hawi. I'd have to battle this headwind north but knew once I turned, a strong tailwind would drive me south. I thought of the family and friends who might be watching at home. With my split I'd be a legend and was determined to hold this pace.

The guy who smoked the bike at Kona!

But I was completely blind to reality, burning my matches and drawing on my reserves. My feet were already starting to get sore, like someone was easing a hot nail into the contact point between the pedal and the shoe. This wasn't a new

216

sensation but I'd never experienced it this early in the bike before. I wiggled my toes to ease the pins and needles. Imperceptibly the heat, conditions and my exuberance were nudging me into the red and I would soon pay the price. The topography of the Queen-K was now painfully familiar with endless, monotonous hills. It undulates relentlessly like an asphalt series of waves and is perfectly designed to absolutely destroy. I'd crest and see the next valley stretching ahead. Fighting the wind to the bottom I'd find no flat, instead the road would arch straight into the next long, grinding climb.

Drinking constantly to keep up with my sweat I went past the settlements of Puako and Kukio. Occasionally I stood on the pedals to relieve my back and get some blood flowing in the shorts area. The heat was rising and with the unrelenting atomic head-on gale I was deep in the blast radius of Ironman Hawaii's thermo-nuclear storm. Passing the Hapuna Beach Resort, the crowds were cheering, screaming and going crazy with horns, bells and handmade signs. This was the World Championship, these folks had come to see their friends. We came to the junction south of Kawaihae and with a quick descent passed through its industrial zone the turn sign read,

'Hawi - 18 miles'

Eighteen miles!

The route north was hell on two wheels and was proving tougher than anything I'd raced before. Wales is bleak with relentless climbing and atrocious weather. Lanzarote has a hot, windy moonscape but the route is varied and nowhere near as humid. Austria is heaven, green, verdant, super-smooth and still. Hawaii's straight north and south route has a pure, mind crushing, monotonous, torturing uniqueness.

Then incredibly as we neared Hawi, the skies turned grey and a gentle drizzle turned to full on rain. It was very heavy but far from cold and I could feel my cells sizzling with the cooling relief. Instantly I was drenched. I'd made it to Hawi.

217

I was over halfway round the bike of the Ironman World Championship. Gingerly making the one-eighty, I accelerated towards the bike 'special needs' bag pick up. With the rain pouring down in torrents I called my number as I approached,

'Fourteen-oh-three!'

The volunteer helped me load my pockets with gels, more bars and two fresh bottles of my own energy mix. With the refreshing rain, my spirits were restored. I'd battled the furnace all the way north and now I was on for a flyer as I headed downwind and south. Pushing off, I relished the long awaited and much anticipated blast back to Kona.

It poured steadily for the next two miles. Then, as quickly as it had started, it abruptly stopped. As if crossing a magical line, the road was bone dry and the endless sky was a vivid azure. The moment the comfortable cool disappeared, I was back in the furnace. It was midday and the temperatures were getting to their fiercest. But something else didn't feel right. My bike wasn't accelerating as I'd hoped, I couldn't feel the push on my back. As I re-overtook a rider who I'd been switching position with for a few miles I called,

'What's going on with this wind?'

'It's flipped! It's gonna be on our noses all the way back too!'

My heart sank. I'd seen and felt the tell-tale signs but my brain couldn't compute. The wind was now blowing in the exact opposite direction! One hundred and twelve miles into a kiln-dry relentless headwind. My positivity wavered and worries washed over me. My over-ambitious plans for a sub six hour bike split evaporated. I had to jolt myself back together.

Push the negativity away.

It's in your head.

This is Kona.

It isn't supposed to be easy!

My mission was to finish. Forget the split, Mr Cowell's words echoed in my head,

The third quarter is always the hardest.

You're the furthest from home.

But actually you have never been closer.

I'd done this nineteen times before and I could do it now. But it's easy to tell yourself to *stay positive*. It's another thing in the fury of the fire fight to keep ahead of your thoughts. With my defences down, in the searingly high thirty degrees Celsius lava fields with a blasting headwind willing me to stop, it was proving almost impossible.

The monotony of the route was doing nothing to distract me. The bike from Hawi back to Kona is a carbon copy of the outward route, only in reverse. Each short descent was followed by its doppelganger climb. My legs were smoked and the wind was trying to stop me in my tracks. A stream of stronger, more powerful riders flew by as if I was standing still. Physically and nutritionally every survival synapse in me screamed that I had to get more liquid and energy in.

Pee by Hawi!

I'd almost forgotten Dave's advice. I didn't feel the urge but pulled over to the verge to relieve myself. I waited, closed my eyes, let out a long breath and waited some more. It took a while, I felt empty. Doubling my efforts I tried to relax. Eventually much to my horror and discomfort, a warm, dark, almost brown, unfamiliar concentrate came out. It was so strong it stung.

Far from looking clear and hydrated I definitely wasn't getting enough liquid in. The sweat had been pouring off me and I'd rung my system dry. Alarmed, I vowed to double my efforts as I pedalled away. The race was torturing me and I could see it was taking its human sacrifices. From my bubble of suffering I was overtaken by official race recovery trucks with their pick-up beds jammed with bikes. The DNFs and casualties were mounting.

219

There is no re-sit.

This is a one-time ticket.

Finish!

Hardening inside, I tried to push back my negative thoughts. I hadn't struggled through the last four years and come all the way to Hawaii to DNF. This was my one shot.

'Is that you babe? Is that you?'

A man's voice jolted me from my darkness as I rode through Kawaihae and started the steady climb to the junction with the Queen-K. Luckily he wasn't talking to me,

'Go babe. Go babe. Oh yeah. Go babe!'

As I passed him he was fumbling with his shorts and then there was whooping and screaming. I looked over my shoulder to see his arms in the air with his shorts lassoing above his head as he ran.

'Babe. I'm so proud. I love you!' he hollered, swinging more than his briefs as he sprinted alongside his true love. I couldn't help smiling, this was Ironman Hawaii, anything goes.

As I made the turn on to the Queen-K with forty miles to go my troubles really started. The temperature hit an intensity I'd never experienced before. I suddenly felt sick and dizzy. I was two hours from Kona and my brain was boiling in my helmet. Unwittingly I'd crossed a red line in conditions I'd never encountered in an Ironman before.

A panic rose inside me. Overheating. I knew this feeling. Sunstroke. It had wiped me out during the first Transalp race. This was serious. I hit the bottom of the next hill and my mind couldn't compute how I'd summon the effort to get to the top without collapsing. With alarm bells ringing, my body was screaming *STOP!* Something deep inside warned me if I pushed my thermostat further it could simply blow.

220

You are on the edge!

System shutdown!

My mind spun as another recovery truck full of bikes sped by. If I red-lined now I'd be on the deck and in the back of one of those pick-ups. A DNF! I had to get to the next summit and then the one after that. I had to get to Kona. I grabbed my water bottle and sprayed it through the vents in my helmet to cool my brain. It helped but I still felt very woozy. Dark thoughts, very dark, consumed me. Not finishing. I could see only black in that direction.

Survive.

Don't over rev the engine.

My temperature gauge was rocketing up and a bottomless unconscious chasm opened in front me. Overheated, dehydrated, on the brink of passing out, a coma or even worse. Every cell shrieked,

STOP!

Things were going south very quickly and my fingers were losing their grip. This was stay-conscious-roulette and I knew the safe option was to pull over and accept defeat. An abyss stretched ahead. Despair. The pain, the bleakness of DNFs, dropping to the sports hall floor, stepping over the tape at Mountain Mayhem, climbing in the ambulance at the Tour de Trigs. Anger rose in me. Everything had conditioned me for this moment. Life beyond Ironman Hawaii without a finish today would be darker than the canyon of potential oblivion in front of me.

I made my choice.

I wasn't going to let go.

If I was going to fail, it would be daggers-up.

Risk everything.

The next climb veered up ahead, the summit impossibly distant. I dropped onto my small chain-ring and went into *get-home-mode*. I drank and poured some more on my head. I desperately needed a feed station and had to conserve what I had. Unbelievably I crested over the rise still upright and conscious. On the down slope, I eased my pace, using gravity to get my head together. The valley stretched ahead, another climb and still no feed station in sight. Pushing on my pedals, I was filled with overwhelming self-doubt. I'd believed I could finish Hawaii and like Icarus, I'd flown too close to the sun. A kaleidoscope of worries and darkness swirled in my baked brain.

'This heat is incredible,' I exclaimed to a fellow competitor as we struggled up the next rise.

'My Garmin is reading forty eight degrees Celsius!'

Dave Scott had been right.

With that 'Oxford-tan' you're gonna get nuked in the lava fields!

He'd had the measure of me. I was out of my lane. It was way too hot for a ginger boy from a rainy Atlantic island off the north west coast of Europe. All I could do was push on until eventually the feed station came into view. Salvation, I had never seen a more welcome site. At the water section, I stopped and took two full refills from the volunteer stowing them on my bike.

'Everything okay?'

Without a word, I emptied a third over my head and shoulders, drinking as it poured.

'Take your time buddy.'

The water sizzled off me. He smiled as I emptied a fourth bottle over my head. This was my oasis in the desert. Kona lay over an hour away in the hazy distance to the south and with a sense of dread I knew I had to leave this sanctuary. I had over twenty miles to ride in this nuclear wind and then I faced a 26.2 mile marathon. Out here on the Queen-K with temperatures nudging the late forties Celsius, I couldn't think that far ahead. The cruel purity of the Hawaii World Championship bike course was crystal clear.

My speed was pitiful as I rode past Puako and Kukio for the second time. My feet were agony and my head was woozy. But it wasn't getting any worse. I was sure I'd hit rock bottom. Or at least I hoped I had. I could feel every cell and nerve cracking and searing with the infernal heat and periodically emptied more water through my helmet vents.

The familiar sites of the southern end of the Queen-K Highway came into view. First the airport, then the welcome sign to the Natural Energy Lab. This is where the bike course and the run overlap. Incredibly there was a steady stream of runners already on the marathon heading out to their final turnaround. They were finishing while I had my final painful miles on the bike to cover. Perhaps today I'd have to adapt the universal wisdom I'd picked up in Lake Placid all those years ago to *Everyone walks the 'entire' marathon!*

I could see my immediate future. This was definitely not going to plan. But I hadn't ended up on the deck. The bike was almost finished and I was still in the game. The marina came into view and we turned right off the Queen-K. We took a few turns and there was the transition. With roaring crowds either side, I freewheeled to the dismount zone. I had never been more relieved to get off my bike and hobble away. My feet were agony. I stopped on the blue matting, and opted to pass through transition in my socks, lent against the rail and slowly took my shoes off. Over the PA system came Mike Reilly's voice and the news,

'And the Wiinneeerrr of the GoPro 2015 Ironman World Championship iiiisssss… Jaannnn Frodeeenoo-h!'

A fellow traveller grinned.

'We're out of the prize money now!'

As I stood nursing my sore feet, Jan Frodeno had crossed the finish line to win the 2015 Ironman World Champion. Our separation in the world of triathlon was exactly the distance of transition and a marathon.

'Yup. No podium for us today.'

We knew what we had to do. With gallows humour we chatted as we limped through transition.

Salt And Glow Sticks

The racing at the front end of the World Championship was over and the winner was across the line. I was still staring down the barrel of a 26.2 mile walk.

As if on eggshells I tottered on the soft carpet, making the large loop to the top of the transition pier. Gradually, no longer locked in the fixed position of the bike, my shoulders, neck and back muscles eased. My gait went from a painful stoop to a weary upright walk. Smoked, sore and nearing the red bike-to-run bag racking area, I called my number,

'Fourteen-oh-three!'

The volunteers directed me to my bag and I went through to the changing area. Oblivious to the soaking floor, I found the nearest free chair and with tired resignation sat down. Time was warping at a different speed now. When I wanted it to go fast, it dragged. When I wanted it to ease up, it flew. In the lava fields the minutes and miles had sucked. Here in the cool changing tent, out of the sun, time wouldn't slow down enough.

On autopilot, before I knew what I was doing, my cycle shirt and bib shorts were off. I pulled on my run shorts, zipped up my vest, replaced my wet cycling socks, carefully pulled on clean ones and slipped on my trainers. I reached for my pot of Vaseline and gave my dangly bits a good once over to minimise any rubbing. Finally I found my hat and my sweat-streaked glasses. My respite from suffering was over in the blink of an eye and I had no other reasons to be sitting there in the shade. I stood and made for the door. I'd been on the rivet, over the red line, in the searing sun and heat for the last eight hours and had absolutely no idea what was going to happen next. I was ready to walk a marathon if that is what it would take to finish. That was the mission. It was 3pm, sunset was at 6. Run, walk or crawl, I'd be finishing in the dark.

As I left the tent and emerged in the merciless sun, the reality of what lay ahead loomed large. At the exit there was water and coke. I drained two cups of water and then mixed a third water with a cup of coke. I finished this last cup five metres into the exit chute and dropped it in the litter zone. Ahead of me the crowds were four deep and going wild up the shallow rise past the Ironman Village and away from the sea.

Automatically, without thinking, I started to *Just f'in run!*

I was staggered. Maybe I could do this and the prospect lifted my spirits. It wasn't fast but it wasn't walking. It was loose, natural and felt good. I was running and hope surged through me. I knew Linds would be waiting within the first mile. The previous night I'd given her my now wildly optimistic splits. She could see I was way behind where I had expected to be. But she also knew the mission and what was at stake. Finishing was binary and there was no chance to come back and vanquish any demons. As I passed, we high fived,

'You're looking really good!'

I knew that wasn't true but it was great to see her holding her familiar Iron-fan vigil. The next section was simple, three miles south to the Pahoehoe Beach Park and then return north to Kona before climbing to the Queen-K. As I ran down Alii Drive, the feed stations were a little over one mile apart. My brain fell into its now familiar and well-worn marathon refrain,

Break it down, get to the next feed station.

Don't think too far ahead.

The volunteers and gazebos came into view. I slowed, grabbing two sponges and carefully drenched my head and shoulders. I knew the dangers of wet socks, soft skinned blisters and wanted to keep my feet dry. As I levelled with the drink tables I stowed the sponges in the front of my top, and took two cups of water and a cup of coke. Mixing them together I drank as quickly and as much as I could but once drained that was my trigger to run.

Never walk with an empty cup!

At the final table, I grabbed two more sponges and stuffed them under the shoulder straps of my vest to slowly release their contents and keep cooling me. The mind games had begun. This was where the difficult questions would be asked and I'd find out how much fight I had left. I'd rehearsed the answers many times before. I gritted my teeth, locked my sights on my short term goal and repeated simple, well-worn instructions,

Get to the next feed station.

That's the game.

You can run a mile.

Any more than that was overwhelming. It would be madness to think about the next twenty plus miles in their entirety. The U-turn at the Pahoehoe Beach Park and the re-tracing of these painful steps back along Alii Drive to Kona would only be six miles done. I'd then be up on to the Queen-K for eight miles out to the Natural Energy Lab, eight miles back to the finish line.

Careful, don't think too far ahead.

Break it down.

One mile at a time.

Incredibly, given how close I'd come to falling into a catastrophic abyss on the bike, I felt okay and was astounded I could actually run. Gradually it dawned on me, it was cooler here. Alii Drive is far from flat, it rolls up and down along the coast. But with the proximity to the water and a refreshing sea breeze, the heat was very different from the lava fields' thermo-nuclear blast. It was still hot enough to melt my DNA and as I passed a shopfront's digital thermometer it read thirty two degrees Celsius. But compared with where it had been, this temperature was a welcome reprieve. I could hear my breathing, the steady padding of my feet, the constant system checks in my mind. I ran on but as with all Ironman marathons I had a sense of no longer being alone as fellow travellers emerged in my consciousness.

'We're living the dream here, eh?'

Time moved quicker with company. Our universal experience was the hellish second half of the bike. We fell into each other's pace, taking collective strength from joint momentum. I'd find out where they were from, where they'd qualified. We were in this together, getting through, surviving. We all had one goal and after hours of lonely suffering we were ready to chat. The next feed station came round and at each oasis I'd drink my cocktail of water and coke and dowse myself with sponges.

I hadn't relieved myself since leaving Hawi hours earlier and was long overdue a comfort break. I didn't feel the urge but thought I should try. Before the Pahoehoe Beach Park turnaround I found a portaloo. Reluctantly and with much coaxing a fiery liquid left me, burning as it met the air. The colour was a shocking dark brown. I had never seen a liquid like weak coffee leave my body. Instantly I recognised I was dangerously dehydrated and had to get fluid in. With over twenty miles still to run, I wasn't out of danger yet. At the next feed station, I drank deeply, switching to four cups, two of water and two of coke.

Eventually the Pahoehoe Beach Park turnaround came into view. It was a beautiful sight and my spirits rose. I had a long way to run, but I was getting closer to the finish of this race. I thanked the volunteers. The support along Alii Drive was incredible. The road was lined either side with houses and hotels but every so often it would open to reveal the Pacific Ocean and a surf beaten rocky coastline. This was the wealthy part of Kona, with large gated rock-star pads, offering glimpses of immaculate gardens stretching down to the waterfront. There were street parties, residents sitting in the shade out for their annual Ironman show.

'Go fourteen-oh-three!'

It felt good to be on my way back to town, every feed station taking me a mile closer to home. The runners heading north and south on Alii Drive shared the lane closest to the Pacific, with cones separating the outbound from those luckier ones who'd already turned and were heading back to Kona.

The other carriageway was full of local traffic queued up and heading north. There were families caught out in their station wagons oblivious to the madness to their left. There were biker gangs on big fat custom sleds, with huge back wheels and throbbing exhausts. They were inching along enjoying the late afternoon heat and non-existent helmet laws in Hawaii. I tried to run with one group that looked like they'd ridden straight out of *American Chopper* but quickly realised their version of inching along was marginally faster than mine. I settled back into my pace.

It was getting later in the day and the intensity of the sun was finally waning. For the first time in hours, it wasn't boiling my brain. At mile four, I saw Gordon Ramsay on his outbound journey from Kona. I was impressed, I'd battled all day and he was a few miles behind me. I was racing my twentieth Ironman and he was a TV chef and restaurant entrepreneur.

Chapeau!

With everything he'd achieved, he clearly had an iron-determination. But the heat was taking its toll. He was sitting in the shade of a gazebo, feet up, not looking in a good place.

With the winner long across the line, the prize money divided up, the racing at the sharp-end was done. We'd all come to Hawaii with one mission, we had to finish. I'd seen from the coverage before the start, he'd looked in great shape and at that moment my heart went out to him. I was anonymous and knew a DNF would crush me beyond anything I'd ever experienced before. Letting go of this bar wouldn't be easy for him, especially with his media profile. I gave him a cheer of encouragement.

'Go on Gordon!'

He was a fellow sufferer and I willed him to get to the finish. My race couldn't stop, and in this heat, I knew it would be hard to come back from where he was.

'Stu!'

A familiar voice.

'Looking great!'

As I ran past Lava Java, the main Ironman Village and back into Kona town, there was Linds doing her cheerleader show.

'I can't believe it. You are flying.'

I felt a lump in my throat, the tears welling and my chin scrunched into a wobble. I couldn't risk losing what already tenuous grip I had left on my hard drive. I was only here because of all her sacrifices. I loved her but didn't dare say the words. It was too soon, not here, with twenty miles to go. I wasn't even in the lava fields of the Queen-K and needed tough thoughts. I'd be in the hurt locker for a while yet.

We high fived and I turned left out of Kona and onto the sharp climb up to the Queen-K. I wanted to keep running, but it was too steep. I dropped to a walk and, after five hundred metres, took the left turn back into Oppenheimer's Hell. The lava fields stretched to the horizon as the road shimmered with mirages. I'd seen this indelible image in *220* as a teenager as I took my first unconscious steps on my road to Kona. Now I was actually running in the world's most iconic moonscape. Eight miles up the road lay the Natural Energy Lab. In total I had sixteen miles to run and was not even halfway through the marathon. This was a long way from over.

No time for thinkers!

Since the near fifty Celsius temperature on the bike two hours earlier, I'd been dreading this moment starting on the Queen-K. But now, to my surprise it was verging on benign. Well maybe benign is too strong a word. It was over thirty

Celsius and the cooling sea breeze didn't make it this far from Alii Drive, but I no longer felt like Captain Cook being boiled in the chief's cooking pot. The Queen-K is never flat, it rolls, goes up and down but incredibly eight miles into Ironman Hawaii's marathon, I didn't really notice the hills. My mind had moved into another dimension. It wasn't that I felt fresh, instead I was so deep, so lost, all I could do was focus on getting to the next feed station. Somehow all thinking, logic, rational thought, sensation were paralysed. I was on autopilot. A deep survival instinct of living for the next short walk, drink and cooling sponge was keeping me going.

In my mind I was flying but the official photographer's race pictures tell the real story. As I neared the turn to the Natural Energy Lab, the sun was sinking, the light fading fast. My gait was short, skin burned, my muscles fighting for every step. I'd pushed my glasses on the top of my cap and my uncovered eyes had a haunted, desperate thousand mile stare. With a twisted face, I was like a horse that had been over-whipped in the final furlong. But I knew none of this. All I saw was the road in front of me, the cones dividing the outbound runners from those heading for Kona and home.

At about mile fifteen they were giving out salt sticks at the feed station.

'How do I use them?

'Easy, lick your finger, put some salt on it, lick it off and drink water.'

I tried it, it was bitter but tasted incredible. My tongue craved it and I took another toke. I'd last relieved myself some twelve miles back at the Pahoehoe Beach Park. I was seriously dehydrated and despite all the coke and water since, aside from sweating, hadn't felt the need to pass any of the copious liquids I was putting in. Over the next twenty minutes the salt seemed to make a miraculous difference. Beyond the turn towards the Natural Energy Lab, I pulled to the side of the road. To my utter relief and amazement I took the longest, clearest pee I

231

had taken in days. Again if I had done my homework I should have been better prepared by taking salt much earlier in the day as part of my nutrition plan.

Mightily relieved I tucked myself back into my shorts and then the most wondrous thing happened. The sun pulled its most spectacular move of the day. It set. Sinking into the ocean with a kaleidoscope of purples, oranges and reds it was swallowed by the horizon. Alone on Makako Bay Drive padding towards the Wawaloli Beach Park, I was on the very edge of the world, looking out into space. It was the most beautiful thing I have ever seen on any Ironman course and one of the absolute highlights of my racing and adventurous life.

As I made my way south for the final time, past the Wawaloli Beach Park and the climb along Makako Bay Drive all I could see was the glow of the next feed station calling in the distance. I had eight miles, a third of a marathon still to run, but I was almost in the fourth quarter and hope surged in me. I realised I'd broken the back of this Ironman. The runners ahead of me and those going the other way had glow sticks looped around their necks like halos bobbing eerily, ghostly circles suspended in the darkness.

At the next feed station in the bright lights, there was a purposeful energy. This was the business end of the world's most famous triathlon. I was given my luminous necklace which I duly clipped together and pulled over my head. As I left the feed station I latched on to two women wearing US Navy tri suits. They were running perhaps a stride faster than was comfortable for me but I stuck with them. I needed a pull, wanted company and a ride home. This was the final stretch. I had covered twenty miles and had just over six to run. The physical suffering wasn't done, but it couldn't touch me. My heart was filled with lightness and I couldn't feel any tension. For the first time, I didn't want this to be over, I was soaring on happiness and waves of joy swept over me. But despite this giddy euphoria, I was conflicted; I wanted to get home, but I longed to stay in this moment forever.

It was so dark even running alongside my new friends I could barely make out their outlines. It hurt but I held their pace, stride for stride. With a steady stream of glow sticks bobbing the other way, some jogging, many walking, we continued to plunge forward, headlong into the pitch black. Shortly after mile 24, the famous point of denouement of Dave Scott and Mark Allen's 'Iron War', as we turned off the Queen-K and descended into Kona town, the US Navy girls lost me. Alone and in utter disbelief, I zig-zagged along through the final turns. Four years of tension were almost at an end, I was going to finish the Ironman World Championship.

I saw Linds standing patiently below a street light. I stopped and could go to my softer place now. We kissed and I told her I loved her. I ran on, making the final turn on to Alii Drive knowing that within five hundred metres I would be home. The crowds were crazy with only a narrow path for runners. My head was spinning as I tried to soak it up. It was numbing, effortless, I was floating, absolutely weightless in an out of body dream. Relief washed over me.

The finish of the Ironman World Championship!

With the roar, energy, lights and noise it was like running in a carnival. Through a wall of cheers I high fived. I passed the boardwalk, the royal palace, the Mokuaikaua Church and on to the seafront. Less than two hundred metres to the barriers and grandstand. There was Linds again beaming and I could hear Mike Reilly's voice,

'You are an Ironman!'

Soak it up. Take it in. This is it.

In the final hundred metres, I looked over my shoulder. I was on my own and had the carpet to myself. I slowed to a jog between the stands, wanting to remember every second of this. Relief, joy, happiness. I'd finished the world's most iconic and gruelling triathlon. The original, the most famous, Ironman

Hawaii. The clock and the arch loomed above me and within seconds I stood, arms in the air.

'Stuart Staples, you are an Ironman!'

The earth stopped on its axis.

The universe juddered to a halt.

Rocking, pivoting, every atom centred on my moment.

Arms up, cameras flashing, bright lights.

All the noise and energy.

A blur.

Time stood still.

I'd done it!

And Then...

With my arms above my head, I closed my eyes, all the tension, anger, worries drained away. There was stillness, silence, absolute inner peace.

Well, at least for a millisecond. This was the finish line in Kona and everything had to rock forwards again. The earth continued spinning, the universe rushed ever onwards.

Flashes of memory. Dave Scott and Mark Allen shaking my hand. I felt giddy, not really there. The 'Catchers' caught me, one on each arm. I was on my feet but not at all steady. Kukui beads were put around my neck and then a massive finisher medal. The 'Catchers' led me through the finish and into transition.

'How are you feeling?'

'Pretty faint.'

They took me to a seating area. Physically I was shelled. Hunched over, completely out of gas, on fumes. The finisher sitting next to me looked equally spent. We caught each other's eyes and smiled,

'Congratulations!'

'And you. That was something else.'

'What a day!'

Minutes later and the world was spinning less. I had to get to Linds and stood feeling much steadier. This was a long way from her first *find-my-delirious-post-Ironman– husband-rodeo* and incredibly through her homing instincts we found each other.

'We did it!'

Opening the door to my soft place, I started to cry. Over the last four years she'd been there with me every step of the way. There was no way I'd have been standing here, my mind blown, a physical wreck with my finisher medal and kukui beads without her love and support. We took some photos and both shed some tears.

I needed to retrieve my finisher pack and the world's most expensive item of clothing, the coveted ace of spades, the Ironman Hawaii Finisher t-shirt. I located my dry bag and changed into my 'street clothes'. Walking gingerly, I collected my blue and red transition bags, got my bike, passed through security and found the ever patient Linds.

We had planned to stay on for the 11.50pm 'cut off' and cheer along the final finishers. But close to collapse and having failed to sync to the eleven hour UK-Hawaii time zone shift, we realised this would be impossible. We walked up the hill to our parked car. Both exhausted and needing to eat, we stopped at an all-day diner to get some easy calories. Waiting for our food with the cool air conditioning and bright lights I relaxed. For the first time in years my brain was still and my infinite battery was drained. I had nothing left inside and my heart felt giddy and light. I looked down at my finisher t-shirt, beads and huge World Championship medal.

The course had humbled me; my swim was 1 hour 27 minutes, the bike 6 hours 25 and the marathon was 4 hours 44. My T1 and T2 transitions had been 6:25 and then 7:35 respectively. My overall time was 12:51:19. The men's winner, Jan Frodeno had finished in 8:14:40 and Daniela Ryf had flown past me in the swim and took the female crown in 8:57:57. I was a *long* way from the podium. But none of this mattered.

Kona, unless you were there, you wouldn't know.

The heat, humidity and wind had been immense, like nothing I had ever experienced before. I hadn't been as prepared as I should have been and the course had nearly crushed me. But I'd finished and every few minutes someone would stop to congratulate me and we'd have a chat. In their eyes I was *someone*, I'd come to Kona and finished the World Championship. They hadn't seen me tottering on the precipice and humbled by the day. I had a medal around my neck and achieved the almost impossible. Dave Scott had been right, I'd been nuked.

The neon brightness of the diner seemed a world away from the deep chasm of semi-consciousness I'd stared into only hours earlier. With a vice-like grip I'd held the wooden bar. With no thought of consequences, risking everything, I'd kicked through the door and stormed the room. Kill or be killed, perhaps I did have *the strength of mind* after all.

There was no rush, I wanted to remember everything, savour the moment and relish being a World Championship finisher. This once in a lifetime moment would never be experienced again. Looking at Linds, with the vivid dance of dark and light memories waltzing invisibly in my mind, I smiled,

'I did it.'

We squeezed each other's hands. Huge tears welled in my eyes.

Discovering My Superpower

I heard the squeak of his stained white crocs on the hospital tiles before I saw him. With a retired rugby forward's girth, his green surgical scrubs were three sizes too small and stretched. There was an unwelcome busyness that left me feeling I was his last appointment of a long day. Recommended as one of the area's lead spinal consultants, for me, it was a conversation that couldn't be rushed. My sense was neither of us really wanted to be there but for very different reasons. He looked me straight in the eye,

'You've broken your back.'

He repeated it slowly,

'Whatever they have told you about *stable fracture*', *'T6*', *protected by the sternum*', it's all true. But you have to remember the most successful way to approach your rehab is never forget you have broken your back!'

He was giving me both barrels which was exactly what I needed.

'The bone will take six to eight weeks to heal and there isn't a lot we can do. You will have to be managed by the pain. Try to keep it as stable and immobile as possible. If it hurts, stop doing it.'

He paused to check it was all sinking in.

'The broken bone will tell you when it's not happy with what you are doing.'

He stopped again and this time picked up a dicta-phone. What attention he'd given me shifted and he mechanically repeated what he'd told me, adding personal details and key points on my medical notes for an invisible secretary to type.

The accident had happened exactly a week earlier on a dawn off-road training ride. It was August 2022 and we'd had a particularly long summer heat wave. I was on my own, fifty minutes in and flying down an overgrown, grassy track. I'd seen lots of dark snaking dry fissures scarring the trails for weeks but caught in the moment, giving it full throttle, I was blind to the risk. The front wheel dropped into a hidden crack. The bike stopped instantly and the back end arched up ninety degrees. Before I had time to think or react, seventy two kilos of me were driven through my head, neck and back.

As I landed, a primordial groan came from deep within. With the force of a sledge hammer in the middle of my spine, the pain was instant, like a supernova. Burning explosions of intense agony paralysed me. Instinctively I knew not to move. There was no unconscious oblivion, my every sense was on high alert. I closed my eyes and breathed, hoping the flares of overwhelming pain would subside.

Time passed. Deep breaths, curled foetal on my side. The fury didn't stop roaring.

Think!

You need help.

Call Linds.

Fortunately my phone had fallen in front of where I lay. I unlocked the screen, it was 7.21am. She'd be awake and I waited for her to pick up.

'I've had a bad crash. My back's not good. I daren't move. I'm very scared'.

I'd put my worst fear into words. Afraid and alone, the enormity of what I might have done hit me. Tears blinded my eyes.

Linds got to me twenty minutes later, the ambulance arrived about an hour after that. Added to all my indignities I'd landed on an ants nest. As the medics cut off my clothes these red devils were crawling everywhere. The crew, Ellie and Barbara, had me strapped to a gurney, with my head and neck taped immobile between two blocks.

'On a scale of one to ten, ten being the worst, how much does it hurt?'

I smiled and wanted to say five but confessed it was nine, touching ten. It was rush-hour and slicing through with blue lights and sirens we didn't stop. I could hear snippets of worried conversations between Ellie who was tending to me and Barbara who was navigating the traffic ahead.

'Have you radioed the trauma team?'

What had I done?

Huge tears of fear filled my eyes and rolled into my ears.

Surely they weren't talking about me.

I'm an Ironman.

In the seven years since I crossed the finish line in Kona in 2015 I'd gone on to bag another ten Ironman medals. And it hadn't stopped there, I'd both finished and ignominiously DNF'd various Tour de Trigs, ridden multiple Tours of Wessex, other local sportifs and discovered the joys of riding with kindred spirits at my local cycling club, Bicester Millenium.

In 2020, through the pandemic lockdown year, when all events were cancelled, I cooked up a hair-brained idea of cycling the equivalent of 29,000 kilometres around the world virtually in twelve months. I captured my obsessive adventure in *The Stravagation*. Probably a story for another time but it's fair to say, things ran a little out of control.

Only four weeks before I was taking this unplanned ambulance ride, I'd stood arms aloft at Ironman UK in Bolton to finish my thirtieth iron-distance race. Every year there was talk of 'surely that's enough' and 'time to do something different' from Simon, but I'd drunk the WTC's kool-aid for too long. Without a challenge stretching ahead in 2023, as soon as I'd received the *early-bird* notification that entry for the next Ironman UK had opened, I'd dutifully submitted my details and payment to active.com.

Putting the dictaphone down, his attention jolted me back to his consultation room,

'Basically you were lucky. You haven't damaged your spinal column but you have fractured T6. It's a back break. The bone will take six to eight weeks to heal, but all the soft tissue, tendons, ligaments and supporting discs that have also been damaged could take much longer. Most people with an injury like this come back one or two fitness cohorts lower.'

We'll see about that! I definitely won't be retiring at thirty Ironman races!

'So when can I start to exercise?'

He looked at me like nothing he'd said had gone in.

'You can't do much aside from stay still and let the bone heal for six to eight weeks. You can do rehab when you feel up for it. Ten minutes on a stepper, an upright exercise bike, a very gentle swim. But it has to be rehab, not exercise.'

He eyed me doubtfully.

'This is a serious injury, don't slow your recovery by overdoing it too soon. You have to be managed by the pain. If it hurts, don't do it, stop.'

But the rehab message did get through over the following weeks and he was right. If I overdid it, I was overwhelmed by a bone moving, grindingly deep, sickeningly sharp, nerve zinging pain. The feedback cycle with a fractured vertebrae is very short. Sneezing was like taking a shotgun blast. The brewing, itching, expectant, helpless seconds before the explosion were terrifying.

For seven weeks I would lie for hours or stand upright, ridged like a pole. I could only sit for short amounts of time. Moving from one prone position to another took elaborate leg levers and arm pushes. Any weight or twist through my trunk shot immediate and lasting agony up my spine. I tried reading paperback books but the slight movement in head angle as I turned the pages sent sharp jolts of fire through my whip-lashed neck. I switched to a Kindle and with days of finger tapping devoured book after book.

My brain felt like it was going to explode. Until the accident I had a second WTC race planned in September 2022 at Ironman Wales. It didn't need a spinal consultant to tell me this would be another expensive DNS. But what hit me even harder was the sudden change in activity. Up to the accident I was consistently doing twenty hour training weeks and soaking my cells in endorphins. In a heartbeat I'd gone from perpetual motion to nothing, dopamine cold turkey. For the first time ever, I had to stay absolutely still and had no way to discharge my infinite battery. With virtually no distraction, my neural butterflies were flitting at warp speed.

What damage had I done?

Would I ever recover?

Is this a life changing injury?

So much of my identity was my indestructible, unstoppable physicality and now I was helpless and vulnerable. I'd gone from swimming, biking and running close to a day per week, to being unable to roll in bed, sit at meals for longer than ten minutes and was hobbling like an old man. I couldn't lift anything or sit at a computer. Even using my phone hurt horribly with the slight forward angle of my neck to read texts and the muscular tug of holding my arms and shoulders off the neutral plain. I couldn't box-set binge, the thought of watching TV abhorred me. It was too passive, at least reading gave me a sense of accomplishment.

'I'm going out of my mind,' I confessed to Linds. 'I'm not achieving anything.'

Patiently she assured me I was recovering and although I couldn't see it, making improvements.

'You don't need to achieve something every day.'

But I did.

Suddenly it occurred to me, neither my brain or my body ever stopped. Every part of the day was filled with distraction and activity. I never sat still from the moment I woke to when I fell asleep. Lying there I could see my flitting, perpetual neural butterflies zipping around the room. *Everything* went through an attention-filter of *interesting-and-captivating-or-not.* Each interaction, conversation and situation I encountered was assessed and in milliseconds and would either grab me or became another *blah* and was instantly lost. My insatiable radio dial was spinning but finding no diverting station to hold it tuned. The lack of movement and ability to satisfy my stimulation seeking was agony, my brain ached.

As I finger clicked page after page of my Kindle, behind the words, thoughts and memories swirled; the yin-yang of my life, the trouble I'd got into at school, fall outs with bosses, search for adventure and challenges and inability to stay still. Slowly it dawned, reflecting on a comment I'd thoughtlessly dismissed from Ben six months earlier as he'd struggled to stay on task with his A-level revision,

'Dad, I think I might have ADHD.'

I lay on my side for days and weeks, for the first time alone with my whirling thoughts, able to see, feel and hear my attention seeking impulses but unable to do anything to distract my spinning mind.

Could it be possible? Was the very smallest of my babushka dolls never really a finisher of thirty Ironman races. But instead hidden deep below my painted veneers an unsophisticated kid with ants in his pants. Had I simply never been diagnosed and survived until nearly fifty years old with undetected ADHD?

A Drive Half Done:

A Stimulation Seeking Brain

And that kind of brings us full circle. I guess the clues were always there. My hand rested lightly on the brushed metal of the car's door handle. With the stillness and quiet, Tom's question floated at the front of my mind. It was early spring of 2023 and we were heading for a pub supper when he dropped the bomb,

Why Dad? Why?

I'd fractured my vertebrae six months earlier and in February I'd sat in another clinician's office. Inexplicably, as I'd climbed to the first floor assessment room the flight of stairs reminded me of Sisyphus, the Corinthian king, and his eternal plight. Sisyphus was punished by Hades, the Greek god of the underworld, for cheating death twice. His sentence was to forever push a boulder up a hill, only for it to roll down as he neared the top. I held the bannister, unsure what I'd discover next. Taking a deep breath, I pulled on the door and went inside to finish the final phase of screening.

Initially I hadn't wanted to get tested and thought merely understanding my life through the prism of the disruptive kid who'd never been diagnosed was enough. Since my Ben-prompted-revelation I'd seen glimpses of the matrix's code, the green letters constantly streaking through my brain. I believed I'd inadvertently discovered a hack by channelling my excess energy into thirty Ironman races. With my Kona World Championship finisher t-shirt, it didn't feel like much of a *disorder* to me.

As the vertebrae healed, my mobility returned. I was sore but training again and started reflecting on my impulsive life. I could see my yin-yang behaviour had certainly brought me upsides, however it had often been my kryptonite. I had made things harder than they needed to be and was sure I hadn't been an easy person to live with. In personal relationships, friendships and at work, I've unwittingly been the bull in the china shop, consistently thoughtless, tactless, self-centred and insensitive. As my back recovered and I came to understand ADHD more deeply, I could see it was a double-edged sword. On the face of it professionally I am a success. I have a beautiful and happy family. Despite everything, Linds has stuck with me and I couldn't be prouder of Ben and Tom. Although nearly fifty and having recently fractured a vertebrae, I'm healthy and in great shape.

Through my research I discovered all the experts agree the brain of someone with ADHD has a duller, more muted response to what are considered neural-typical levels of dopamine. Put simply, the neurons are constantly seeking stimulation and looking for their next hit. It's been compared to having a sports car mind, with the brakes of a bicycle. There is a tendency towards exciting and compulsive behaviours. Risky and thrill-seeking activities are common, especially adrenaline-fuelled pastimes, as well as drug use, alcohol abuse, gambling, infidelity and over-exercise.

Clearly the current ubiquity of screens in our lives and infinite nature of social media, gaming and online apps raises health and ethical questions. With manipulative AI algorithms designed to keep us hooked, these micro-dosing dopamine machines are a subject of intense research. In our always-on, never-bored world, it is feared by many that the onset of ADHD symptoms are being accelerated and magnified. Perhaps it is no coincidence that legions of scrollers are starting to worry about previously unnoticed behaviours and ways of thinking that are strong indicators of ADHD. Like the invisible, long-term harm of smoking we may never understand the neural risks of our digital world for decades due to commercial greed and vested interest.

As I listened to experts, absorbed books and research materials, the jigsaw pieces I'd struggled with for years started moving into place. I could see from my own experience why when someone with ADHD finds a satisfying stimulation level and distraction it can be obsessively pursued with extraordinary focus. When something grabbed me, my challenge wasn't the attention deficit, but how to channel my over-abundance of it once I'd locked on to a goal. What's more, I'd felt first-hand how boredom and lack of stimulation can squeeze and hurt the ADHD mind. I'd often been perplexed by an overwhelming feeling of wanting to explode. Before I got my assessment results I'd constructed the edges of the puzzle and now the middle was revealing itself. I could see the decades of micro-decisions, the gradual building of habits and neural pathways to constantly feed my insatiable search for stimulation.

I could also recognise the downside of this frenetic-no-off-switch synaptic wiring and how it had fuelled my stress. I'd drifted into almost permanent survival mode and lost the ability to distinguish between real and imagined danger. It was clear my fight or flight responses had been magnified further by past trauma and hurt. My nerves were drawn tight, holding previous wounds and stresses, instinctively and misguidedly defending against all future harm. The insomnia and IBS I had experienced were certainly down to anxiety. The last pieces of the puzzle were falling into place.

Many people wonder what brings it on. In a minority of cases it can be triggered by environmental and social conditions, such as smoking and drinking during pregnancy, a child's low birth weight or simply being premature. It can also be activated by trauma, a brain injury or epilepsy. But these causes are the exception rather than the rule.

Research indicates that in most cases ADHD is hereditary. Nine times out of ten when parents are sitting with their disruptive child in the head teacher's office, one or both of them could well have had similar brushes with school authorities or employers in their past. The apple clearly doesn't fall far from the tree, ADHD is a generational game all the family can play.

The yin and yang of my life were definitely revealing themselves; the comments and jokes that had tumbled out at school, the irritation of teachers and later less patient bosses. I'd spent my life bumping into people who couldn't cope with my boundless and sometimes less than subtle enthusiasm for everything. I'd been lucky to find some who saw it as a strength. But also profoundly hurt by others who found it too much, disruptive and easier to expel.

From my teenage-headmaster-inspired-drive with Dad I'd found a way to satisfy my dopamine hungry mind and drain my infinite energy. In TaeKwonDo, swimming, biking, running and the gym I'd built an addictive habit of vigorous daily exercise. The escalation from the unpredictable weather dependence of windsurfing to the Tour de Trigs, the London Marathon, triathlon and Ironman all made sense. Each time I became dose tolerant I simply upped the intensity with two or three Ironman races a year, mountain biking, 24-hour solo challenges, ultra-events, TaeKwonDo championship, the UCI multi day Transalp and the Legacy Programme.

When running the family business, I was blind to the risks and all I could do in our bid for independence from working for someone else was 'twist'. The five years of self-employment went in the blink of an eye. But even heading a start-up couldn't satisfy my stimulation seeking brain. Alongside this and my sport I'd failed to learn the guitar, successfully trained a gundog and taught myself the basics of Spanish, German and Italian, whilst also brushing up my rusty A-level French. Nothing in any of that struck me as strange. I simply couldn't understand why everyone else wasn't trying to fill their days.

Once on a ride Simon and I talked about the Marshmallow Test. It's a famous Harvard experiment where kids were filmed to measure their response to delayed gratification. It assessed whether they would take one marshmallow now or wait

247

twenty minutes for two. The hypothesis being that the kids who waited twenty minutes and got two pink chewy treats went on to experience better life outcomes. Smiling I'd declared,

'I'd take the first one and then smash the glass and have the other two!'

Simon looked at me frustrated,

'No Stu,' he explained patiently, 'there are only ever two marshmallows. They bring out a second one if you don't eat the first!'

But I've approached life thinking there was always more than two. Smash the glass and grab what you can. For me, there's *now* or *never*, and I rarely see hidden consequences. In long work meetings when I am a passive participant I struggle to sit still, so I pace the room and stand behind my chair. The filter between warp-speed synaptic leaps, actions and words is very porous. I blurt out what comes first into my mind. Most of the time it makes me look witty and smart. Occasionally it's blunt, hurtful, and insensitive.

The startling truth is that ADHD is more common than most people think. Current estimates from the scientific community agree that Attention Deficit Hyperactivity Disorder is one of the most prevalent cognitive conditions that affects approximately one in twenty children and one in thirty adults in the developed world. It's hard to picture what these numbers mean but put simply it's a lot of people. It is believed there are two to three million children and adults in the United Kingdom that show symptoms consistent with ADHD. In the United States the number could be between ten and fifteen million people whose brains are constantly seeking stimulation. What's more, these numbers tell us the symptoms only resolve in a third of cases of children with ADHD. Two thirds of these boisterously frenetic kids will live their entire lives on a yin-yang rollercoaster with its many gifts and curses.

The medical world is divided on what to do with these millions of people. Some experts see the ADHD's dopamine hungry brain function as an 'impairment' and a 'disability'. They are forceful proponents that an ADHD life without pharmacological help is untenable. Research shows these medicines do help some people.

I learnt it's only recently with MRI brain scanning that science's understanding of ADHD has started to deepen. Needless to say, it's also a very divided field of research and medicine. The fact ADHD is labelled a 'disorder' and uses very negative, pejorative terms like 'attention deficit' and 'hyperactivity' hardly embraces neuro-diversity and the potential upsides of this dopamine craving synaptic wiring. The voices calling for a redefinition and a focus on the positives rather than the negatives are becoming louder and more vociferous.

***

After a few days the assessment results came through. I opened the attachment with some trepidation and of course skim read looking for the short answer. If I'm honest I was hoping for a big fat tick,

Yup, you've aced the test. Gold Medal. Take the top step of the ADHD podium!

It would have rounded this story off beautifully and made the explanation of my flaws and mistakes much easier. But the findings, like life, were nuanced and not so clear cut,

'Assessment summary - Our assessment of your cognitive and behavioural difficulties may be supportive of ADHD.'

I read and reread the findings. I'd gone through a three stage screening process and for the self-evaluation and interview parts I'd smashed the test, scoring maximum points. I'd landed at the far end of the spectrum for symptoms of inattention and hyperactivity. But on the third element, the twenty minute Qb computer testing, the results were merely suggestive of ADHD and in the main consistent with adults of my age.

And that is perhaps the rub, all the indicators of ADHD are magnified traits of what it is to be human. Over the years I have got myself into some difficult situations personally and professionally. I've made mistakes, lost friends, jobs and missed countless opportunities. But I'm nearly fifty and have learned, mainly through trial and error, how to survive in a sophisticated adult world. I can see through my approach how the Qb computer screening yielded the outcome it did. As I sat in the room, was wired up and my heart beat faster, I made a decision, took responsibility and focused. I told the boisterous boy inside,

Now isn't the right time.

Readying myself in front of the desktop, clicker in hand and a motion camera tracking a table tennis ball strapped to my forehead, I slowed the neural butterflies down. I kept completely still, coaching myself to not take my eyes off the screen. I'd been told it would take twenty minutes and although the shapes sped by at near impossible speed, I'd endured much worse than this and knew I couldn't give up. I relied on the mature and rational me. But perhaps I couldn't take all the credit. This format of computer testing can be unreliable in isolation without interviews and more contextual assessment. As subjects are strapped in, the stimulating circumstance can frequently trigger hyperfocus, smooth the symptoms of ADHD and as a result will often yield false negatives.

Experience has shown me, I am most vulnerable to the negative side of my dopamine hungry, stimulation seeking mind when; I am stressed or under pressure; if my beliefs are challenged, something conflicts with my worldview or my self-image; or simply I am bored, tired and my logical thinking is off guard. When I am in these cognitive states I find it is nearly impossible to keep perspective or rationalise. But my sense is that this is true for most of us. The vast majority of people are vulnerable to impulsive behaviours and the less constructive sides of our personalities when in these emotionally agitated

250

situations. I have learned coping strategies, ways to compensate and am getting better at identifying high-risk triggering situations.

And this brings me to perhaps the hardest dilemma of the screening process. As I sat in the assessment centre's reception, I stood out like a sore thumb in a cohort of adolescents. It was like looking back in time and remembering those quiet school corridors regretting my words and actions. As I watched my disruptive doppelgangers anxiously pace and play with their phones, I thought of my own teenage drive with Dad. I wondered whether an early diagnosis of ADHD would have helped or hindered me. If someone had told this over-exuberant kid he had a *disorder* would my life have been different?

It's an impossible quandary because I wasn't assessed. Instead I was told by people who I loved and held as heroes that they *believed* in me and I was *normal*. As the trees and hedges had sped past, I was given a dose of reality that there was no free-pass and nobody would hand me any breaks in life. I heard words about the ability to achieve most things if I worked hard and applied myself and that life wasn't predetermined. As our drive ended I was in no doubt only I could take responsibility for how things played out. I was in charge and controlled the choices of what I did next. I will never know the answer of how things may have been different if I'd been diagnosed decades ago. My sense is I would have carried it like a mill stone and subconsciously used the label to absolve myself of failures. My strong suspicion is knowing it wouldn't have helped me achieve my life outcomes.

Maybe I have ADHD, maybe I don't. I'm uncertain I will ever find out for sure. The reality is we are all complex, on some kind of cognitive behavioural spectrum and to varying degrees can sometimes struggle. There is little doubt that millions of people learn, interact and work in different ways but can be as intelligent, productive, creative and inspiring as a so-called *normal* person, and in some cases more so. Maybe it's time to be more accepting, tolerant and flexible towards this diversity rather than seize upon diagnosis, chemical sedation and stigmatising a sizeable proportion of the population. Perhaps we should be careful with the current trend to put a 'disorder' label on what is in actual fact the richness of being extraordinary, flawed and of course human.

On current estimates this stimulation seeking brain function could be affecting up to 5% of the population. What might help more is; education and awareness of how to recognise the symptoms in ourselves and others; guidance on how to thrive with a distraction seeking brain; and critically for those, like me, with minds like popcorn machines, ways to compensate, recognise high risk trigger situations and advice on how to develop coping strategies when most vulnerable to its downsides.

'Disorder!' my mum had snorted when I'd chatted about the assessment with her. 'Generations ago, you'd have been a hunter. Your stamina and drive would have fed the tribe.'

Instinctively I know her ancestral diagnosis is right and they had inadvertently prescribed the best medicine for *my* dopamine craving grey matter. All these years on as I pull though the water, take those first pedal turns on my bike or hear the steady pad of tarmac under my feet, I feel like a teenager again and remember the surge of joy and euphoria as I called,

Mum. Just going for a run.

What has never changed through the telescope of time is the chemistry and electricity that zings in my blood when I exercise. Everything settles, relief washes over me and I start to recharge my depleted resilience battery. The natural remedy I have found through impulsive and obsessive adventures has been intoxicating. I'm glad no-one gave the teenage me, full of boundless energy and an innate desire to squeeze the most out of life, anything other than wholesome activity. If they had, I may never have swum with light rays dancing through the water in

Kailua Bay, been nuked in Oppenheimer's Hell or watched the sun vanish at the world's end as I ran towards the Pacific Ocean down Makako Bay Drive.

Through my adventures, all powered by my stimulation-seeking brain, I have finally seen just how close to the sun I can fly. The smallest of my Russian dolls isn't a kid battling a disorder but instead a friend I like and who makes me laugh. We do some crazy stuff together. He's a dreamer, who inspires and stretches me. He displays extraordinary resilience and has near indomitable strength of mind. Occasionally we get into some real scrapes but even these yield rich lessons.

Perhaps I am doomed to never be content with stillness or likely to find anything other than fleeting inner peace. Maybe it will always be the drive rather than the destination for me. Possibly all my satisfaction, fulfilment and spiritual quietness will be found in distraction, movement and travelling along the next absorbing road. But as I'd descended those stairs from the assessment centre I certainly didn't feel I'd been condemned by Hades to live Sisyphus' tortuous sentence. But I wonder whether, for those who share my life, I'm possibly their boulder forever rolling back down the hill.

Another tap on the window, they were waiting, hungry for their Friday night meal. I bathed in the silence one last time, my fingers hovering by the door. I had to launch from my perch, soar and see where the thermals would take me next. With a deep breath, I pulled the brushed metal handle. The outside rushed in and the world lurched forwards again.

Why Dad? Why?

Linds, Ben and Tom, I hope that goes some way to answering the question.

If you enjoyed this book, please give it a positive review and tell your friends.

My other books in the Flawed but Resilient Series:

The Stravagation: Cycling Around the World in Lockdown

and

Not Normal Behaviour: Becoming an Ironman
20th Anniversary Edition

can also be found on Amazon.

Of course, Stuart isn't done yet with mad adventures. Join him for the next instalment in the Flawed but Resilient Series:

PB@50

In 2004, aged 30, Stuart recorded a personal best, PB, at Ironman Austria of 10 hours 53 minutes 54 seconds.

Ten years later, aged 40, he bettered this by 15 seconds to post a PB of 10.53.38.

Many consider the athletic decline of the late 40s to be irreversible. What's more, in August 2022, aged 48, Stuart crashed his bike and fractured his spine.

After a long rehab, aged over 50, Stuart is setting out to try and beat his PB at Ironman Austria.

Follow Stuart on his journey as he explores the latest training, nutrition, recovery and technological innovations to help him achieve his quest. Can the most cutting-edge endurance breakthroughs help him achieve his goal, overcome the complications of a broken back and the inevitable atrophy of age? Perhaps most critically, can he achieve his PB@50 ambition without falling into the self-destructive traps that have snared him before?

Is his first mistake to go back on Strava…?

Connect with Stuart on Strava, Instagram and Facebook to follow the story as it unfolds.

Acknowledgements

Single-mindedness and selfishness are often two sides of the same coin.

There is no doubt through my adventures that I have embodied both. I'm not saying either state of mind is right or wrong but I suspect many of those we admire in the world of endeavour have needed to be uncomfortably single-minded and selfish to succeed.

Some of my early proofreaders and friends suggested that I temper down the honesty to help readers 'like me'. I opted not to. For me, there are already too many books from those that achieve extraordinary feats where we perhaps only see the likeable side of the narrative. These books paint the hero in a favourable light, rarely giving a peek into their soul or innermost thoughts. Invariably their stories paper over the flaws, the collateral damage and fail to give a satisfactory answer to the question of 'why'.

Therefore, I took my proofreaders' advice on structure and grammatical mistakes but didn't alter my openness and honesty. I think the book is better for it and I hope they forgive me. What's more, my single-mindedness stands in stark contrast to their selfless patience in helping me polish and complete this book.

I must give special thanks to my friend and writing mentor, Sarah Mackie. Her insight, energy and guidance were an incredible tonic as I went through my darkest time recovering from my back accident. Without you Sarah, this book would never have got beyond T1.

Huge thanks to my army of proofreaders, in no particular order of pedantry, although I am sure you know who you are: Karl Ralph, James Harrison, Debbie Aust, Claire Lindley, Paul Emanuel, Pip Pearson, Lynne Pearson, Luke Pillinger, Nicola 'von Mulhaire' Jensen, Luke Chen and Paul Corso.

Finally, there are three people that none of this would have been possible without. Ben and Tom, Tom and Ben, my mini-mes. I love you and am so proud of the brilliant human beings you have become. More than anything you make me laugh and keep my feet firmly on the ground. And it goes without saying, we all know I would be in a crumpled heap if it wasn't for the 'Lucky' Linds, the true hero of all my adventures. Every one of my early readers wanted to hear these stories from Linds' perspective. To save my blushes, I hope she remains stoically silent. Linds, you know how much you mean to me and my life would be empty without you.

I wrote this book as a manifesto for energetic and boisterous kids, their parents and teachers. My love and respect for my mum and dad goes without saying. But I was also lucky enough to be believed in by some extraordinary teachers. They persisted in trying to find my potential when others had written me off:

Mr Jones (PE in Henley)

My Payne (PE and Geography in Henley)

Mr Philipps (PE and History in Henley)

Mis Cartwright (English in Henley)

Liam and Dave (TaeKwonDo in Stratford and Warwick)

Mr Cowell (PE in Alcester)

Mr Woodcock (History in Alcester)

Dr Bernard (History in Southampton)

This is a book for teachers who believe in energetic, boisterous and sometimes disruptive kids and their potential.

And a final huge thank you for reading my book. If you enjoyed it, please tell your friends, spread the word and give it a positive review on Amazon.

Printed in Great Britain
by Amazon